It Is All About You

From Eden to Eternity
How God Never Forgot His Creation

ALSO BY DAVID G. BROWN

Miracles, Signs, Symbols, and Judgment
God's Plan for the End Times

Prophecy Fulfilled
Jesus is the Messiah

It Is All About You

From Eden to Eternity
How God Never Forgot His Creation

David G. Brown

ISBN 979-8-9995981-0-3 (HARDCOVER)
ISBN 979-8-9995981-1-0 (PAPERBACK)
ISBN 979-8-9995981-2-7 (EBOOK)

Printed in the United States of America

Cover design by Iz Scheerer
Interior design and typography by Iz Scheerer
WWW.BADAPPLESTUDIODESIGN.COM

Acknowledgment

To those who lend their support,
and to the ones I have the privilege of teaching.

Whenever a project like this moves forward, there are always others who lend their support. I want to especially thank my wife. Though she often jokes that no one will ever read the books I write, she continues to support me in countless ways. I'm also deeply grateful to my granddaughter Izzy for her incredible artwork in designing the cover and other enhancements for this book. Her Bad Apple Studio consistently produces amazing work. Finally, I want to express my appreciation to my church family, Bonnie Brae Church of Christ, especially the class I have the privilege of teaching, for their ongoing encouragement and support in all of my efforts.

Preface

It's remarkable how God sometimes guides us into unexpected journeys. About a year and a half ago, while preparing for a weekly Bible class I teach, an unexpected thought struck me: Has God forgotten His creation? This question emerged seemingly out of nowhere. For some time, I pondered it, uncertain where it would lead. However, a few months later, the realization that I needed to explore this further became unmistakable. I began to sense that this question was not just a fleeting thought—it was a calling.

My wife underwent a scheduled knee replacement surgery—routine in nature, with no anticipated complications. The procedure went well, and I brought her home expecting a couple of months of recovery and physical therapy. Yet, as we all know, life can change in an instant. She was prescribed an opioid for pain management, and tragically, she had an adverse reaction that evening. Unknown to me until the following morning, she had vomited and aspirated, which caused her to go into cardiac arrest in her bedroom.

By God's providence, our daughter—a trained nurse—was only a few minutes away. She immediately began CPR while I spoke with the 911 operator. What followed was a whirlwind of events: eleven days in the ICU, seventeen total days in the hospital, and another twenty-three days in a physical rehabilitation facility. Initially given only a very small chance to survive, it became a harrowing, faith-testing ordeal. With the support of literally thousands praying for her recovery, I can now say—praise God—she made it. Today, she's doing well, and we are deeply grateful for all who came to our aid and lifted her up in prayer.

During those intense weeks, my focus was entirely on my wife's recovery. Yet even amidst that trial, I couldn't shake the question that had sparked this project. It continued to resonate within me: Has God forgotten His creation?

Looking back now, I realize that what I experienced—what we experienced—only confirmed the truth I was beginning to write about. No, God has not forgotten. Not even close.

In fact, it is in the valleys—those uncertain, painful, and fragile places—that we come to understand just how near God truly is. From the moment of humanity's fall in Genesis to this very day, God has been actively engaged with His creation. He has never withdrawn His presence, nor has He ceased to love what He made. His heart has always been inclined toward redemption, restoration, and relationship.

Life will always bring its share of surprises. Some are joyful; others are nearly unbearable. But through it all, we have the unwavering assurance that the God who made us has neither forgotten us nor abandoned us to our circumstances. He walks with us in the fire, speaks to us in the silence, and anchors us in His love when the storm rages hardest.

And that is the very heart of this book—It Is All About You. Not in a self-centered sense, but in the truth that God's divine plan has always been about reaching you. Loving you. Redeeming you. And restoring you to Himself.

Table of Contents

ADDITIONAL MATERIAL

It Is All About You

From Eden to Eternity
How God Never Forgot His Creation

CHAPTER

1

God Never Stopped Loving You

The phrase "*It's not all about you*" is often used to promote humility and counteract the self-centered tendencies of modern culture. There have even been books written on this subject, such as *It's Not About You: A Brief Guide to a Meaningful Life* by Tom Rath. While this message is valuable—especially in an age of personal branding and self-promotion—it doesn't fully capture the depth of God's relationship with humanity as revealed in Scripture. Yes, the Christian life is ultimately about glorifying God, but the biblical narrative also shows that, in His sovereign love, God has made this relationship profoundly personal.

From the opening verses of Genesis to the final promises in Revelation, the Bible reveals a profound and beautiful tension—a dual reality at the heart of the Christian understanding of God. On one hand, God is **God is supreme: majestic, holy, all-powerful, and utterly distinct from His creation.** supreme: majestic, holy, all-powerful, and utterly distinct from His creation. He speaks the cosmos into existence with a word. He commands the seas, the stars, and the course of human history. He is enthroned above time and space, and nothing escapes His sovereign will. On the other hand, this same God is immanent: near, tender, and intricately involved in our lives. He walks in the garden with Adam, hears Hagar's cry in the wilderness, and weeps at the tomb of Lazarus.

This divine tension—what theologians call the **transcendence and immanence** of God—is not a contradiction but a comfort. In His transcendence, God possesses the power to govern the universe; in His immanence, He exhibits the love to care for our souls. The God who holds galaxies in place is the same God who notices when a single sparrow fall (Matthew 10:29) and knows every hair on your head (Luke 12:7). He is present both in the sweeping drama of nations and in the quiet ache of a lonely heart.

This is exemplified in the person of Jesus Christ, where divinity and humanity are perfectly united. He calms storms with His command, demonstrating divine authority, yet also touches the sick and blesses children with tender compassion. Jesus, "God with us" (Emmanuel), makes the immanence of God tangible while revealing the holiness of the Father.

Throughout the Bible, God's transcendence inspires awe and reverence. Isaiah trembles in His presence, exclaiming, "Woe to me! I am ruined!" (Isaiah 6:5). The mountains melt before Him, the heavens declare His glory, and angels cover their faces in worship. Yet, Scripture also reminds us that He is "close to the brokenhearted" and "saves those who are crushed in spirit" (Psalm 34:18). He binds wounds, forgives sins, and speaks in a still, small voice to those willing to listen.

Balancing these truths is essential. If we emphasize only God's transcendence, we may perceive Him as distant and detached. Conversely, if we focus solely on His immanence, we might treat Him too casually, forgetting His majesty. The biblical portrait, however, holds both in perfect harmony: God is above us and yet with us; He is holy and yet approachable.

When life feels chaotic or uncertain, we can trust in a God who is sovereign over all things. This paradox is not meant to confuse us but to ground us. When life feels chaotic or uncertain, we can trust in a God who is sovereign over all things. When life feels lonely or painful, we can find refuge in a God who is near, who listens, and who understands. In a world that often feels impersonal and indifferent, the God of the Bible stands in stark contrast—He is the Almighty who also calls us friend (John 15:15).

Ultimately, this dual nature of God invites us into a deeper relationship. We worship Him with awe, yet we also walk with Him in intimacy. He is not just the God of the universe—He is the God who sees you, knows you, and invites you into the eternal story of His love and redemption.

In Genesis, we see a Creator who forms humanity intentionally, breathing His very breath into Adam. In Psalm 139, David celebrates God's detailed knowledge of him, stating, **"You knit me together in my mother's womb... I am fearfully and wonderfully made."** In the Gospels, we encounter Jesus, the incarnate Son of God, who walks among us, touches lepers, weeps with the grieving, and dines with sinners. These actions reflect not the behavior of a distant deity, but of a God who profoundly cares about each individual.

However, this personal concern is not indulgent. God's love for us is not about validating our self-importance; it's about inviting us into something greater than ourselves: His eternal redemptive story. While the modern mantra might be, *"You do you,"* the gospel calls us to *"Die to yourself, and live for Christ."* Yet in doing so, we do not lose our identity; we discover who we were always meant to be.

So yes, in one sense, *it's not all about you.* Life isn't centered on your comfort, fame, or success. But in a greater sense, *it is about you*—not because you are the center of the universe, but **because** the God who **is** the center has chosen to make you the object of His love. Jesus didn't die for vague abstractions—He died for people. He died for you.

This is why Revelation concludes with breathtaking intimacy: **"God's dwelling place is now among the people, and He will dwell with them. They will be His people, and God Himself will be with them and be their God"** (Revelation 21:3). The culmination of the biblical narrative is not merely God's triumph over evil—it is His restoration of relationship with His people.

While humility remains essential, and while the Christian life should always point toward the glory of God rather than the glory of self, we must also affirm this astonishing truth: you matter deeply to God. You are seen, known, and loved. In Christ, you are called to walk not just in obedience, but in fellowship with the One who made you for Himself.

In that sense, it may not be **all** about you—but God has certainly made it very much about you, for your good and for His glory. God's love is not distant or abstract; rather, it is a self-giving, sacrificial love that defines His relationship with us. This love is deeply rooted in the very nature of God Himself, as 1 John 4:8 affirms, "**Whoever does not love does not know God, because God is love.**" Love is not merely one of God's attributes—it is His very essence. Everything He does, from creation to redemption, is an outpouring of this divine love. The clearest and most profound demonstration of this love is found in John 3:16-17, which states, "**For God so loved the world that he gave his one and only Son, that whoever believes in him shall not perish but have eternal life. For God did not send his Son into the world to condemn the world, but to save the world through him.**" This passage emphasizes the personal and sacrificial nature of God's love—He did not merely express affection from a distance but took decisive action, giving His Son as the ultimate sacrifice so that we might have eternal fellowship with Him.

The theological context of this love is seen in the doctrine of atonement, which reveals how Christ's sacrifice reconciles sinful humanity to a holy God. The Old Testament foreshadowed this act of redemption through the sacrificial system, where the shedding of blood was required for the forgiveness of sins (Leviticus 17:11). Yet, these sacrifices were only temporary, pointing forward to the ultimate sacrifice of Christ, who, as Hebrews 9:12 states, "**did not enter by means of the blood of goats and calves; but he entered the Most Holy Place once for all by his own blood, thus obtaining eternal redemption.**" Jesus' death on the cross was not only an act of divine love but also an act of divine justice, where the penalty for sin was paid so that those who believe might receive grace instead of judgment (Isaiah 53:5). This demonstrates that God's love is not a passive or permissive love, but a holy love that satisfies both His justice and mercy.

This love is not based on our merit or worthiness, as Romans 5:8 declares, "**But God demonstrates his own love for us in this: While we were still sinners, Christ died for us.**" Unlike human relationships, where love is often conditional and dependent on behavior, God's love is freely given, even when we are in rebellion against Him. This reflects the biblical theme of grace, which Paul explains in Ephesians 2:8-9, "**For it is by grace you have been saved,** through faith—and this is not from yourselves, it is the gift of God—not by works, so that no one can boast." God's love is not something that can be earned or deserved; rather, it is a divine gift, offered freely to all who receive it. This unconditional love is at the heart of the gospel, revealing that God sees each person as valuable, regardless of their past or failures.

The love of God, as revealed in Christ, is also transformative. It is not only about salvation from sin but about restoration into the fullness of life that God intended for humanity. 2 Corinthians 5:17 affirms this by stating, "**Therefore, if anyone is in Christ, the new creation has come: The old has gone, the new is here!**" God's love does not leave us in our brokenness but renews and restores us. This is why Jesus calls His followers not only to receive His love but also to reflect it in their lives. John 13:34-35 instructs, "**A new command I give you: Love one another. As I have loved you, so you must love one another. By this everyone will know that you are my disciples, if you love one another.**" The love of God is not just a theological concept; it is the very foundation of Christian living, calling believers to embody that same love in their relationships with others.

Ultimately, the love of God is eternal and unbreakable. Romans 8:38-39 provides one of the most powerful assurances of this truth: "**For I am convinced that neither death nor life, neither angels nor demons, neither the present nor the future, nor any powers, neither height nor depth, nor anything else in all creation, will be able to separate us from the love of God that is in Christ Jesus our Lord.**" This passage affirms that God's love is steadfast and secure, unaffected by external circumstances or personal failures. It is a love that remains constant, holding us fast even in the midst of trials, doubts, and struggles.

To rephrase, God's love is sacrificial, unconditional, transformative, and eternal. It is the foundation of the gospel and the heart of His redemptive plan for humanity. Through Christ's atoning work, we understand that love is not **God's love is sacrificial, unconditional, transformative, and eternal.** just a feeling; it is an active pursuit of reconciliation and restoration as we journey toward eternal fellowship with Him. The invitation of God's love is extended to all, and for those who receive it, it changes everything including our identity, our purpose, and our destiny.

Beyond viewing us as His creation, God calls us His children. 1 John 3:1 proclaims, "**See what great love the Father has lavished on us, that we should be called children of God! And that is what we are!**" This identity as *children of God* is not figurative; it is a profound spiritual reality. Through faith in Christ, believers are adopted into God's family, as confirmed in Galatians 3:26, "**So in Christ Jesus you are all children of God through faith.**" This adoption means that we are not distant subjects of a divine ruler but beloved members of God's household, invited to approach Him as a loving Father.

And as our Father, God does not merely tolerate His children; He actively desires intimacy with them. This is beautifully illustrated in Revelation 3:20, where Jesus says, "**Here I am! I stand at the door and knock. If anyone hears my voice and opens the door, I will come in and eat with that person, and they with me.**" The imagery of a shared meal speaks to close personal engagement, and deep fellowship. In biblical times, eating together was an act of *hospitality and relationship-building*, signifying mutual acceptance. Here, Jesus extends an invitation to every individual, expressing His desire to commune with them in a personal and meaningful way.

The concept of divine friendship further deepens this relationship. John 15:15 records Jesus' words, "**I no longer call you servants, because a servant does not know his master's business. Instead, I have called you friends, for everything that I learned from my Father I have made known to you.**" This statement is profound in that Jesus, the Son of God, does not reduce His followers to mere servants but elevates them to friends. This speaks of shared intimacy, trust, and personal investment. Likewise, James 4:8 assures us, "**Come near to God and he will come near to you.**" The call to draw near suggests that while God is always present, He desires a voluntary search from us, a response to His open invitation.

God's faithfulness is not merely an attribute; it is the foundation of His character and the anchor of our hope. In a world characterized by shifting loyalties, broken promises, and unpredictable circumstances, God's constancy stands in stark contrast. While human faithfulness may falter under pressure, wane over time, or be compromised by weakness, God's faithfulness is absolute. It is not based on emotions, obligations, or fleeting moments of favor; it is rooted in His unchanging and eternally good nature.

Throughout Scripture, God's faithfulness is linked to His covenant love—a love that is independent of our merit or performance and anchored in His will and purpose. From His promises to Abraham, to the deliverance of Israel, to the fulfillment of His redemptive plan in Christ, God's unwavering commitment to His people weaves through the biblical narrative. His word never returns void, and His promises are everlasting.

This truth is beautifully expressed in Deuteronomy 31:8, which provides both comfort and courage: "**The Lord himself goes before you and will be with you; he will never leave you nor forsake you. Do not be afraid; do not be discouraged.**" This is not a distant deity offering detached reassurance; it is the personal promise of a God who goes before us, stands beside us, and supports us when we cannot stand. He is not merely waiting at the finish line; He is actively involved in our journey, preparing the way and strengthening us along the path.

Importantly, God's faithfulness is unconditional. It is not revoked when we stumble or withdrawn in our weakness. As Paul writes in 2 Timothy 2:13: "**If we are faithless, He remains faithful, for He cannot deny Himself.**" His presence does not fluctuate with our emotions. Whether we are experiencing spiritual victories or facing despair, He remains the same—a refuge and strength, "**an ever-present help in trouble**" (Psalm 46:1).

This unshakeable faithfulness brings both reassurance and invitation. It reassures us that we are never alone, never abandoned, and never beyond His reach. It invites us to rest—not in our own strength, but in the arms of a faithful God who keeps His word and fulfills His promises. He secures His people from beginning to end. In a world filled with uncertainty, God's faithfulness is the one certainty we can always rely on.

Beyond merely being with us, God's faithfulness is rooted in His infinite knowledge of us. His omniscience is beautifully expressed in Psalm 139:1-4, which states, "**You have searched me, Lord, and you know me. You know when I sit and when I rise; you perceive my thoughts from afar. You discern my going out and my lying down; you are familiar with all my ways. Before a word is on my tongue, you, Lord, know it completely.**" These words reveal an intimate and deeply personal connection between God and His people. Unlike human relationships, where misunderstandings or miscommunications can arise, God knows us fully and perfectly. He understands our deepest thoughts, our hidden fears, and even the words we will speak before they leave our lips. This level of divine awareness confirms that we are never insignificant or forgotten in His sight.

This intimate knowledge does not lead to distance or disinterest, but rather to deeper love and care. Many may fear being fully known, believing that their flaws and failures would lead to rejection. Yet, the God who knows every detail about us chooses to love us still. Isaiah 49:15-16 captures this beautifully: **"Can a mother forget the baby at her breast and have no compassion on the child she has borne? Though she may forget, I will not forget you! See, I have engraved you on the palms of my hands."** The imagery of being engraved on God's hands conveys permanence and intentionality; a love that is indelible and unbreakable.

In light of this, believers can rest in the security of God's faithfulness, knowing that His presence is not based on merit but on His unchanging character. Lamentations 3:22-23 reassures us: **"Because of the Lord's great love we are not consumed, for his compassions never fail. They are new every morning; great is your faithfulness."** Even in seasons of uncertainty, pain, or wandering, God remains constant. Whether we are in the heights of joy or the depths of despair, His faithfulness endures.

The reality that God is faithful, present in our lives, and unchanging should profoundly transform the way we live. It is not merely a distant theological concept for intellectual agreement; it is a deeply personal, transformative truth that permeates our daily lives. If we genuinely believe that God walks beside us, and stands behind us as our rear guard, then anxiety about the unknown loses its grip. The future, no matter how uncertain or daunting it may appear, is securely held in the hands of the One who is both sovereign and good.

Because God is already in our tomorrow, we are liberated from the crippling need to control every outcome or anticipate every threat. Faith in His presence allows us to move forward in peace rather than panic. We no longer need to perform or earn acceptance, for we are already beloved—redeemed, and called His own. This freedom releases us from the exhausting pursuit of approval from others, circumstances, or even ourselves. Our identity is not something we must construct; it is a gift from the God who created and knows us intimately, and delights in calling us His children.

Moreover, the fear of being forgotten, overlooked, or left behind loses its power in light of God's unwavering attention toward us. To be known by God is not simply to be recognized, but to be entirely understood and personally loved according to His divine knowledge. Every burden, every unspoken prayer, and every hidden ache is seen by the One who neither slumbers nor sleeps. In Isaiah 49:16, God declares, **"See, I have engraved you on the palms of my hands."** This is not poetic exaggeration; it is a divine affirmation that we are never out of His sight or heart.

God's faithfulness is not theoretical; it is the steady presence that sustains us amid chaos, the gentle whisper that calms us in the storm, and the firm foundation that supports us when all else falters. It empowers us to endure suffering without despair and to wait in hope rather than fear. Every challenge becomes an opportunity to trust and love more deeply, and walk more closely with the One who has proven Himself faithful in every generation.

When we truly grasp the closeness and dependability of God, our perspective on life transforms. By choosing trust over toil, we discover that faith is not just belief—it is the bridge to abiding fellowship with God. His faithfulness stabilizes our steps and illuminates our path home. In Him, we discover the courage to live—not with anxiety or aimlessness, but with a sense of confidence and security.

God's love also extends beyond knowledge and presence. It is an invitation to transformation. Matthew 11:28-30 presents one of the most tender appeals of Jesus: **"Come to me, all you who are weary and burdened, and I will give you rest. Take my yoke upon you and learn from me, for I am gentle and humble in heart, and you will find rest for your souls. For my yoke is easy and my burden is light."**

This invitation speaks directly to those who are burdened by sin, tress, or struggles. Jesus does not simply offer sympathy; He offers rest, renewal, and purpose to those who turn to Him.

Even in moments of doubt or insecurity, Scripture affirms our worth and value to God. Psalm 8:4-5 marvels, **"What is mankind**

> **Even in moments of doubt or insecurity, Scripture affirms our worth and value to God.**

that you are mindful of them, human beings that you care for them? **You have made them a little lower than the angels and crowned them with glory and honor.**" This passage highlights the significance God has placed on humanity, despite our frailty. Jesus reinforces this truth in Matthew 10:29-31, saying, "**Are not two sparrows sold for a penny? Yet not one of them will fall to the ground outside your Father's care. And even the very hairs of your head are all numbered. So don't be afraid; you are worth more than many sparrows.**" If God is attentive to the smallest details of creation, how much more does He value and care for each person?

The overarching narrative of Scripture is that God longs for a restored relationship with humanity. From creation to redemption, His love is woven throughout history. Sin has disrupted this relationship, but God, in His mercy, has provided a way back through Jesus Christ. Romans 3:23 acknowledges, "**For all have sinned and fall short of the glory of God,**" yet 2 Corinthians 5:18-19 assures us that through Christ, we are reconciled to God: "**All this is from God, who reconciled us to himself through Christ and gave us the ministry of reconciliation: that God was reconciling the world to himself in Christ, not counting people's sins against them.**"

Remaining connected to God is the key to spiritual growth and fulfillment. John 15:4-5 instructs, "**Remain in me, as I also remain in you... Apart from me you can do nothing.**" This passage illustrates the necessity of ongoing relationship, emphasizing that our spiritual vitality comes from abiding in Christ. The ultimate fulfillment of this relationship is found in eternal fellowship with God, expressed in Revelation 21:3-4: "**Look! God's dwelling place is now among the people, and he will dwell with them. They will be his people, and God himself will be with them and be their God. He will wipe every tear from their eyes. There will be no more death or mourning or crying or pain, for the old order of things has passed away.**"

As we journey through Scripture, exploring the profound and consistent ways God engages with humanity, we arrive at a powerful truth: God has never forgotten you—not for a moment. From Genesis to Revelation, the biblical narrative reveals not a distant deity but a faithful Father who relentlessly seeks a relationship with His creation. The entire arc of Scripture testifies to a divine love that endures, a presence that remains steadfast, and a purpose that never fails.

From the moment of the Fall in Eden, God began to lay the groundwork for restoration. He did not turn away in indifference or abandon humanity to despair. Instead, He clothed Adam and Eve, made a covenant with Noah, called Abraham, guided Israel, and ultimately sent His own Son for reconciliation. Each step in this redemptive story has been intentional, marked by both justice and mercy, with one central aim: to bring His people back to Himself—to bring *you* home.

This path, forged by grace and walked by faith, is neither abstract nor impersonal. It is paved with God's promises, made real through the life, death, and resurrection of Jesus Christ. As Jesus stated in John 14:2–3: **"I go to prepare a place for you... And I will come again and take you to be with me so that where I am, you may be also."** This reveals the heart of God: not only saving us from sin but drawing us into eternal fellowship with Him.

Every page of Scripture bears witness to this relentless pursuit. The wilderness wanderings, the prophetic pleadings, the coming of the Messiah, and the sending of the Holy Spirit all echo the same divine heartbeat: I am with you. I have not forgotten you. I am preparing a place for you.

As we delve deeper into the biblical evidence of God's faithfulness, we recognize that this is more than a story—it is an invitation. An invitation to trust that your life is not unnoticed, your struggles are not overlooked, and your journey is not aimless. God has charted the way, marked the path, and promised to walk it with you.

So, as we continue through the pages of Scripture, may your heart be encouraged and your spirit lifted. Every signpost along this journey points to one profound truth: you are being led home—not to a place built by human hands, but to a dwelling fashioned by the eternal God, where love never ends and His presence fills all in all.

These truths form the foundation of the Christian life: we are known, loved, and called by the eternal God—not as distant subjects in a cosmic plan, but as cherished sons and daughters. The God who spoke the universe into existence stoops low to call us friends, as seen in John 15:15: **"I no longer call you servants, because a servant does not know his master's business. Instead, I have called you friends, for everything**

> **The God who spoke the universe into existence stoops low to call us friends...**

that I learned from my Father I have made known to you." We have been adopted into His family, as Paul writes in Romans 8:15: "**The Spirit you received does not make you slaves, so that you live in fear again; rather, the Spirit you received brought about your adoption to sonship. And by him we cry, 'Abba, Father.'**" This invites us into a relationship characterized not by fear, but by love, security, and purpose. This is no impersonal religion but the heartbeat of the gospel—a divine pursuit of intimacy with His people.

Understanding that God's love is *personal* changes everything. It means you are not just a face in the crowd or a name in a ledger. You are seen, heard, and pursued by the One who knit you together in your mother's womb. His love is not based on your performance, past, or potential; it is rooted in His unchanging nature.

Recognizing that His love is *eternal* provides unshakeable security. In a world of shifting loyalties and fleeting affections, the steadfast love of the Lord never ceases (Lamentations 3:22). His commitment is not seasonal or circumstantial; it endures forever. From your first breath to your final heartbeat and beyond, we are held in His everlasting arms.

Understanding that His love is *transformative* reminds us that the Christian life is not about remaining as we are. God loves us too much to leave us unchanged. His grace meets us in our brokenness, while His Spirit leads us into healing, growth, and maturity. As we walk with Him, we are renewed day by day (2 Corinthians 4:16), shaped into the likeness of Christ, and called to live out His purposes in the world.

This doesn't elevate us to the center of the universe, nor does it reduce us to insignificant particles in a grand design. Instead, it places us exactly where we belong—in the embrace of the Father, as participants in His mission and reflections of His love. The Christian life is not about self-glorification; it is also not about insignificance. We matter because *He* says we matter. Our lives have weight and meaning because they are anchored in the eternal love of the One who created us.

This recognition should evoke a profound response: instead of pride, we offer praise while seeking to serve in ways that bring satisfaction to God and benefit to humanity. Gratitude becomes the melody of our lives, and devotion becomes our natural response. We no longer chase identity in lesser things, for we have found our true name in Him. To be loved so deeply by God is not a cause for complacency; it is a catalyst for transformation. We love because He first loved us (1 John 4:19), and in that love, we are called to pursue Him with all our hearts—faithfully and wholeheartedly. When we live from this foundation, our faith becomes more than belief; it becomes belonging. And in belonging, we flourish.

As we continue this journey through the biblical evidence, remember that God has never forgotten or failed to engage in our relationship with Him. Now, we will explore the path He has laid out to lead you to the home He has prepared.

CHAPTER
2

What was God's Purpose in Creating the World and What was His Purpose in Creating Us?

Before we begin to answer this, it would be best to break the questions down into its basic components, as the answer to the first part will significantly impact the second. No one can be absolutely certain about a profound question such as this, but one can gain insight from the very nature of God as presented through His holy Scriptures. While we, as Christians, are primarily concerned with the answer from a biblical perspective, we must acknowledge that this question pertains to all of humanity and religious traditions.

The question of what was God's purpose in creating the world and humanity is one that touches on theology, philosophy, and the essence of existence. Various religious and philosophical traditions provide different interpretations and explanations for this mystery. As I explore this question, I will briefly discuss other religious traditions outside of Christianity, not because I believe they hold a unique key to the puzzle, but rather to highlight that nearly all belief systems recognize a higher power or divine entity.

God's creation of the world is a profound testament to His glory, love, and divine purpose. The beauty and complexity of the universe reflect God's supreme power and wisdom, inviting all creation to recognize and praise Him. As expressed in Psalm 19:1, **"The heavens declare the glory of God; the skies proclaim the work of his hands."** This act of creation was not random but rather a deliberate expression of God's boundless generosity and His desire for a relationship with humanity.

Humanity holds a special place in creation; after all, we are made in the image of God (Genesis 1:27). This unique status signifies an everlasting connection with the Creator, where humans are entrusted with the stewardship of the earth. This role, in turn, reflects God's own creative and sustaining nature. Genesis 1:28 emphasizes this responsibility: "**God blessed them and said to them, 'Be fruitful and increase in number; fill the earth and subdue it. Rule over the fish in the sea and the birds in the sky and over every living creature that moves on the ground.'**"

The creation account reveals God's longing for fellowship with humanity. In the Garden of Eden, God walked and communed with Adam and Eve, illustrating His desire for a loving relationship with His creation (Genesis 3:8-9). This relational aspect is central to understanding humanity's purpose in God's plan. Even after humanity's fall into sin, God's purpose for creation remained steadfast. The Bible tells the story of God's redemptive plan, culminating in the work of Jesus Christ. Colossians 1:16 affirms this: "**For in him all things were created: things in heaven and on earth, visible and invisible, whether thrones or powers or rulers or authorities; all things have been created through him and for him.**" This verse highlights that all creation, including humanity, exists "for Him," implying that our very existence is part of God's divine intention.

Even after humanity's fall into sin, God's purpose for creation remained steadfast.

Creation serves as the stage for this unfolding redemption, highlighting God's enduring love and commitment to restoring all things. God created the world to manifest His glory, share His love, provide humanity with a meaningful role, foster a deep relationship, and reveal His redemptive plan. This overarching purpose invites all creation to know God while experiencing His goodness, and participate in His eternal plan.

God's creation of the world and humanity is a comprehensive expression of His divine nature and His purpose, demonstrated through His love. At the heart of creation is the manifestation of His glory and the invitation to a deep, personal relationship with Him. As the Bible reveals in 1 John 4:8, "**God is love,**" and love, by its very essence, desires to be shared and experienced. This intrinsic nature of God compelled Him to create the world, an act that stands as a testament to His boundless love and the desire to share His goodness.

The heavens and the earth, in all their complexity and beauty, declare the glory of God. Psalm 19:1 states, "**The heavens declare the glory of God; the skies proclaim the work of his hands.**" Every aspect of creation, from the vastness of the universe to the intricate details of nature, reflects God's power, wisdom, and beauty. Through creation, God reveals Himself, inviting all of humanity to marvel at His works and worship Him. The vastness of space, the movement of celestial bodies, and the intricate balance of life on Earth all point to an intelligent designer whose wisdom surpasses human understanding.

Humanity, created in the image of God, holds a unique place in this divine order. The imago Dei, Latin for "image of God," signifies a special relationship and purpose. Humans are entrusted with the stewardship of the earth, reflecting God's own creative and sustaining nature. Psalm 8:6 reinforces this concept: "**You made them rulers over the works of your hands; you put everything under their feet.**" This verse highlights humanity's responsibility to reflect God's rule and dominion over creation.

Beyond being stewards, humans were created to have a relationship with God. In the Garden of Eden, there was a close fellowship between God and the first humans, Adam and Eve (Genesis 3:8-9). This intimate relationship reflects God's desire for a deep and personal connection with humanity. He longs for His creation to know Him, experience His love, and walk in close fellowship with Him. Even after the fall of humanity into sin, God's purpose for creation remained unwavering. The Bible tells the story of God's redemptive plan, a plan fulfilled in Jesus Christ. John 1:3 confirms this: "**Through him all things were made; without him nothing was made that has been made.**" This verse asserts that Christ Himself is the agent of creation, reaffirming the interconnectedness of God's divine plan for humanity.

God's purpose in creation extends beyond mere existence. The imago Dei is not just about stewardship but also about moral, spiritual, and relational aspects. Being made in God's image means humans are endowed with reason, morality, creativity, and the capacity for love and worship. Ecclesiastes 3:11 affirms this:

"He has made everything beautiful in its time. He has also set eternity in the human heart; yet no one can fathom what God has done from beginning to end." This verse speaks to humanity's intrinsic longing for eternity and purpose, a desire placed in us by our Creator.

Additionally, God's original plan contrasts with other religious views on creation. In Hinduism, creation is often viewed as cyclical, with the universe undergoing endless cycles of creation and destruction. In contrast, the Judeo-Christian view sees creation as a singular, purposeful act leading toward ultimate redemption. Buddhism, which does not emphasize a creator deity, instead views existence as a cycle of suffering that must be transcended. These differing perspectives highlight the uniqueness of the biblical creation narrative, which emphasizes relationship, purpose, and divine intentionality.

This expansion highlights the depth of God's intent in creation and humanity's role within it. God's creation is not arbitrary; rather, it is purposeful and deliberate, while infused with divine love. As humanity navigates its existence, recognizing this divine purpose leads to a life of worship, reverence, and a greater understanding of our relationship with the Creator.

With all of this in mind, it is helpful to examine what other religions and philosophical traditions have to say about this subject, as nearly all religions are based on a belief in a divine deity or creator figure. Looking at the "big five" religions—Islam, Christianity, Judaism, Hinduism, and Buddhism—these five collectively comprise nearly five billion people, making up over 62 percent of the world's population.

In Islam, the deity at the head of the religion is "Allah," which is the Arabic word for "God." While God is central to Islam, Christianity, and Judaism, this does not mean that their conceptions of God or their relationships to creation are identical. Although these three religions share the belief in a supreme being who is worshiped, they differ in how they encapsulate distinct theological concepts and cultural understandings.

Islam, Christianity, and Judaism—collectively known as the Abrahamic faiths—are unified by a foundational commitment to monotheism: the belief in one sovereign God who is the creator, ruler, and sustainer of all existence. This shared conviction weaves a critical theological thread that historically and conceptually links these three religions, tracing their roots back to the patriarch Abraham, revered in each tradition as a model of faith and obedience to the one true God.

In Judaism, monotheism is central to its identity, clearly expressed in the Shema, a significant declaration of faith found in Deuteronomy 6:4: "Hear, O Israel: The Lord our God, the Lord is one." This verse underscores the absolute oneness and indivisibility of God, a foundational truth that has shaped Jewish worship, law, and worldview throughout history. God, or Yahweh, is perceived as wholly other—transcendent, eternal, and morally perfect—yet also deeply involved in the lives of His chosen people.

Islam, which emerged in the 7th century on the Arabian Peninsula through the prophet Muhammad, also upholds strict monotheism, known in Arabic as *Tawhid*. The opening chapter of the Qur'an states, "Say: He is Allah, the One and Only; Allah, the Eternal, Absolute; He begets not, nor is He begotten; and there is none like unto Him" (Surah Al-Ikhlas 112:1–4). This uncompromising monotheism is the cornerstone of Islamic theology and permeates every aspect of Muslim belief and practice, with any association of partners with God (*shirk*) considered a grave theological error.

Christianity, while sharing this monotheistic foundation, offers a unique and more complex understanding of God's nature through the doctrine of the Trinity. Christians affirm that there is one God who exists eternally in three persons: God the Father, God the Son (Jesus Christ), and God the Holy Spirit. This is not a belief in three gods (tritheism), nor is it modalism (the belief that God merely appears in different modes). Instead, it expresses the belief that within the singular divine essence, there are three distinct, co-equal, and co-eternal persons who are fully and truly God.

The doctrine of the Trinity developed from the early Christian community's experiences with Jesus and the Holy Spirit, as they sought to remain faithful to Jewish monotheism while recognizing the divinity of Christ and the presence of the Holy Spirit. The formulation of Trinitarian theology evolved over several centuries, particularly through church councils such as the First Council of Nicaea (325 AD) and the First Council of Constantinople (381 AD), which helped codify the understanding of Jesus as fully God and fully man, and the Holy Spirit as a distinct person within the Godhead.

This Trinitarian view is supported by various passages in the New Testament. For example, in Matthew 28:19, Jesus instructs His followers to baptize "**in the name of the Father and of the Son and of the Holy Spirit.**" Similarly, John 1:1–14 describes the Word (Logos), who was with God and was God, becoming flesh in the person of Jesus. The Holy Spirit is portrayed as a divine person who guides, empowers, and indwells believers (John 14:16–17; Acts 1:8).

> **The Holy Spirit is portrayed as a divine person who guides, empowers, and indwells believers.**

Though the Trinity is a mystery that transcends full human understanding, it illustrates how God is inherently relational and how Christians experience Him in distinct yet unified ways—as Father, Redeemer, and Sustainer. The theological nuance of the Trinity is often misunderstood by followers of other monotheistic religions, leading to accusations of polytheism. However, Christians firmly uphold the oneness of God, asserting that the three persons do not represent separate beings but one essence expressed in a tri-personal form.

While all three Abrahamic faiths are monotheistic, Christianity's doctrine of the Trinity introduces a distinctive theological perspective that reflects both the early Christian encounter with Jesus Christ and the unfolding of divine revelation in Scripture. This belief affirms the oneness of God while revealing the richness and depth of God's nature as eternally existing in perfect unity and relational love.

This supreme being possesses attributes such as omnipotence, omniscience, omnipresence, immutability, mercy, justice, and eternal existence. The sacred texts of these religions—the Qur'an for Muslims, the Bible Old and New Testaments for Christians, and the Old Testament for Jews—describe these attributes and provide guidance for their followers. Though these three religions share some similarities, there are significant differences in language, terminology, and theological doctrines.

As previously noted, the Arabic term "Allah" simply means "God", and it is used by Arabic-speaking Muslims, Christians, and Jews alike. However, within Islamic theology, "Allah" is uniquely associated with the God of Islam. In contrast, in English-speaking contexts, the term "God" is more commonly used to refer to the deity of Christianity and Judaism. Depending on how one counts—whether considering unique names, titles, or compound forms—Christians recognize 30 to over 100 different names and titles for God throughout the Old and New Testaments. These include names such as Yahweh (or Jehovah), Elohim, El Shaddai ("God Almighty"), Adonai ("Lord" or "Master," often used in place of YHWH), Jehovah-Jireh ("The LORD will provide"), and Jehovah-Rapha ("the LORD who heals"), particularly when referring to God in the Old Testament.

A core distinction in Islam is the concept of Tawhid, which emphasizes the absolute oneness and uniqueness of God. Allah is strictly singular, without partners, offspring, or equals. This strict monotheism explicitly rejects the Christian doctrine of the Trinity and the divinity of Jesus. Conversely, in Christianity, as mentioned earlier, God is understood as a Trinity, comprising God the Father, God the Son (Jesus Christ), and God the Holy Spirit. Christians believe that Jesus is both fully divine and fully human—the Son of God who came to Earth to redeem humanity.

There are other significant differences as well. Muslims believe that Allah's final and most complete revelation is the Qur'an, which was revealed to the Prophet Muhammad in the seventh century. This in contrast to the Old and the New Testament that was written as early as 1445 B.C. This revelation is regarded as the ultimate guidance for humanity. Christians, on the other hand, believe that God's revelation is found in both the Old and New Testaments, with the ultimate revelation being Jesus Christ Himself, whom Christians believe is God incarnate.

In Islamic theology, the creation of the world and humanity is deeply interconnected with the purpose and will of Allah, who is both Almighty and Most Merciful. This understanding is fundamentally rooted in the sacred texts of Islam, especially the Qur'an and Hadith (sayings and traditions of the Prophet Muhammad).

The Qur'an clearly articulates the purpose of creation in Surah Adh-Dhariyat (The Winnowing Winds), 51:56, where Allah declares: "I did not create the jinn and mankind except to worship Me." This verse succinctly encapsulates the primary reason for the existence of all rational beings—humans and jinn—emphasizing that their essence is to engage in the worship ('ibadah) of Allah. Jinn in Islamic theology (Arabic: *jinn*, plural of *jinni*) are supernatural beings created by God from "smokeless fire" (*Qur'an 55:15*)—distinct from both humans, who are created from clay, and angels, who are created from light. The concept of jinn is deeply woven into Islamic belief and culture, and they are mentioned frequently in the Qur'an and Hadith. Worship in Islam is a multifaceted concept that extends far beyond ritualistic practices such as: Prayer (salat). Fasting (sawm), Almsgiving (zakat) and Pilgrimage (*hajj*). It also includes ethical conduct, social justice, the pursuit of knowledge, and even everyday activities, which become acts of devotion when performed with the right intention. As long as an action aligns with Allah's guidance, as revealed in the Qur'an and exemplified by the Prophet Muhammad, it is considered an act of worship.

Thus, in Islam, 'ibadah' (worship) is not confined to religious rituals but instead integrates into all aspects of a believer's life, transforming ordinary actions into expressions of devotion when carried out in accordance with divine commandments.

The creation narrative in Islamic theology is deeply intertwined with the concept of worship and the manifestation of divine attributes. The purpose of creation, according to Islam, is for humans and jinn to worship and serve Allah, reflecting His divine will. Worship is a holistic concept, encompassing both religious rituals and daily conduct, emphasizing submission to Allah's commandments.

Islam, Christianity, and Judaism—collectively known as the Abrahamic faiths—share a fundamental commitment to monotheism: the belief in a single, sovereign God who is the creator, ruler, and sustainer of all existence. This shared conviction serves as a significant theological thread that connects the three religions historically and conceptually, tracing their lineage back to the patriarch Abraham, revered in each tradition as a model of faith and obedience to the one true God.

In Judaism, monotheism is central to its identity, clearly articulated in the Shema, a foundational declaration of faith found in Deuteronomy 6:4: **"Hear, O Israel: The Lord our God, the Lord is one."** This verse emphasizes the absolute oneness and indivisibility of God, a core truth in Jewish theology that has influenced worship, law, and worldview throughout history. God, or Yahweh, is seen as wholly other—transcendent, eternal, and morally perfect—yet intimately involved in the lives of His chosen people.

The opening chapter of the Qur'an states, *"Say: He is Allah, the One and Only; Allah, the Eternal, Absolute; He begets not, nor is He begotten; and there is none like unto Him"* (Surah Al-Ikhlas 112:1–4). This unwavering monotheism is the foundation of Islamic theology, reflected in every aspect of Muslim belief and practice. Associating partners with God (shirk) is deemed a serious theological error in Islam.

Historically, both Islam and Christianity claim spiritual descent from Abraham, yet their portrayals of God diverge significantly when examining their source texts and theological developments. In the Bible, God reveals Himself as a personal, covenant-making being who enters into intimate relationships with His creation. From Genesis, we encounter a God who walks in the garden with Adam and Eve, speaks directly to Noah, Abraham, and Moses, and binds Himself to His people with promises of enduring faithfulness. This covenantal relationship is characterized by interaction, emotional expression (such as grief, compassion, jealousy, and joy), and a proactive divine initiative to redeem and restore His people despite their failures.

In contrast, the Qur'anic portrayal of Allah emphasizes transcendence, distance, and absolute authority. While Allah is described as merciful and compassionate, He does not engage in personal, relational covenants as Yahweh does throughout the Hebrew Bible. The Qur'an depicts God as sovereign and majestic, yet largely unknowable in essence. He reveals His will but not His heart. The dynamic between Allah and humanity is one of master and servant, primarily rooted in obedience and submission to divine law. There is no equivalent in the Qur'an to the biblical theme of God seeking the lost, mourning rebellion, or rejoicing over repentance.

The God of the Bible, apart from Christian claims about Jesus, consistently expresses a desire to dwell with His people. From the Tabernacle in the wilderness to the Temple in Jerusalem, and through the writings of the prophets, we see a God longing to be near, to forgive, to teach, and to transform. The language employed is deeply relational: He is a shepherd to His flock, a husband to His bride, and a father to His children. These metaphors convey closeness and affection. The Qur'an, by contrast, avoids such imagery, with Allah not depicted as a Father, nor seeking personal intimacy with individual believers.

> **...We see a God longing to be near, to forgive, to teach, and to transform.**

Furthermore, the biblical narrative emphasizes a theme of grace—undeserved favor given by God not based on merit, but out of His love and compassion. The Hebrew Scriptures abound with stories of divine mercy extended to those who have faltered, from King David to the people of Israel as a whole. The God of the Bible is portrayed as slow to anger, abounding in steadfast love, and willing to forgive. While forgiveness is also present in the Qur'an, it is typically granted to those who first demonstrate their devotion through righteous acts, prayer, and obedience. Forgiveness is possible but not central to Allah's self-revelation, lacking the foundational role it holds in the Bible.

Although both Islam and Christianity affirm the existence of only one God, their respective portrayals of that God differ profoundly. The God of the Bible is intensely personal, relational, and redemptive. He interacts with humanity not just as Creator, but as Lover, Shepherd, Redeemer, and Friend. In contrast, Allah is transcendent, sovereign, and focused solely on submission to His will. The emotional, covenantal, and redemptive intimacy found in the Bible is absent from the Qur'anic depiction. These are not merely different names for the same being; they represent fundamentally different understandings of God.

This perspective on creation differs significantly from Christian and Jewish teachings, where the purpose of humanity is also tied to stewardship, divine relationship, and participation in God's eternal plan. While there are shared elements between these Abrahamic faiths—such as monotheism and the recognition of a supreme Creator—their theological frameworks shape vastly different understandings of God's nature, human purpose, and salvation.

Judaism and Jewish thought, in particular, often view creation as a purposeful and ordered act by God. The world was created with specific intentions, and humanity's role is to fulfill God's commandments and work towards tikkun olam, the repair of the world. This concept implies aligning the world with divine will through ethical and moral actions. Moreover, Judaism sees humans as partners with God in the ongoing process of creation, emphasizing a collaborative relationship expressed through adherence to the Torah (the first five books of the Old Testament) and active engagement in bettering the world.

I will return to discussing other religions shortly, but it's important to recognize that beyond religious perspectives, philosophical viewpoints also delve into the question of creation's purpose. Some philosophical perspectives, influenced by thinkers such as Plotinus, suggest that creation is the natural expression of an infinite and perfect being. Just as the sun radiates light, an infinite divine being manifests the universe as a natural consequence of its nature. Existential and humanistic philosophies, on the other hand, propose that the meaning and purpose of existence are not predetermined but rather constructed by individuals through their actions and choices. These perspectives highlight human agency and responsibility in shaping one's own life and meaning.

The reasons for the creation of the world and humanity vary widely across different traditions and philosophies, each reflecting deeper theological, metaphysical, and ethical principles. Religious traditions provide frameworks rooted in divine purpose, love, and relationship, while philosophical perspectives explore broader implications of existence and meaning. These diverse interpretations invite ongoing reflection and dialogue, contributing to the rich tapestry of human thought and belief.

But the question remains, why did God create man in His image? From a Christian perspective, God's intent is primarily derived from the Bible, specifically Genesis 1:26-27, which states: **"Then God said, 'Let us make man in our image, after our likeness. ... So God created man in his own image, in the image of God he created him; male and female he created them.'"** The reason for creating man in God's image is to establish a relationship and communion with His creation and to facilitate a deep, meaningful connection between God and humanity. Being made in God's image implies a unique capacity to know, love, and interact with God in a way that reflects a personal and relational nature. This capacity for relationship is central to many religious teachings, suggesting that humans are designed to engage in a reciprocal relationship with the divine.

In ancient Near Eastern cultures, kings often placed images of themselves in distant parts of their kingdoms to signify their authority and presence. Similarly, being made in God's image implies that humans are meant to represent God's rule and care over creation. This idea is closely connected to the concept of stewardship, where humanity is entrusted with the responsibility to manage and care for the world in a way that reflects God's character and intentions. Being created in God's image also endows humans with moral and rational capacities. This includes the ability to discern right from wrong, to reason and make decisions, and to create and appreciate beauty. These capacities reflect aspects of God's nature and enable humans to live in a way that mirrors divine attributes. This moral and rational likeness underscores the dignity and value of human life, establishing a foundation for ethical behavior and justice.

The belief that humans are created in God's image confers intrinsic worth and dignity to every individual. This idea is foundational to many concepts of human rights and equality, asserting that every person possesses inherent value regardless of status, abilities, or achievements. This **...Rooted in the** intrinsic worth is rooted in the divine image, **divine image,** emphasizing that all people are deserving **emphasizing that** of respect and honor. Finally, being made **all people are** in God's image points to a purpose and **deserving of** destiny that transcends mere existence. **respect and honor.** It suggests that humans are called to grow into greater likeness to God, embodying virtues such as love, justice, mercy, and wisdom. This purpose involves both personal development and communal responsibility, aiming toward the fulfillment of a divinely intended potential. The idea of humans being created in God's image encompasses a rich tapestry of meanings and implications. It highlights the potential for a unique relationship with the divine, the role of humans as representatives and stewards of creation, and the endowed capacities for moral and rational thought. Furthermore, it underscores the intrinsic worth and dignity of every individual, grounding fundamental principles of human rights and equality. Ultimately, this concept speaks to a profound purpose and destiny for humanity, inviting individuals and communities to reflect and embody divine characteristics in their lives.

The creation narrative in Genesis is seen as a testament to God's wisdom and purposeful design. The idea of a covenant is central to Jewish understanding. God's original plan involved entering into a covenant relationship with humanity, starting with Adam, then Noah, Abraham, the people of Israel, and finally with David. This

Davidic covenant continues down to Jesus, who is in the line of David. It is through this covenantal agreement that humanity has direct access to God. This covenant signifies a mutual commitment and a framework for living according to divine principles. For Jews, following God's commandments (Torah) is a way to live in accordance with God's original plan. The Torah provides guidance on how to live a life that honors God and maintains the order and harmony of creation.

In Islam, God's original plan is understood as the creation of a world in which humans worship and serve Allah, reflecting His divine attributes through their lives. Worship in Islam is a comprehensive concept that extends beyond ritual acts; it encompasses living a life in accordance with Allah's will and guidance. Humans are regarded as khalifah (stewards) of the earth, entrusted with its care and management. This stewardship involves upholding justice, compassion, and order in the world, thereby reflecting God's attributes in their actions. Across various religious traditions, God's original plan is seen as one of order, goodness, and harmony, with humanity playing a significant role as caretakers and representatives of the divine. This concept highlights the importance of a close relationship with God, the responsibility to care for creation, and the call to live in alignment with divine principles. Whether through Christianity's emphasis on the imago Dei (image of God), Judaism's covenantal relationship with God, or Islam's principle of stewardship, a common theme emerges: humanity is called to align with God's purpose, contribute to the flourishing of creation, and fulfill divine intentions.

However, when humanity disrupts God's original plan, religious traditions offer different interpretations of the consequences and God's response. These perspectives often center on themes of sin, redemption, and restoration. In Christianity, the disruption of God's plan is primarily seen through the "Fall", where Adam and Eve disobeyed God, bringing sin and brokenness into the world. The primary consequence of this disobedience was separation from God, characterized by both spiritual and physical death, suffering, and a world that was no longer in perfect harmony. The corruption of creation, brought about by sin, led to pain, toil, and disorder, disrupting the peace and order originally intended by God.

Despite this fall, Christianity teaches that God has the final word. Even in humanity's brokenness, God promised redemption, first seen in Genesis 3:15, where He foretold the eventual defeat of evil. Central to Christian belief is the advent of Jesus Christ, the Son of God, who came to restore the broken relationship between humanity and God. Through His life, death, and resurrection, Jesus provided a path for humanity to be reconciled with God, offering forgiveness and the hope of eternal life (John 3:16). Christians also believe in the ultimate restoration of all things, as described in the Book of Revelation, where God promises a new heaven and a new earth, a future free from sin and suffering, in which God will dwell among His people (Revelation 21:1-4).

In Judaism, the disruption of God's plan is often understood through the lens of human disobedience and the subsequent need for atonement and reconciliation. The Hebrew Bible recounts numerous instances in which the Israelites strayed from God's commandments, resulting in consequences such as exile, suffering, and national calamities. These events are interpreted as both natural consequences of disobedience and acts of divine discipline meant to bring the people back to God. Departing from God's laws leads to moral and social decay, affecting individuals, communities, and the nation as a whole. However, Judaism emphasizes God's ongoing efforts to renew His covenant with Israel. Through the prophets, God continuously calls His people to repentance and a return to covenantal faithfulness (Isaiah 1:18; Jeremiah 31:31-34). The Day of Atonement (Yom Kippur) plays a central role in seeking forgiveness and restoring one's relationship with God. Additionally, there is a strong belief in a Messianic Age, in which a descendant of David will reign, bringing peace, justice, and the fulfillment of God's promises to Israel and the world (Isaiah 11; Micah 4:1-4).

In Islam, the disruption of God's plan is understood as humanity's failure to live according to divine guidance, leading to sin and moral decay. Sin results in both spiritual separation from Allah and societal corruption. The Qur'an 30:41 states: "*Corruption has appeared throughout the land and sea by what the hands of people have earned so He may let them taste part of [the consequence of] what they have done that perhaps they will return.*" This passage highlights how deviation from divine guidance leads to disorder and suffering. Life's hardships, trials, and difficulties are often interpreted as reminders for individuals to return to the right path (Qur'an 29:69).

Islam teaches that Allah responds to human disobedience with continuous guidance. He sends prophets to call people back to righteousness, culminating in the final revelation given to Prophet Muhammad and recorded in the Qur'an (Qur'an 16:36). A core principle in Islamic theology is tawbah (repentance), which emphasizes Allah's Mercy and Forgiveness. The Qur'an 39:53 reassures believers: *"Say, 'O My servants who have transgressed against themselves [by sinning], do not despair of the mercy of Allah. Indeed, Allah forgives all sins. Indeed, it is He who is the Forgiving, the Merciful."* However, Islam also teaches that there will be a Day of Judgment, in which every individual's deeds will be assessed. The righteous will be rewarded with Paradise, while those who persist in disobedience will face divine justice (Qur'an 99:6-8). Across these traditions, the disruption of God's original plan results in significant consequences, affecting both the spiritual and physical realms. However, each tradition also emphasizes divine mercy, guidance, and the possibility of redemption. Christianity highlights the redemptive work of Jesus Christ, Judaism focuses on covenant renewal and atonement, and Islam stresses continuous guidance and forgiveness from Allah. Ultimately, all these perspectives underscore the hope for restoration and the possibility of realigning with God's original purpose. It is easy to ascertain the clear difference between Islam and Christianity. In Christianity, mankind is not dependent on their good deeds to attain salvation. Instead, salvation is purely a gift of grace through the work of Jesus Christ on the cross. One becomes justified by Christ's substitutionary death, which, in turn, saves us from spiritual death and sets us on a path of service in this life and eternity in the future.

Despite differences in interpretation, a common thread among these faiths is the understanding that human sin has profound consequences, yet God's mercy and justice provide a path for restoration. Whether through the sacrifice of Christ, the renewal of the Jewish covenant, or the Islamic call to repentance and obedience, each tradition ultimately offers hope for redemption and a return to divine alignment.

Central to Christian belief is the embodiment of Jesus Christ, God's Son, who came to restore humanity's broken relationship with God.

Through His life, death, and resurrection, Jesus provides a way for humans to be reconciled with God, offering forgiveness and the hope of eternal life. This act of redemption is regarded

Jesus provides a way for humans to be reconciled with God...

as the ultimate expression of God's love and mercy, providing humanity with a path to overcome the consequences of sin. The Judeo-Christian tradition holds that God's plan includes the ultimate restoration of all things. Prophetic writings in the Hebrew Bible and the New Testament describe a future reality in which God will create a new heaven and a new earth, free from sin and suffering. In this renewed creation, God will dwell among humanity in perfect harmony, fulfilling His original intention for a world characterized by justice, peace, and the fullness of life. While the Judeo-Christian belief system emphasizes that while humanity's disobedience brings profound consequences, God's response is marked by His continuous effort to redeem and restore. Through covenants, prophetic guidance, and the redemptive work of Jesus Christ, God offers humanity a path back to harmony and fulfillment, underscoring a hopeful vision of ultimate restoration in accordance with His divine plan.

There are two additional religions that I want to touch on briefly; they are Hinduism and Buddhism. In Hinduism, the concept of creation is deeply embedded in its cyclical worldview, which contrasts with the linear perspective of Judeo-Christian traditions. Hindu cosmology teaches that the universe undergoes endless cycles of creation, preservation, and destruction, governed by the three principal deities of the Trimurti: Brahma (the creator), Vishnu (the preserver), and Shiva (the destroyer and transformer). This cycle, known as Samsara, suggests that creation is not a one-time event but a continual process of rebirth and dissolution. Unlike the Abrahamic view of a personal God creating the world for relationship and redemption, Hinduism often presents creation as a manifestation of Brahman, the ultimate, formless, and all-encompassing divine reality. Some Hindu texts, like the Rig Veda, describe creation as arising from a cosmic sacrifice, while others, like the Puranas, speak of Brahma emerging from the navel of Vishnu to create the world. In this sense, creation is seen as divinely orchestrated but impersonal, unfolding according to dharma (cosmic law) and karma (moral causation) rather than an intentional relationship with humanity.

Hinduism also emphasizes that human beings, while part of the divine reality, are caught in the cycle of birth, death, and rebirth (reincarnation) due to their past actions (karma). Unlike the Christian and Jewish view that humans are created once in the image of God, Hindu thought suggests that the soul (Atman) is eternal and takes on different physical forms across multiple lifetimes. The ultimate goal in Hinduism is not salvation through a personal redeemer, but moksha, or liberation from the cycle of rebirth, which is achieved through self-realization and union with Brahman. While stewardship and moral responsibility exist in Hinduism, the emphasis is placed on spiritual enlightenment and transcendence of the material world rather than dominion over it.

Buddhism, which emerged as a reformist movement from Hinduism, takes a different approach to the question of creation and divine purpose. Unlike Christianity, Judaism, and Islam, Buddhism does not focus on a creator deity but rather on the nature of existence and suffering. The Buddha, Siddhartha Gautama, largely avoided discussions about the origin of the universe, considering them irrelevant to the ultimate goal of enlightenment (nirvana). Instead of attributing creation to a divine being, Buddhist teachings emphasize dependent origination (pratītyasamutpāda meaning "dependent origination" or "dependent arising"), the idea that all things arise due to interdependent causes and conditions, rather than a singular divine act. This philosophical stance shifts the focus away from creation and instead teaches that the world, suffering, and human existence are all part of a vast web of causes and effects that are in constant flux.

In Buddhism, human beings are not seen as divinely created in God's image, as in Judeo-Christian belief, but as sentient beings caught in Samsara, the cycle of birth, suffering, death, and rebirth driven by karma. The goal of life is not to seek redemption from sin but to attain liberation from suffering through enlightenment. The Buddhist perspective aligns less with the idea of a fallen creation requiring redemption and more with the notion that suffering is an intrinsic part of existence that must be overcome through wisdom, ethical living, and meditation. While Christianity, Judaism, and Islam emphasize a relationship with God, Buddhism teaches that awakening to the true nature of reality leads to the cessation of suffering. Thus, Buddhism does not emphasize divine creation, a final judgment, or salvation through grace, but rather focuses on personal spiritual development and enlightenment as the path to transcendence.

Hinduism and Buddhism, despite their rich philosophical inquiries and spiritual disciplines, diverge significantly from the biblical worldview regarding God, human purpose, and the ultimate destiny of the soul. From a biblical perspective, these systems are fundamentally flawed because they do not recognize a sovereign, personal God who has intentionally created humanity out of love, nor do they provide a clear and assured path to eternal communion with Him. Instead, they depict a cyclical and impersonal existence that relies entirely on individual effort.

Historically, Hinduism is founded on the belief in samsara, the endless cycle of birth, death, and rebirth. The soul, or *atman*, remains trapped in this cycle until it attains *moksh*a, or liberation, achieved through righteous living, spiritual discipline, and ultimately union with *Brahman*, the impersonal ultimate reality. The caste system, historically endorsed by Hindu texts, enforces a rigid social hierarchy, assigning individuals to predetermined roles and often restricting spiritual access based on birth rather than personal faith or divine calling. This structure leaves little room for divine grace or relational redemption, burdening the individual with the task of self-perfection over countless lifetimes.

Buddhism, which arose in response to Hinduism's ritualism and caste divisions, also embraces the doctrines of rebirth and *karma*. While it completely rejects the idea of a personal creator God, it teaches that suffering is inherent in life and that liberation (*nirvana*) is attained by extinguishing desire and the illusion of the self. However, this liberation does not restore a divine relationship; rather, it signifies an escape from existence itself. In Buddhism, there is no ultimate sovereign being guiding creation or offering reconciliation; salvation relies solely on adherence to the Eightfold Path, with no guarantees—just effort and hope.

From a Christian theological perspective, the lack of a personal, redeeming God—often found in other world religions—leaves humanity in a state of constant spiritual striving without the assurance of relational restoration or eternal hope. Traditions like

Hinduism and Buddhism place the responsibility for salvation on human effort, through mechanisms such as karma, detachment, or ritual, without guaranteeing reconciliation with the divine. In contrast, the God of the Bible is neither distant nor impersonal. He actively engages in human history, extends grace, and initiates redemption through the sacrificial work of Jesus Christ. Christianity reveals a God who does not wait for humanity to reach Him but descends in mercy to rescue, restore, and dwell with His people. This sets Christianity apart not only from Eastern philosophies but also from any worldview that relies on human merit for salvation. In the biblical narrative, God's self-revealed purpose is evident: to draw near, redeem those made in His image, and establish an eternal relationship through covenantal love. In this divine initiative, fulfilled in Christ and sustained by grace, we find our true identity and ultimate destiny—eternal communion with the God who created us, knows us, and desires to be with us forever.

CHAPTER
3

Genesis:
God's Original Plan

In the beginning, God created the heavens and the earth, establishing a world characterized by order, beauty, and harmony. This act of creation, as described in the Book of Genesis, was deemed **"very good"** by God (Genesis 1:31), signifying His wisdom, power, and intentional design. Every component of the universe, from celestial bodies to aquatic life, was meticulously crafted with purpose and positioned within a carefully balanced ecosystem. The vastness of the heavens, the richness of the earth, and the depths of the oceans all testify to God's glory and His sovereign role in orchestrating life. As expressed in Psalm 19:1, **"The heavens declare the glory of God; the skies proclaim the work of his hands."** This original creation was not a consequence of randomness but an embodiment of divine intentionality, illustrating the perfect order and goodness that emanates from the Creator.

At the apex of His creative endeavor, God fashioned humanity in His own image, a remarkable distinction that differentiates human beings from all other forms of creation. The doctrine of the imago Dei, Latin for "image of God," represents one of the most essential theological principles, influencing our understanding of human dignity, purpose, and our relationship to the divine. In contrast to other elements of creation, which were generated according to their kind (Genesis 1:11, 21, 24), humanity was uniquely created in God's likeness, reflecting His attributes, character, and moral nature. This divine imprint endows humanity with intrinsic dignity, moral consciousness, relational capacity, and a sacred purpose within the world.

The assertion found in Genesis 1:27 is among the most profound in all of Scripture: "**So God created mankind in his own image, in the image of God he created them; male and female he created them.**" I aim to delve deeper into this profound proclamation throughout this chapter, as it forms the foundational belief system presented here and in the initial chapters of Genesis. This declaration indicates that every human being, irrespective of status, background, or ability, possesses inherent worth and is capable of mirroring God's character. Unlike animals, which were created to inhabit and populate the earth, human beings were designed to exercise stewardship over creation with wisdom, care, and responsibility. One is not merely another species within the ecosystem but are endowed with a distinct role as image-bearers, representing God's authority on earth.

One is not merely another species ... But are endowed with a distinct role as image-bearers...

In the context of the ancient Near East, the assertion that all humans bear the image of God constitutes a radical proposition. In contemporary pagan cultures, kings were often regarded as divine or as exclusive representatives of their gods, exercising absolute authority over their subjects. In contrast, the book of Genesis introduces a transformative concept: that all human beings, male and female, affluent and impoverished, ruler and servant, are created in the image of God. This revelation elevates human worth beyond societal hierarchies, asserting that all individuals possess equal dignity before their Creator. Unlike the myths of Mesopotamia and Egypt, which frequently depict humanity as an afterthought created to serve the gods, the biblical narrative presents a God who intentionally creates humanity for relationship, purpose, and stewardship over the earth (Genesis 1:28; Psalm 8:5-6).

The implications of being made in the image of God extend beyond mere status or privilege; they address the fundamental essence of humanity. This divine likeness is manifested in various ways. Humanity possesses intellect and reason, reflecting God's infinite wisdom and capacity for thought. Unlike animals, which primarily operate on instinct, human beings possess the ability to reflect, analyze, and engage in moral reasoning. Isaiah 1:18 invites individuals into this divine characteristic, stating, **"Come now, let us reason together, says the Lord."** This intellectual capacity, distinctive to humanity, facilitates the pursuit of knowledge, philosophy, and artistic expression, all of which echo God's creative nature.

Moral awareness constitutes another essential element of the imago Dei. Unlike any other creature, humanity is endowed with an intrinsic understanding of right and wrong, reflecting God's holiness. Romans 2:15 affirms this fact of God's law when it says, **"They show that the requirements of the law are written on their hearts, their consciences also bearing witness, and their thoughts sometimes accusing them and at other times even defending them. inscribed on the human heart."** This enables the discernment of moral truth, even in the absence of direct revelation. This moral capacity is an inherent aspect of what it means to be human, distinguishing individuals from the rest of creation. Similarly, creativity and innovation emerge from the divine image. Just as God is the ultimate Creator, humanity is endowed with the ability to create, build, and cultivate. Whether through art, music, engineering, or storytelling, this creativity reflects God's joy in producing beauty and functionality. Exodus 35:31-32 describes Bezalel, the craftsman of the tabernacle, as being **"filled with the Spirit of God, with wisdom, with understanding, with knowledge and with all kinds of skills."** The capacity to innovate and shape the world is not merely a human characteristic but a reflection of God's own creative power.

Beyond intellect and creativity, humans are inherently relational beings, designed for community and love. The nature of God is understood as existing in eternal relationship—Father, Son, and Holy Spirit in perfect unity as seen in John 17:21-23 **"that all of them may be one, Father, just as you are in me and I am in you. May they also be in us so that the world may believe that you have sent me. ²² I have given them the glory that you gave me, that they may be one as we are one—²³ I in them and you in me—so that they may be brought to complete unity. Then the world will know that you sent me and have loved them even as you have loved me."** Humanity was created for fellowship, companionship, and love. This divine relationship is reflected in human interactions, encompassing marriage, family, friendships, and societal structures. The creation of male and female in the image of God underscores this relational

Humanity was created for fellowship, companionship, and love...

aspect, indicating that humanity was never intended to exist in isolation. Genesis 2:18 affirms this notion when God declares, "**It is not good for the man to be alone.**" Humanity was created for fellowship, companionship, and love, all of which mirror God's own relational nature.

Accompanying this divine image is a sense of responsibility. Humanity was bestowed dominion over creation, a mandate characterized not by exploitation but by stewardship. Genesis 1:28 commands humans to "**fill the earth and subdue it. Rule over the fish in the sea and the birds in the sky and over every living creature that moves on the ground.**" This role as caretakers of the earth reflects God's own sovereignty and provision. Humanity is entrusted with the cultivation and governance of creation, tasked with maintaining its goodness and ensuring it flourishes. Psalm 8:6-8 reinforces this calling: "**You made them rulers over the works of your hands; you put everything under their feet.**" This responsibility is understood not as oppression but as wise and compassionate leadership, reflecting God's own care for His creation.

However, despite being created in God's image, sin entered the world and marred that reflection. The Fall, as described in Genesis 3, introduced corruption, brokenness, and spiritual separation from God. Nevertheless, even in humanity's fallen state, the image of God was not erased; rather, it was distorted. Genesis 9:6, "**Whoever sheds human blood, by humans shall their blood be shed; for in the image of God has God made mankind,**" written after the Fall, continues to affirm that humans are made in God's likeness, underscoring that human dignity remains intact despite the presence of sin. The New Testament presents Jesus Christ as the perfect image of God Colossians 1:15 says "**The Son is the image of the invisible God, the firstborn over all creation.**", sent to restore what was lost. Through faith in Christ, believers experience transformation, being renewed in the image of their Creator. As articulated in 2 Corinthians 3:18, "**And we all, who with unveiled faces contemplate the Lord's glory, are being transformed into his image with ever-increasing glory, which comes from the Lord, who is the Spirit.**"

The fulfillment of the imago Dei will ultimately be realized in eternity, when believers are fully conformed to the image of Christ. 1 John 3:2 states, "**Dear friends, now we are children of God, and what we will be has not yet been made known. But we know that when Christ appears, we shall be like him, for we shall see him as he is.**" In the new creation, redeemed humanity will fully reflect God's image, existing in perfect communion with Him.

The assertion that humanity bears the image of God transcends mere theological doctrine; it constitutes the foundation of human identity, ethics, and purpose. This truth delineates our relationship with God, our obligations toward one another, and our role within the world. It compels us to honor, be a good steward, and restore both creation and human's dignity, recognizing that every individual is a reflection of the divine. Acknowledging this truth informs our perspectives on justice, morality, and the inherent value of life. As Isaiah 43:7 affirms, humanity was "**created for [God's] glory, whom I formed and made.**" Being in the image of God is not merely a characteristic of our nature; it represents a calling to reflect God's love, wisdom, and holiness in the world, ultimately drawing all things back to Him.

God's plan entrusted humanity with dominion over the earth, yet this was not a mandate for exploitation but rather a call to stewardship; a sacred responsibility to care for creation as God's representatives. From the outset, humanity's role was not characterized by unrestrained power but rather by harmonious governance, mirroring the benevolence, wisdom, and justice of the Creator. In Genesis 1:28 that I mentioned earlier, establishes this divine commission, stating, "**God blessed them and said to them, 'Be fruitful and increase in number; fill the earth and subdue it. Rule over ...**'" The Hebrew term for "subdue" (kabash) does not mean destruction or tyranny but rather the ordered cultivation of the earth, ensuring that it flourishes in accordance with God's design. Similarly, the term for "rule" (radah) is frequently employed in Scripture to describe the wise and just reign of a king, indicating that humanity's dominion is to be modeled after God's righteous and caring rule rather than self-serving exploitation.

The placement of Adam and Eve in the Garden of Eden further underscores this principle. Genesis 2:15 states, "**The Lord God took**

the man and put him in the Garden of Eden to work it and take care of it." The terms "work" (abad) and "take care" (shamar) connote cultivation and preservation, indicating that humanity's relationship with creation was intended to be one of service rather than domination. The Garden of Eden symbolizes the ideal relationship between humanity and nature—a space characterized by abundance, beauty, and harmony, where Adam and Eve functioned not as owners but as caretakers of God's creation. This model of stewardship reflects God's own character as a sustainer, reinforcing the notion that creation was intended to be cultivated and not exploited.

Throughout Scripture, the theme of creation care is consistently reiterated. Psalm 24:1 declares, "**The earth is the Lord's, and everything in it, the world, and all who live in it.**" This verse serves as a reminder that, while humanity may be entrusted with authority, ultimate ownership resides with God alone. As stewards, individuals are called to manage creation in a manner that reflects God's glory rather than their own selfish ambitions. The Sabbath laws in Leviticus 25:1-7 further illuminate this principle, as God commanded Israel to allow the land to rest every seventh year, ensuring that creation itself would not be depleted by continuous exploitation. This demonstrates that the land is not merely a resource to be consumed but a sacred trust to be honored and preserved.

The prophetic writings also emphasize God's concern regarding the mistreatment of creation. Hosea 4:1-3 illustrates how Israel's sin and corruption led to environmental degradation: "**There is no faithfulness, no love, no acknowledgment of God in the land… Because of this the land dries up, and all who live in it waste away; the beasts of the field, the birds in the sky, and the fish in the sea are swept away.**" This passage reveals that when humanity fails in its stewardship, creation itself suffers, serving as a poignant reminder that our relationship with the natural world is deeply interwoven with our obedience to God.

In the New Testament, Jesus frequently employed agricultural imagery to convey spiritual truths, thereby reinforcing the notion that creation and divine revelation are intricately interconnected. Matthew 6:26-28 emphasizes God's care for the natural world, asserting, "**Look at the birds of the air; they do not sow or reap or store away in barns, and yet your heavenly Father feeds them… See how the flowers of the field**

grow. They do not labor or spin." If God attends to even the smallest elements of His creation, how much more should humanity, as His image-bearers, engage with the natural world with reverence and care?

The ultimate realization of God's plan for creation will manifest through the restoration of all things in Christ. Romans 8:19-21 articulates how creation itself yearns for liberation from corruption, stating, **"For the creation waits in eager expectation for the children of God to be revealed... The creation itself will be liberated from its bondage to decay and brought into the freedom and glory of the children of God."** This passage affirms that humanity's redemption is profoundly linked to the redemption of the world, underscoring that God's ultimate plan is not the obliteration of creation, but its renewal.

> **God's ultimate plan is not the obliteration of creation, but its renewal.**

The final vision of renewal is the New Heaven and New Earth in Revelation 21:1 unveils a restored world where God resides among His people, fulfilling the original intent of Genesis 1-2. This eschatological hope serves as a reminder to believers that faithful stewardship in the present reflects the reality of God's forthcoming kingdom. The obligation to care for creation transcends mere environmental concern; it is a theological mandate, deeply entrenched in God's design, His commands, and His promise of restoration.

Consequently, the dominion bestowed upon humanity in Genesis 1:28 does not serve as a justification for unrestrained exploitation; rather, it constitutes a sacred calling to embody God's care, wisdom, and justice within the world entrusted to us. To exercise dominion in God's image is to serve creation, not to exploit it; to cultivate, protect, and be good stewards to the earth in a manner that honors the Creator and anticipates the forthcoming renewal of all things.

Beyond their role in creation, humanity's relationship with God represents the foundational basis of their existence. From the very beginning, God designed human beings not merely as caretakers of the earth but as entities intended to engage in intimate fellowship with Him. In Genesis 3:8, **"Then the man and his wife heard the sound of the Lord God as he was walking in the garden in the cool of the day"** in this verse there is a poignant depiction of God's presence in the Garden of Eden, as He walked among Adam and Eve in the cool of the day. This passage illustrates a profound and personal communion, sharply contrasting with subsequent generations who would seek God from a distance. Adam and Eve experienced Him directly, engaging with His presence in a manner unclouded by sin, separation, or fear. This divine fellowship was intended to be the source of their joy, wisdom, and ultimate fulfillment, for in God alone resides life that is abundant and complete.

However, this relationship was characterized not by coercion but by free will; a reality that underscores the understanding of God's love and trust. True love cannot exist without choice; therefore, God did not create humanity as mere robots programmed for obedience but as moral agents capable of freely choosing Him. This capacity for voluntary devotion lies at the core of God's desire for humanity, as compelled love is not love at all. Just as God exists in relational unity, Father, Son, and Holy Spirit, humanity was designed to reflect that love through voluntary worship and obedience.

Jesus affirmed this foundational truth when He stated, "**Love the Lord your God with all your heart and with all your soul and with all your mind**" in Matthew 22:37. This command, echoing the Shema, a Hebrew word meaning "**hear**" or "**listen**", in Deuteronomy 6:5, encapsulates the very purpose for which humanity was created: to love, know, and serve God with the entirety of their being. In the Garden of Eden, Adam and Eve were intended to exist in complete and joyful communion with their Creator, reflecting His character in their lives and stewarding the world as co-regents under His sovereign rule.

The significance of this original divine fellowship cannot be overstated. Humanity was not merely placed in the Garden as tenants or laborers but as beloved children in the presence of their Creator. Psalm 16:11 encapsulates this truth eloquently, stating, "**You make known to me the path of life; you will fill me with joy in your presence, with eternal pleasures at your right hand.**" The nearness of God constituted the very source of their joy and peace, for their identity and purpose were deeply rooted in Him. Unlike the rest of creation, which operated according to instinct and natural law, human beings were uniquely designed to think, love, and engage in personal relationships with God, thereby reflecting His image in their actions, relationships, and stewardship of the earth.

However, this divine fellowship also encompassed moral responsibility. The presence of the Tree of the Knowledge of Good and Evil in the Garden was not a trap but a necessary aspect of human free will. Genesis 2:16-17 records God's command to Adam: **"You are free to eat from any tree in the garden; but you must not eat from the tree of the knowledge of good and evil, for when you eat from it you will certainly die."** This instruction was not arbitrary but constituted a test of trust and love. To obey God's word was to affirm that His wisdom was perfect, His authority just, and His love sufficient. The choice to follow or reject God was inherently embedded in humanity's design; only through the act of freely choosing God could love be deemed genuine.

In a tragic turn, Adam and Eve's decision to heed the serpent rather than God shattered this perfect communion. Genesis 3:23-24, **"So the LORD God banished him from the Garden of Eden to work the ground from which he had been taken. ²⁴ After he drove the man out, he placed on the east side of the Garden of Eden cherubim and a flaming sword flashing back and forth to guard the way to the tree of life."**, this verse describes their expulsion from the Garden, a consequence not of cruelty but of justice and grace, for a sinful humanity could no longer dwell in the holy presence of God. The exile from Eden represented more than a physical removal; it signified a spiritual rupture, a separation that humanity would endure for generations to come. Yet, even amid this moment of judgment, God's desire for relationship with His people remained unwavering. The entire biblical narrative, from Genesis to Revelation, unfolds as the story of God restoring what was lost, culminating in the work of Jesus Christ, the perfect mediator who bridges the gap between fallen humanity and a holy God.

Although Adam and Eve were expelled from the Garden of Eden, the presence of God has persisted in the world. Throughout history, He has consistently engaged with His people, inviting them to return to Him. He communicated with Abraham, wrestled with Jacob, revealed His laws to Moses, and dwelled among the Israelites in the Tabernacle and later in the Temple. However, these instances were merely foreshadowing of the ultimate restoration to come. The complete reconciliation between God and humanity was achieved in Jesus Christ, who is referred to in John 1:14 as **"the Word [who] became flesh**

and made his dwelling among us." Through Christ, God once again interacted with His people, restoring the divine fellowship lost in Eden.

The invitation to walk with God remains accessible to all who seek Him. James 4:8 asserts, "**Come near to God and he will come near to you.**" The call to return to intimacy with the Creator is fundamental to the gospel message, as Christ's atonement has dismantled the barriers of sin. Contemporary believers are not merely forgiven but are reconciled, restored, and invited into a relationship that is even deeper than that experienced in Eden, for through the Holy Spirit, God resides within His people. 1 Corinthians 3:16 reinforces this notion, stating, "**Don't you know that you yourselves are God's temple and that God's Spirit dwells in your midst?**"

> The call to return to intimacy with the Creator is fundamental to the gospel message...

Ultimately, the complete restoration of this divine fellowship remains a future promise. The vision of the New Heaven and New Earth in Revelation 21:3 proclaims, "**Look! God's dwelling place is now among the people, and he will dwell with them. They will be his people, and God himself will be with them and be their God.**" What was lost in Eden will be fully restored, and humanity will once again walk with God in eternal joy.

The narrative of Adam and Eve in the Garden functions as both a cautionary tale and a foundational promise within the theological discourse. It clarifies the consequences of disobedience while simultaneously revealing the profound nature of the divine desire for intimacy with creation. The endowment of free will to humanity should not be construed as a deficiency in the divine design but rather as a fundamental component of authentic love and trust. The imperative to love God with all one's heart, soul, and mind remains the central tenet of human existence. Through faith in Christ, this original design is not only restored but also brought to its fullest realization, as believers are transformed into the likeness of the Son, thereby re-entering the presence of their Creator.

The purpose assigned to humanity extends significantly beyond mere survival; it constitutes a divine calling to multiply, populate the earth, and exercise dominion over it. The command articulated in Genesis 1:28 is not solely an exhortation for biological reproduction but a mandate for cultural, intellectual, and societal advancement under divine authority. Humanity is tasked not only with populating the earth but also with cultivating, shaping, and stewarding it, thereby creating societies that reflect the order, wisdom, and righteousness of their Creator. Each domain of human life—family, knowledge, governance, industry, and creativity—should operate in harmony with God's original design, ensuring that the world flourishes as a manifestation of divine goodness.

This divine commission underscores that civilization itself is integral to the divine plan. Humanity was not intended to exist in primitive isolation but to cultivate art, science, philosophy, and governance as expressions of the divine image inherent within them. The Cultural Mandate, as it is frequently termed, implies that humanity is to actualize the potential of creation by establishing societies that mirror the harmony and justice of the divine kingdom. The act of subduing the earth is not an exercise in oppression but rather an expression of responsible dominion, shaping the world in accordance with divine wisdom and creative order. This responsibility is further emphasized in Genesis 2:15, which states, **"The Lord God took the man and put him in the Garden of Eden to work it and take care of it."** This verse accentuates humanity's cooperative role in sustaining and advancing creation, tending to it as a gardener tends to his garden—not through exploitation but through nurturing, ensuring that it may thrive.

The biblical perspective on human purpose is multifaceted, encompassing spiritual, relational, and societal dimensions. The family unit, considered the foundational element of society, was instituted by God, and the formation of communities is regarded as an extension of divine order. Proverbs 11:10-11 affirms the societal impact of righteousness, stating, **"When the righteous prosper, the city rejoices; when the wicked perish, there are shouts of joy. Through the blessing of the upright a city is exalted, but by the mouth of the wicked it is destroyed."** This verse underscores how godly living and justice sustain the stability and prosperity of communities, reinforcing the notion that civilization flourishes when aligned with divine moral law.

As societies developed, the pursuit of knowledge, advancements in industry, and the establishment of governance became essential aspects of God's purpose for humanity. The pursuit of wisdom and understanding is repeatedly emphasized in Scripture as a means of glorifying God. Proverbs 4:7 asserts, **"The beginning of wisdom is this: Get wisdom. Though it cost all you have, get understanding."** Similarly, Exodus 31:2-5 describes how God endowed Bezalel with the Spirit of God, granting him skill, ability, and knowledge in various crafts; demonstrating that human creativity and innovation are gifts from the Creator. The construction of civilizations, technological advancement, and the establishment of just laws were intended to be pursuits intertwined with divine purpose, serving as acts of worship that reflect His divine nature through human ingenuity and moral governance.

Conversely, Scripture cautions that when human civilization diverges from God, disorder and corruption ensue. The narrative of the Tower of Babel in Genesis 11:1-9 illustrates the consequences of human ambition detached from divine purpose. Rather than laboring for God's glory, humanity sought self-exaltation, resulting in confusion and division. This account highlights the perils of cultural and technological progress that lacks submission to God's authority. Absent His guidance, human civilization descends into decay, oppression, and self-destruction, a theme that recurs throughout biblical history. Psalm 127:1 encapsulates this truth: **"Unless the Lord builds the house, the builders labor in vain."**

Despite humanity's propensity for the misuse of power and the distortion of divine design, the ultimate realization of the Cultural Mandate is found in Jesus Christ. He came not only to redeem individuals but also to restore all of creation. Colossians 1:16-17 asserts, **"For in him all things were created: things in heaven and on earth, visible and invisible, whether thrones or powers or rulers or authorities; all things have been created through him and for him. He is before all things, and in him all things hold together."** This passage explains that Jesus serves as the source, sustainer, and purpose of all creation; through His redemptive work, the original design of God's kingdom is being restored. The vision of the New Heaven and New Earth articulated in Revelation 21:1-4 further substantiates that God's plan for creation transcends individual salvation. The restored world will manifest as a perfected civilization characterized by righteousness, wherein humanity fulfills its ultimate purpose in communion with God. The New Jerusalem, as depicted in Revelation 21:2, is not merely a return to Eden but represents a glorified, redeemed society. This illustrates that God's design for human flourishing has always encompassed a transformed world. One instilled with His glory and order.

Consequently, the divine calling bestowed upon humanity in Genesis 1:28 is not an obsolete relic but rather an ongoing commission that attains its fullest expression in Christ. The flourishing of civilization, when aligned with God's righteousness and wisdom, serves as a testament to His sovereign purpose. Human beings are summoned not merely to exist, but to create, govern, and promote, ensuring that all dimensions of life reflect the goodness and justice of God's kingdom.

God's original plan, as articulated in Genesis, envisioned a world replete with order, beauty, and harmony, with humanity occupying a central role in governing and cultivating creation under His divine authority. The universe is not a result of chance; **The universe is not** instead, it has been intentionally crafted by God, **a result of chance;** with every element carefully arranged to showcase **instead, it has** His wisdom and sovereignty. Humanity was **been intentionally** not merely another creation among many; they **crafted by God...** were uniquely fashioned in the image of God, designated to govern the earth as His representatives. The opening chapters of Genesis portray a world in which humanity is to exist in communion with their Creator, stewarding creation in perfect alignment with His will.

The concept of being created in the image of God suggests that individuals are not merely passive observers of creation; rather, they are active participants in embodying God's righteousness, love, and wisdom across all dimensions of life. Genesis 1:27 articulates this notion: **"So God created mankind in his own image, in the image of God he created them; male and female he created them."** Distinct from all other facets of creation, humanity possesses the capacity for moral reasoning, relational depth, creativity, and spiritual communion with the Divine. This imago Dei represents not merely a designation but a profound calling, but an invitation to reflect God's character and to govern creation with wisdom. Humanity's stewardship of the earth is intended to be characterized by care, and creativity, rather than control or reckless exploitation, thus ensuring that the earth flourishes in accordance with God's purpose. Genesis 2:15 further emphasizes this role: "**The Lord God took the man and put him in the Garden of Eden to work it and take care of it.**" From the inception of creation, humanity was designed to be co-laborers with God, tending to the world not for selfish gain but as an expression of worship and obedience.

Moreover, the ultimate purpose of humanity transcends mere survival or existence; it encompasses the pursuit of an intimate relationship with the Creator, through which individuals discover their joy, purpose, and identity. Isaiah 43:7 reinforces this divine calling, affirming, "**Everyone who is called by my name, whom I created for my glory, whom I formed and made.**" Humanity is not an afterthought in the divine narrative of creation but rather the apex expression of God's love and intention. God did not create humanity out of necessity or loneliness, but rather from an abundance of love, desiring to share His presence, wisdom, and joy with them.

This divine relationship is exemplified in the Garden of Eden, where Adam and Eve engaged in direct communion with God. Genesis 3:8 illustrates that God walked in the garden during the cool of the day, signifying that His presence among humanity was intended to be personal and immediate rather than distant or abstract. In contrast to later generations who would seek God from afar, Adam and Eve experienced Him as a loving Father, existing in a state of unbroken fellowship with their Creator. This relationship constituted the foundation of their wisdom, fulfillment, and ultimate purpose. Importantly, it was characterized by free will rather than coercion, a critical component of love and trust. Humanity was designed to choose God, walk in obedience, and reflect His character within the world.

The perfection of creation extended beyond the natural world; it was meant to reflect divine order in every aspect of human existence. Humanity was entrusted with a mandate to be fruitful, expand across the earth, and exercise stewardship over all living things. This charge went beyond simple biological growth—it was a call to spread God's glory throughout the world. People were given the responsibility of building communities, advancing knowledge, shaping culture, and governing with justice and wisdom, ensuring that every dimension of life aligned with the divine design for creation. The flourishing of human civilization was intended to align with God's moral law, manifesting the heavenly kingdom on earth. However, the advent of sin in Genesis 3 disrupted this divine order. The intimate relationship between God and humanity was fractured, resulting in a distortion of creation's purpose due to human rebellion. Rather than exercising righteous dominion, individuals sought selfish power; instead of wise stewardship, they engaged in exploitation and corruption. Nevertheless, despite this tragic fall, humanity's original purpose was not obliterated—only marred. The plan of redemption was initiated, with God actively working throughout history to restore what was lost.

The ultimate realization of God's original design is epitomized in Jesus Christ, who came not only to redeem individuals but also to restore the entirety of creation. Colossians 1:16-17 states, **"For in him all things were created: things in heaven and on earth, visible and invisible, whether thrones or powers or rulers or authorities; all things have been created through him and for him. He is before all things, and in him all things hold together."** Jesus, regarded as the perfect image of God (Hebrews 1:3), arrived to restore the divine relationship between humanity and their Creator, fostering reconciliation and renewal in a fractured world. Through His life, death, and resurrection, He has established a pathway for humanity to return to their original purpose, inviting individuals back into communion with God and the realization of their divine calling.

This restoration extends beyond the spiritual realm, encompassing the entire universe. The New Heaven and New Earth signify the fulfillment of God's original design, where humanity will be fully restored to perfect harmony with their Creator. The vision of the New Jerusalem transcends a mere return to Eden; it depicts a glorified, eternal abode where God's people will reside in His presence, fully reinstated to their intended purpose. Consequently, the Genesis account should be interpreted not merely as a narrative of human origins but as the blueprint for God's eternal plan. Humanity was created for God's glory, designed to reflect His nature, and commissioned to steward His creation in righteousness. Although sin temporarily disrupted this divine purpose, it did not ultimately thwart it; through Christ, all things will be made new, and the original beauty, order, and harmony of creation will be fully restored. From the outset, His purpose was to establish a

> **Although sin temporarily disrupted this divine purpose, it did not ultimately thwart it...**

realm characterized by harmony, order, and communion, wherein humanity would reside in His presence and manifest His glory in all facets of existence. The perfection of Eden was not merely a transient state but rather a paradigm for eternity, offering insight into the intended relationship between God and His creation. Despite the intrusion of sin, which disrupted this divine order, God did not forsake His original purpose. Instead, He initiated a redemptive plan aimed at restoring what was lost and achieving an even greater fulfillment through Christ.

Although the Fall introduced pain and separation, God's immutable character and faithfulness ensured that sin would not prevail. His redemptive mission, has meticulously been woven throughout the entire biblical narrative, and points toward a future reality in which His kingdom is fully restored. Beginning with the first prophecy of redemption in Genesis 3:15—where God proclaims that the offspring of the woman will crush the serpent's head. Scripture chronicles a God who persistently seeks His people. The entirety of the Old Testament sacrificial system, the prophetic assurances of restoration, and the advent of the Messiah collectively illustrate a God actively engaged in redeeming creation from the consequences of sin.

This redemptive plan ultimately culminates in Jesus Christ, who came not only to save individuals but also to restore the entire created order. Colossians 1:19-20 emphasizes this universal redemption, stating, **"For God was pleased to have all his fullness dwell in him, and through him to reconcile to himself all things, whether things on earth or things in heaven, by making peace through his blood, shed on the cross."** Christ's sacrificial work was not merely a means of personal salvation; rather, it marked the inception of the renewal of all things. His resurrection serves as the firstfruits of this new creation, providing assurance that sin and death will ultimately be eradicated.

The Book of Revelation articulates a compelling vision of ultimate restoration, wherein God's eternal purpose is fully realized. One sees in the final two chapters of the book of Revelation a mirroring of the original paradise of Eden, affirming that God's ultimate intention for humanity remains unchanged; to dwell with Him in eternal joy and communion. The barriers of sin that previously separated God from His people will be entirely removed, and His presence will once again define the essence of existence.

In the Old Testament we see a contrast between the creation story and the original design of Genesis. Mankind in the form of the Jews sort and obtained on a limited bases a temporary manifestation of God's presence in the Tabernacle during Israel's wilderness journey (Exodus 25:8) or the Temple in Jerusalem. Rather, God Himself has chosen to implement a temporary design as He shifted to His dwelling place to His people. However, this in no way should be considered the final habitat because does not deal a complete destruction of sin. This placeholder is just a way for God to keep us close until a new creation is complete and we are will inhabit this new creation devoid of sin, suffering, and decay. This eternal state represents not merely a return to Eden but a glorified reality in which the entire universe is renewed under Christ's reign. 2 Peter 3:13 asserts, **"But in keeping with his promise we are looking forward to a new heaven and a new earth, where righteousness dwells."**

This promise of renewal underscores the steadfastness of God's love for His people. Despite human rebellion, He remains committed to restoring what was lost, thereby ensuring that His creation ultimately fulfills its original purpose. The Apostle Paul echoes this hope in Romans 8:21, asserting that **"the creation itself will be liberated from its bondage to decay and brought into the freedom and glory of the children of God."** This passage explains that redemption is not solely personal but also universal, as all of creation anticipates the day of complete restoration.

The overarching narrative of Scripture—encompassing creation, fall, redemption, and ultimate restoration—illustrates a God who is sovereign over history, faithful to His promises, and steadfast in His love. What began in Genesis with the paradise of Eden culminates in Revelation with the eternal communion of God among His people. The restoration of all things is not merely a theological aspiration but a guaranteed reality that believers anticipate with eagerness. As articulated in 1 Corinthians 2:9, **"What no eye has seen, what no ear has heard, and what no human mind has conceived—the things God has prepared for those who love him,"** this passage assures us of a glorious future.

Consequently, God's ultimate intention for humanity remains unchanged. He created individuals for His glory, designed them for fellowship with Him, and, despite the disruption caused by sin, provided a means for restoration through Christ. The eventual reality of God's presence dwelling with His people not only fulfills His original plan but also serves as a testament to His unwavering faithfulness. The narrative of redemption reassures us that the brokenness of this world is not the conclusion; rather, God is actively restoring all things, leading to an eternal kingdom characterized by righteousness, joy, and communion with Him that will endure forever.

CHAPTER
4

When Humanity Disrupts the Divine Plan:
What Follows?

The previous chapters examined humanity's relationship with the divine and the purpose behind human creation. They explored the original divine plan and its theological implications as interpreted by the five major world religions. Now, we must consider the consequences of humanity's disruption of that plan and its profound effects on existence. This rupture between humanity and its divine purpose initiates a cycle of disorder, suffering, and alienation. As a result of disobedience, the harmonious order intended by the Creator is shattered, leading to a world marred by sin and marked by both spiritual and physical separation from God.

As with many facets of existence, actions are accompanied by consequences. In the beginning, God created humanity in His own image and placed them in the Garden of Eden to cultivate and care for it. He issued a directive in Genesis 2:17, stating, "**but you must not eat from the tree of the knowledge of good and evil, for when you eat from it you will certainly die.**" This command was unequivocal: they were to abstain from consuming the fruit of a single tree, specifically, "**the tree of knowledge of good and evil.**" The rationale underlying this command has been the subject of extensive theological inquiry and historical analysis, aimed at expounding its purpose and implications.

From a theological perspective, the prohibition against eating from the tree can be interpreted as a test of obedience and trust. By

By refraining from the fruit, Adam and Eve would demonstrate their willingness to submit to God's authority...

refraining from the fruit, Adam and Eve would demonstrate their willingness to submit to God's authority and acknowledge His sovereignty. This act of obedience was pivotal for maintaining the intended harmony between humanity and the divine. It is plausible that God was delineating the boundary between divine knowledge and human limitation. By instructing them to abstain, God emphasized that certain forms of knowledge, particularly the moral discernment necessary to define good and evil, were reserved for His divine prerogative. Their ensuing disobedience resulted in an experiential understanding of evil, culminating in shame and estrangement from God, as illustrated in Genesis 3:7-8. From a historical perspective, scholars have provided various interpretations of this command. Some argue that the prohibition was designed to preserve human innocence and mitigate the burdens associated with moral discernment. Others contend that the command functioned as a means to foster free will, thereby allowing humans to choose obedience and engage in a genuine relationship with God.

The command to abstain from the tree of the knowledge of good and evil serves as a foundational element in the relationship between God and humanity, emphasizing obedience, trust, and the acknowledgment of divine sovereignty. Its transgression resulted in profound consequences, altering the trajectory of human history and transforming the nature of human-divine interaction. Genesis 3:1-3 states: "**Now the serpent was more crafty than any of the wild animals the Lord God had made. He said to the woman, 'Did God really say, 'You must not eat from any tree in the garden'? The woman replied, 'We may eat fruit from the trees in the garden, but God did say, 'You must not eat fruit from the tree that is in the middle of the garden, and you must not touch it, or you will die.' The serpent countered, 'You will not certainly die... For God knows that when you eat from it your eyes will be opened, and you will be like God, knowing good and evil.'**"

In biblical and mythological traditions, the serpent embodies dual symbolism, functioning both as a literal snake and as a representation of Satan or a malevolent force. In the Book of Genesis, the serpent appears as a cunning creature that engages Eve in conversation, tempting her to partake of the Tree of Knowledge. At first glance, it appears to be an ordinary animal, part of God's creation. However, following its deception of Eve, the serpent is cursed to crawl on its belly and consume dust, suggesting that it was once something more than merely a snake.

Subsequent biblical texts, such as Revelation 12:9, explicitly identify the serpent with Satan, referring to him as "**The great dragon was hurled down—that ancient serpent called the devil, or Satan, who leads the whole world astray. He was hurled to the earth, and his angels with him.**" This connection implies that Satan either utilized the serpent as a vessel or that the serpent itself serves as a symbolic representation of deception and rebellion against God.

Beyond the biblical narrative, serpent symbolism is prevalent in various ancient cultures, often representing concepts such as wisdom, chaos, or duality. In Mesopotamian and Canaanite traditions, serpents were frequently associated with divine beings or tricksters, thereby reinforcing the biblical depiction of the serpent as a deceiver. Conversely, other traditions, such as Hinduism, regard serpents as powerful entities that are not inherently malevolent.

The serpent's role in the fall of humanity further solidifies its association with Satan. By leading Eve and Adam into disobedience, it acts as the catalyst for sin and suffering, mirroring Satan's role as the ultimate adversary. The prophecy in Genesis, which articulates enmity between the serpent and the "seed of the woman," is often interpreted as a foreshadowing of Christ's eventual triumph over sin and evil.

Consequently, the serpent serves as both a physical entity and a profound symbol of evil and deception. This dual identity enables it to function as both an earthly and spiritual antagonist within the biblical narrative, significantly shaping its enduring importance in religious discourse. Eve's fascination with the serpent's words in Genesis 3 marks a critical juncture in the fall of humanity. Captivated by the serpent's reasoning, she engaged in a dialogue that ultimately led to a transformative decision. Had she sought divine counsel regarding this encounter, the trajectory of human history might have been altered. However, she did not. Instead, she permitted the serpent's words to resonate in her consciousness, thus influencing her perspective and judgment.

This shift in perspective is evident in Genesis 3:6-7, where Eve's perception of the forbidden fruit undergoes a transformation. The passage states, **"When the woman saw that the fruit of the tree was good for food and pleasing to the eye, and also desirable for gaining wisdom, she took some and ate it. She also gave some to her husband, who was with her, and he ate it. Then the eyes of both of them were opened, and they realized they were naked; so they sewed fig leaves together and made coverings for themselves."**

Prior to this moment, Eve had likely passed by the tree numerous times without yielding to temptation. However, following her encounter with the serpent, her perception of the tree was transformed. Was her decision motivated by ambition, a desire for wisdom, or merely the allure of the fruit itself? The text suggests a confluence of all three—she recognized that it was good for food, aesthetically pleasing, and capable of imparting knowledge. This newfound desire compelled her to take and consume the fruit, an act that signified the initial step in humanity's decline.

Although Eve was the first to succumb to the serpent's deception, Adam was by no means an innocent bystander. The text specifies that Adam was present with her when she consumed the fruit. This raises significant questions: Had he witnessed the entire exchange between Eve and the serpent? If so, why did he not intervene? Even if he arrived later, he still opted to participate in the same act of disobedience, fully aware of God's command. His silence and subsequent decision to eat the fruit indicate a failure of leadership and discernment, rendering him equally culpable for their collective transgression.

Another profound consequence of this event is the sudden awareness of their nakedness. The knowledge they acquired did not yield the enlightenment they may have anticipated; rather, it resulted in an abrupt recognition of their vulnerability and shame. Their initial instinct was to cover themselves with fig leaves, an act that symbolized the estrangement that now existed between them and God. The innocence they once possessed was forfeited, supplanted by guilt and fear.

This passage not only underscores the deceptive nature of sin but also illuminates the broader issue of humanity's propensity to rely on its own judgment rather than seeking divine wisdom. The fall was not merely about consuming a piece of fruit; it represented a shift in allegiance—preferring the words of the serpent over the word of God. In that moment, both Eve and Adam chose independence over obedience, and the ramifications of that decision resonate throughout history.

> The fall was not merely about consuming a piece of fruit; it represented a shift in allegiance...

Following the pivotal encounter with the serpent, the narrative assumes a somber tone as God enters the scene, traversing the garden in the cool of the day. Genesis 3:8-10 delineates the reaction of Adam and Eve upon hearing the sound of the Lord approaching. Instead of eagerly welcoming His presence, as they may have done previously, they now respond with fear and shame, concealing themselves among the trees. The Lord, fully aware of the events that have transpired, calls out, **"Where are you?"**—Not out of ignorance regarding their whereabouts, but as an invitation for them to confront their predicament. Adam's response reveals the profound nature of their transformation: **"I heard you in the garden, and I was afraid because I was naked; so I hid."**

This moment is deeply significant. Adam and Eve, who once stood before God in a state of innocence, now experience fear for the first time. Their relationship with Him has altered, not due to any withdrawal on God's part, but because their perception of Him has fundamentally changed. The knowledge they sought, which they believed would elevate their status, has instead burdened them with guilt, preventing them from approaching their Creator with confidence.

With their disobedience laid bare, God pronounces the consequences of their actions. To Eve, He declares that childbearing will be characterized by pain, and that her relationship with her husband will become one of tension, marked by intertwined desires and subjugation. To Adam, the ground itself is cursed as a result of his transgression. The earth will no longer yield its bounty freely; rather, he will labor under hardship, contending with thorns and thistles to secure sustenance for his survival. The reality of mortality is also articulated: **"For dust you are, and to dust you will return."** This pronouncement starkly contrasts their original existence, where life was sustained effortlessly in communion with God. Henceforth, their days will be defined by toil and, ultimately, death. Nevertheless, even amidst this moment of judgment, there is an indication of divine grace. The Lord God, in an act of mercy, garments Adam and Eve with skins. This gesture is significant—it represents the first shedding of blood to cover human shame, foreshadowing the sacrificial system that would later be instituted as a means of atonement. Additionally, it underscores God's continued care for them, even as He enforces the consequences of their sin.

The final pronouncement determines their fate: they must be prohibited from consuming from the Tree of Life and living eternally in their fallen state. While this may appear to be a severe punishment, their expulsion from the garden serves as an act of protection. To exist perpetually in sin and separation from God would constitute a far greater curse. Consequently, the Lord banishes them, sending them into the world beyond the garden, where they are compelled to toil upon the very ground from which they were formed. This moment signifies a pivotal juncture in human history. The perfect harmony between God and humanity has been disrupted, and the ramifications of this rupture will resonate through subsequent generations. Nevertheless, even as they depart from Eden, a semblance of hope persists. The promise inherent in God's declaration—the enmity between the serpent and the seed of the woman—suggests a future redemption. Although sin has entered the world, it will not ultimately prevail.

Following their expulsion, God stationed cherubim on the eastern side of the Garden of Eden, along with a flaming sword that flashed back and forth to guard the pathway to the Tree of Life. This reference to cherubim warrants further exploration, as their significance as divinely fashioned beings and their role within the heavenly realm is profound. An insightful resource on the subject of angels is Terry Law's *The Truth about Angels*, which I highly recommend.

Cherubim occupy a unique and significant position in biblical theology, symbolizing both the holiness of God and His divine presence. Throughout Scripture, they emerge in critical moments of revelation, acting as guardians of sacred spaces, attendants at God's throne, and embodiments of divine worship. Their presence highlights both the majesty of God and the separation that sin engenders between humanity and Him. From the Garden of Eden to the Tabernacle, from the prophetic visions of Ezekiel to the throne room of God in Revelation, cherubim serve as a powerful representation of God's holiness, sovereignty, and redemptive plan.

This act signified the profound separation between fallen humanity and the divine presence, underscoring that sin established an insurmountable barrier between humankind and God. This theme of separation and divine guardianship persisted in the construction of the Tabernacle, wherein cherubim were prominently incorporated. In Exodus 25:18-22, God instructed Moses to create the Ark of the Covenant adorned with two cherubim of hammered gold overshadowing the Mercy Seat. Their wings were to be outstretched over the ark, facing one another, thereby forming the locus of God's presence and the point of communion with Moses. This sacred space between the cherubim became the focal point for divine communication and atonement. The cherubim symbolized God's enthronement and the reality that His presence was both magnificent and inaccessible to sinful humanity absent mediation.

Moreover, cherubim were intricately woven into the veil that demarcated the Holy Place from the Most Holy Place within the Tabernacle. Exodus 26:31 articulates this elaborate design: "**Make a curtain of blue, purple, and scarlet yarn and finely twisted linen, with cherubim woven into it by a skilled worker.**" This curtain reinforced the concept that the presence of God was not to be approached casually and that a mediator was requisite for entering His holiness. Only the high priest, once annually on the Day of Atonement, could traverse this veil to intercede on behalf of the people.

The presence of cherubim extended beyond the Tabernacle to the edifice of Solomon's Temple. In 1 Kings 6:23-28, Solomon commissioned the creation of two colossal cherubim fashioned from olive wood and gilded in gold, each standing fifteen feet tall with an outstretched wingspan of the same dimensions. These cherubim were situated in the inner sanctuary, overshadowing the Ark of the Covenant, thereby reinforcing their role as divine attendants to God's presence. This grand representation elevated their symbolic function, highlighting the awe-inspiring nature of God's dwelling on earth.

The prophetic visions of Ezekiel provide one of the most striking representations of cherubim. In Ezekiel 1:4-14, the prophet describes a vision of four living creatures, each possessing four faces—those of a man, a lion, an ox, and an eagle—symbolizing intelligence, strength, service, and majesty. These entities move in unison, support the throne of God, and are enveloped in fire and lightning, highlighting their supernatural essence. Subsequently, in Ezekiel 10:15, the prophet explicitly identifies these beings as cherubim: "**Then the cherubim rose upward. These were the living creatures I had seen by the Kebar River.**" Ezekiel's vision portrays the cherubim as potent, enigmatic beings that function as divine agents of God's will.

The apex of biblical references to cherubim occurs in Revelation 4:6-8, where the Apostle John describes the throne room of God. Surrounding the throne, four living creatures engage in continuous worship, proclaiming, "**Holy, holy, holy is the Lord God Almighty, who was, and is, and is to come.**" Their six wings and multitude of eyes exemplify their unceasing vigilance and eternal adoration of the Almighty. This portrayal solidifies their role not merely as guardians but as active participants in the divine worship of heaven.

The climactic significance of the cherubim within the biblical narrative is manifest at the crucifixion of Jesus Christ.

The climactic significance of the cherubim within the biblical narrative is manifest at the crucifixion of Jesus Christ. Upon Christ's death, Matthew 27:51 records that the veil of the Temple, adorned with the imagery of cherubim, was torn in two from top to bottom. This dramatic occurrence signified the removal of the separation between God and humanity through Christ's atoning sacrifice. Hebrews 10:19-20 elucidates, "**Therefore, brothers and sisters, since we have confidence to enter the Most Holy Place by the blood of Jesus, by a new and living way opened for us through the curtain, that is, his body...**" Consequently, cherubim were no longer necessary to guard the divine presence from sinful humanity, for through Christ, believers were granted direct access to God.

The cherubim, once emblematic of separation, now signify the ultimate reconciliation between God and His people. As a result of Christ's atonement, the pathway into God's presence has been opened, transforming what was once safeguarded by celestial beings into a reality accessible to all who place their trust in Him. This transformation from guardians of exclusion to symbols of redemption illustrates the unfolding narrative of God's grace and His longing to dwell with His people for eternity.

The act of disobedience in the Garden of Eden was the beginning of sin in the world, resulting in physical death becoming the inevitable consequence for all humanity, as all have sinned and fallen short of the glory of God. As Scripture asserts, "There is no one righteous, not even one." The repercussions of this original sin are evident throughout human history, manifesting in the destructive tendencies of mankind, which include acts of the flesh such as sexual immorality, idolatry, hatred, jealousy, rage, selfish ambition, and various forms of corruption. Those who persist in such behaviors are cautioned that they shall not inherit the kingdom of God.

Nevertheless, even in the midst of this spiritual turmoil and moral decay, God, in His mercy, has provided a pathway to redemption. Romans 6:23 informs **"For the wages of sin is death, but the gift of God is eternal life in Christ Jesus our Lord."** Although sin creates a chasm between humanity and God, His faithfulness remains steadfast as written in 1 John 1:8, **"If we claim to be without sin, we deceive ourselves and the truth is not in us. ⁹ If we confess our sins, he is faithful and just and will forgive us our sins and purify us from all unrighteousness."** This promise of redemption reveals the essence of God's character, who desires not destruction but restoration, calling His people back into a reconciled relationship with Him.

Therefore, believers are encouraged to approach the throne of grace with confidence, trusting that in their time of need, they will receive mercy. As stated in 1 John 5:4, **"For everyone born of God overcomes the world. This is the victory that has overcome the world, even our faith."** Within the overarching narrative of Scripture, one can observe both the profound effects of human rebellion and the persistent pursuit of God to redeem His creation. Throughout history, God's responses to sin have been characterized by both justice and mercy, reflecting His intention not for condemnation, but for reconciliation.

God's justice necessitates that sin be addressed, as He is inherently holy and righteous. Nevertheless, His mercy extends forgiveness and restoration to those who demonstrate repentance. Psalms 103:8 articulates this balance with eloquence: **"The Lord is compassionate and gracious, slow to anger, abounding in love. He will not always** accuse, nor will He harbor His anger forever; He does not treat us as our sins deserve or repay us according to our iniquities." This passage clarifies that while God embodies justice, His nature is also one of abundant grace, thereby offering hope to the repentant.

This theme is further reinforced in the proclamations of the prophet Isaiah, who expresses God's willingness to heal and guide those who return to Him in Isaiah 57:18, "**I have seen their ways, but I will heal them; I will guide them and restore comfort to Israel's mourners, creating praise on their lips. Peace, peace, to those far and near,**" says the Lord, "**And I will heal them.**" However, this same passage cautions that the wicked, akin to a restless sea, will experience no peace, thereby highlighting the consequences of unrepentant rebellion. God's justice is inescapable; however, His mercy remains perpetually accessible to those who seek Him.

The historical narrative of Israel exemplifies this dynamic interplay between divine justice and mercy. The book of Hosea illustrates Israel's unfaithfulness through the metaphor of the prophet's marriage to Gomer, symbolizing God's steadfast love for His wayward people. Despite their spiritual infidelity, God remains unwavering in His commitment to restoration as found in Hosea 2:19-20, "**I will betroth you to me forever; I will betroth you in righteousness and justice, in love and compassion. [20] I will betroth you in faithfulness, and you will acknowledge the LORD.**" This declaration encapsulates God's essence—a relentless pursuit of His people, beckoning them back to a covenant relationship despite their transgressions.

In Christian theology, the parable of the Prodigal Son serves as a profound illustration of divine mercy. The father's joyous reception of his wayward son, who returns in a state of repentance, embodies the grace that welcomes sinners back into communion with God. The father's declaration in Luke 15:32, "**We had to celebrate and be glad, because this brother of yours was dead and is alive again; he was lost and is found**"—underscores the transformative nature of genuine repentance. It transcends mere forgiveness; it entails restoration.

The doctrine of atonement, as articulated by theologians such as Anselm and Aquinas, reinforces this principle. The satisfaction theory of atonement suggests that Christ's sacrificial death fulfilled divine justice, thereby allowing God's mercy to be imparted to humanity without restraint. Romans 3:25-26 affirms this doctrine:

"**God presented Christ as a sacrifice of atonement, through the shedding of His blood—to be received by faith. He did this to demonstrate His righteousness, because in His forbearance He had left the sins committed beforehand unpunished—He did it to demonstrate His righteousness at the present time, so as to be just and the one who justifies those who have faith in Jesus.**" This passage expounds the intricate balance between justice and grace—God does not overlook sin; rather, through Christ, He offers the means for humanity to attain justification.

Consequently, throughout Scripture, one observes a God who, in response to human rebellion, administers justice while simultaneously extending mercy. He embodies both judge and redeemer, holding humanity accountable while providing a pathway back into His presence. From the fall in Eden to the redemption through Christ, His overarching purpose remains unequivocal: to restore His people to Himself, reclaiming what was lost through sin. The invitation to salvation is extended to all, and through faith in Jesus, the fractured relationship between God and humanity is mended, heralding the promise of eternal life.

His overarching purpose remains unequivocal: to restore His people to Himself...

Sin, like a contagion, spread from the initial act of disobedience in the Garden of Eden, corrupting the human heart and alienating humanity from God's presence. This spiritual defilement did not remain confined to Adam and Eve; it became the inherited condition of all humankind. As Scripture states in Romans 3:10: "**There is no one righteous, not even one,**" highlighting the universal nature of sin and humanity's moral inability to achieve righteousness on its own.

This indicates that sin is not merely an external behavior but a fundamental condition of the human soul—a distortion of the divine image within us. The Fall introduced both guilt and spiritual death, severing humanity's relationship with its Creator (Genesis 3:22–24; Ephesians 2:1).

Early Church Fathers, including Augustine of Hippo, emphasized the doctrine of original sin, characterizing humanity's inherent tendency to rebel against God. He argued that without divine grace, the human will is enslaved to sin, a perspective that significantly influenced Western Christian theology. The Reformers, particularly Martin Luther and John Calvin, echoed this sentiment, emphasizing the total depravity of man—our complete inability to choose God without His intervention.

Therefore, the universality of sin presents not just a moral issue but a theological crisis that demands divine rescue. Recognizing the pervasive reach of sin lays the groundwork for understanding the necessity of Christ's redemptive work. It is not through human effort or religious rituals that we are reconciled to God, but solely through His grace, extended to us through Jesus Christ, the only one who was without sin (Hebrews 4:15).

The reality of this fallen condition is evident in various aspects of human existence—manifesting through behaviors categorized as the acts of the flesh, which encompass immorality, selfishness, envy, strife, and rebellion against God. Such behaviors serve as manifestations of a deeper, intrinsic brokenness that humanity is incapable of rectifying independently. Individuals who persist in these behaviors are cautioned in Galatians 3:19-21 about their eternal consequences: **"The acts of the flesh are obvious: sexual immorality, impurity and debauchery; [20] idolatry and witchcraft; hatred, discord, jealousy, fits of rage, selfish ambition, dissensions, factions; [21] and envy; drunkenness, orgies, and the like. I warn you, as I did before, that those who live like this will not inherit the kingdom of God."**

Amidst this depravity, God's mercy shines as a beacon of hope. He did not abandon humanity to the burden of sin; instead, He provided a path to redemption through His Son, Jesus Christ. This divine plan, in which Christ bore the punishment for our sins, allows humanity to attain eternal life and to once again walk in the presence of God, demonstrating His unwavering faithfulness. While sin causes separation, God's love brings reconciliation. His promise remains steadfast, as stated in 1 John 1:9: **"If we confess our sins, he is faithful and just and will forgive us our sins and purify us from all unrighteousness."** Thus, forgiveness is not only attainable but assured for those who approach Him with humility.

With this assurance, believers are invited to approach the throne of grace with confidence. They are no longer required to cower in fear as Adam and Eve did in the Garden of Eden. Rather, they may stand boldly in faith, assured by the assertion that **"for everyone born of God** overcomes the world. This is the victory that has overcome the world, even our faith" as found in 1 John 5:4. This victory is not attained through human effort but through faith in Christ, who triumphed over sin and death on behalf of all who believe. Consequently, the narrative of Scripture is not merely a chronicle of humanity's rebellion; more significantly, it is a testament to God's unwavering pursuit of redemption. God's justice necessitates that sin be addressed, for He is holy and righteous. Nevertheless, His mercy extends an invitation for restoration to those who repent. Psalms 103:8-10 encapsulates this paradox eloquently: "**The Lord is compassionate and gracious, slow to anger, abounding in love. He will not always accuse, nor will he harbor his anger forever; He does not treat us as our sins deserve or repay us according to our iniquities.**" This theme of restoration is intricately woven throughout Scripture. The prophet Isaiah articulates God's readiness to heal and guide those who return to Him in Isaiah 57:18, "**I have seen their ways, but I will heal them; creating praise on their lips. I will guide them and restore comfort to Israel's mourners.**" However, Isaiah also issues a solemn warning in Isaiah 57:21, "**There is no peace,**" says my God, "**for the wicked.**" This passage reinforces the reality that peace is reserved for those who seek God, while unrest is the fate of those who persist in rebellion.

Thus, throughout the grand narrative of Scripture, we observe a God who does not overlook sin but instead offers a pathway to redemption. He serves as both judge and redeemer, calling humanity to accountability while extending the promise of grace. From the moment sin entered the world in Eden to the moment Christ triumphed over death on the cross, God's overarching mission has been unequivocal; to restore His people to Himself. The invitation remains open to all, as articulated in Matthew 11:28, "**Come to me, all you who are weary and burdened, and I will give you rest.**" Through faith in Christ, the fractured relationship between God and humanity is mended, and the hope of eternal life is assured.

> **Through faith in Christ, the fractured relationship between God and humanity is mended...**

In Christianity, the concept of redemption extends far beyond mere forgiveness of sins; it represents a profound transformation that reshapes the core of an individual's heart, mind, and purpose. Stemming from the Greek term *apolutrōsis*, which means "a release by payment of ransom," redemption signifies that humanity has been reclaimed from the bondage of sin and death through the sacrificial death of Jesus Christ (Ephesians 1:7; Colossians 1:13–14).

This transformation is closely linked to the biblical concept of metanoia, often translated as repentance. More than just feeling remorse, *metanoia* involves a complete reorientation of the mind and will—a radical turning away from sin and self-centeredness, and a deliberate turning toward God. As Paul states in Romans 12:2, believers are called to **be transformed by the renewing of [their] mind,** indicating that true redemption results in fundamental changes in one's thinking, desires, and values.

Moreover, this renewal is not solely behavioral; it is spiritual and covenantal. Through the indwelling of the Holy Spirit (Titus 3:5; Ezekiel 36:26–27), the redeemed receive new hearts and are empowered to live in obedience. This journey involves sanctification—a lifelong process of becoming holy and Christlike— illustrating that redemption is both a one-time act of divine grace and an ongoing process of divine shaping.

Historically, Church Fathers like Athanasius emphasized that redemption not only forgives humanity but also restores individuals to the divine image lost in the Fall. Similarly, Augustine taught that redemption restores the proper ordering of one's loves—so that God becomes the supreme object of human affection and purpose.

Ultimately, Christian redemption leads to a reconciled relationship with the Creator, not merely as forgiven sinners, but as adopted sons and daughters, heirs with Christ (Romans 8:15–17). It represents a complete reclaiming of the human person for God's glory, characterized by renewed intimacy, restored purpose, and eternal hope.

Throughout Scripture, God consistently articulates His profound desire for humanity's return to righteousness. He does not take pleasure in punishment but yearns for restoration. In Isaiah 1:18, He extends an invitation imbued with hope: **Come now, let us settle the matter... Though your sins are like scarlet, they shall be as white as snow.** This imagery of scarlet sins being rendered white as snow illustrates the boundless mercy of God, who is willing to cleanse even the most egregious stains of sin. It serves as a divine assurance that no individual is beyond redemption if they turn to Him with sincerity.

Similarly, in Ezekiel 18:31, the Lord implores His people, "**Rid yourselves of all the offenses you have committed, and get a new heart and a new spirit.**" This passage emphasizes the necessity of inner renewal. God does not merely advocate for external changes; He seeks to transform the very essence of a person by granting them a new heart and a new spirit. It is insufficient to alter behavior; true redemption demands an internal transformation that subsequently manifests outwardly in a life characterized by righteousness.

The theme of renewal persists throughout the New Testament, where Jesus asserts that redemption is accessible to all who repent and believe in Him. In John 3:3, He proclaims, "**Very truly I tell you, no one can see the kingdom of God unless they are born again.**" This notion of being born again signifies the radical nature of spiritual transformation—an entirely new beginning that arises through faith in Christ. The Apostle Paul echoes this sentiment in 2 Corinthians 5:17, affirming, "**If anyone is in Christ, the new creation has come: The old has gone, the new is here!**" Therefore, redemption transcends mere abandonment of past mistakes; it entails embracing a completely new identity as a child of God.

The process of transformation is not achieved solely through human effort, but rather through the power of the Holy Spirit. Titus 3:5-6 articulates this theological concept, stating, "**He saved us, not because of righteous things we had done, but because of His mercy. He saved us through the washing of rebirth and renewal by the Holy Spirit, whom He poured out on us generously through Jesus Christ our Savior.**" It is through this divine renewal that believers are empowered to walk in righteousness and resist the temptations associated with their former selves. Moreover, redemption is not a singular event but rather a lifelong journey. Following initial salvation, believers are called to engage in continual growth in faith, shedding their old ways to become more Christ-like. Romans 12:2 exhorts, "**Do not conform to the pattern of this world, but be transformed by the renewing of your mind.**" This transformation constitutes an ongoing process that necessitates daily surrender to God's will, immersion in His Word, and reliance on His Spirit.

Ultimately, redemption represents a divine invitation extended to all individuals. No sin is too great, nor any heart too hardened, for God to restore. His grace is sufficient to cleanse, renew, and transform every person who turns to Him. As Joel 2:13 reminds: **"Return to the Lord your God, for He is gracious and compassionate, slow to anger and abounding in love, and He relents from sending calamity."** This encapsulates the essence of redemption—a call to return, to be transformed, and to embrace the newness of life that God freely offers through Jesus Christ.

The path to redemption has been characterized by God's unwavering pursuit of humanity, expressed through prophetic messages, divine interventions, and ultimately, the sacrificial work of Jesus Christ. Throughout the Old Testament, God consistently reached out to His people, calling them back to righteousness through His prophets. Despite Israel's recurrent straying, the voice of the prophets served as a reminder of God's enduring mercy and the ever-present opportunity for restoration. These divine warnings, despite Israel's cycles of rebellion, were intended not merely as condemnations but as invitations to return to God's grace.

The theme of redemption attains its ultimate realization in the New Testament, epitomized in the life and mission of Jesus Christ. Central to Jesus' ministry was the emphasis on repentance and the advent of God's kingdom. His message was both direct and urgent: "The time has come," he proclaimed. **"The kingdom of God has come near. Repent and believe the good news!"** as expressed in Mark 1:15. Through His teachings, miracles, and acts of compassion, Jesus manifested God's desire to reconcile humanity to Himself. Nonetheless, it was through His sacrificial death and triumphant resurrection that the pathway to redemption was fully actualized. As articulated by the apostle Paul in 2 Corinthians 5:18, **"All this is from God, who reconciled us to himself through Christ and gave us the ministry of reconciliation."** Through Christ, the barriers of sin were dismantled, establishing a new covenant between God and His people.

This profound transformation did not escape the attention of early Christian theologians. The Church Fathers, such as Irenaeus, endeavored to articulate the significance of Christ's redemptive work. Irenaeus introduced the concept of recapitulation, which presents Christ as the new Adam; one who retraced the path of human disobedience with perfect obedience, thereby restoring humanity's relationship with God. This idea is congruent with Paul's teaching in Romans 5:19, "**For just as through the disobedience of the one man the many were made sinners, so also through the obedience of the one man the many will be made righteous.**" Thus, Jesus' life, death, and resurrection are perceived not merely as isolated occurrences but as the reversal of Adam's fall, facilitating renewal and restoration for all who believe.

Over the centuries, various theological interpretations have emerged to clarify the nature and scope of Christ's atoning work. One of the earliest and most enduring models is Christus Victor, which was particularly significant in early Church theology. This perspective views Christ's death and resurrection not simply as a legal transaction or moral example, but as a cosmic victory—His decisive triumph over sin, death, and the devil.

Rooted in themes of divine conflict and deliverance, Christus Victor emphasizes humanity's captivity under hostile spiritual forces. By entering into our mortal condition and dying a victorious, substitutionary death, Christ broke their power and liberated humankind from bondage. This idea is powerfully expressed in Hebrews 2:14–15, where the author states: "**Since the children have flesh and blood, he too shared in their humanity so that by his death he might break the power of him who holds the power of death—that is, the devil— and free those who all their lives were held in slavery by their fear of death.**" Thus, redemption encompasses not only the forgiveness of sins but also a universal liberation from evil's tyranny.

> ...Redemption encompasses not only the forgiveness of sins but also a universal liberation from evil's tyranny.

Early Church Fathers, such as Irenaeus of Lyons and Gregory of Nyssa, championed this model. Irenaeus, in his *Recapitulation* theory, portrayed Christ as the second Adam, reversing the first Adam's failure and leading humanity back to communion with God. Gregory likened Christ to bait on the hook of humanity, concealing divine power within human weakness to deceive and defeat Satan. These vivid metaphors highlight the early Christian belief that Christ's incarnation and passion were part of a divine strategy to overthrow the spiritual forces of darkness.

The *Christus Victor* model also emphasizes the incarnational aspect of salvation. Christ's participation in our humanity was not incidental; it was essential—He entered our condition to redeem it from within. As Athanasius stated in *On the Incarnation*, "He became what we are that He might make us what He is." This victory is not only external and cosmic but also internal and personal, breaking the chains of sin that bind each individual heart.

In contrast to later models that focus primarily on legal guilt or penal substitution, *Christus Victor* presents a comprehensive vision of salvation: not just reconciliation with God, but the defeat of every power opposing God's kingdom. As Paul affirms in Colossians 2:15, it is a public spectacle in which Christ **"disarmed the powers and authorities"** and **"triumphed over them by the cross."**

Thus, redemption in this framework transcends individual forgiveness. It announces the beginning of a new creation and a restored cosmic order, where Christ reigns as the victorious King. His resurrection is not merely a validation of innocence, but the firstfruits of a new humanity liberated from fear, futility, and death.

The Christian concept of redemption represents a dynamic and transformative journey, initiated by God's persistent call to repentance and culminating in the redemptive work of Christ. This journey transcends the mere avoidance of punishment; it is fundamentally about realigning one's existence with God's will, embracing righteousness, and restoring communion with the Divine. Although the path to redemption is fraught with trials and challenges, it is simultaneously illuminated by the promise of hope. Through the voices of the prophets, the testimony of Scripture, and the ultimate revelation of Christ, God continuously invites humanity toward Him. Redemption is not merely a historical event; it constitutes an ongoing process of spiritual renewal, characterized by a continuous turning away from sin and a movement toward the source of all goodness and truth. In this lifelong journey, individuals who accept God's invitation will experience not only forgiveness but also transformation, becoming what Paul describes as "new creations" in Christ, restored and renewed in the love of God.

In Christian theology, the disruption of God's original plan through human sin does not signify the conclusion of the divine narrative. Scripture unfolds a comprehensive narrative of redemption and restoration, culminating in a renewed creation devoid of sin and suffering. This promise calls humanity toward a future characterized by reconciliation and wholeness. Central to this redemptive narrative is the sacrificial act of Jesus Christ. In John 3:16, it is proclaimed, **"For God so loved the world that he gave his one and only Son, that whoever believes in him shall not perish but have eternal life."** This verse encapsulates the profound depth of God's love and the provision of a pathway back to Him. Through Christ's sacrifice, believers are extended the gift of forgiveness and the promise of eternal communion with God.

The Apostle Paul further explains this transformation in 2 Corinthians 5:17, asserting, **"Therefore, if anyone is in Christ, the new creation has come: The old has gone, the new is here!"** This statement signifies that through divine grace, individuals experience a profound renewal, realigning with God's original intent for humanity. Throughout history, this promise of renewal has served as a cornerstone of Christian hope, inspiring countless individuals and communities to persevere through trials, anchored in the assurance of God's redemptive plan. The anticipation of a restored creation has significantly influenced theological discourse, religious practices, and the missionary endeavors of the Church, all aimed at aligning with and participating in God's ongoing work of reconciliation and restoration.

The concept of a renewed creation is vividly depicted in Revelation 21:1-4, where John articulates his vision, **"Then I saw 'a new heaven and a new earth,' for the first heaven and the first earth had passed away... 'Look! God's dwelling place is now among the people, and he will dwell with them... He will wipe every tear from their eyes. There will be no more death'..."** This prophetic imagery provides believers with hope for a future in which the brokenness introduced by sin is entirely eradicated, and perfect harmony with the Creator is restored.

Through the sacrificial love of Jesus Christ and the outpouring of divine grace, a pathway back to God is offered; a journey characterized by forgiveness, healing, and the assured hope of eternal communion in a renewed creation. In the aftermath of humanity's disruption of God's plan, the path forward is fraught with challenges and trials. Nevertheless, amidst the darkness of sin, the light of divine love illuminates the way, offering hope, redemption, and the promise of a future restored. As humanity navigates the complexities of its fractured existence, the invitation to return to God persists as a beacon of hope guiding humanity back to the embrace of its Creator and the fulfillment of His divine purpose.

CHAPTER
5

The Long Road Home:
How God Repeatedly Called His People Back
by the Signs Along the Way

Throughout the biblical narrative, one enduring theme emerges: God's unwavering pursuit of reconciliation with humanity. Despite repeated acts of rebellion and failure, His response is not abandonment but mercy. Rather than turning away, God actively engages His creation—calling, covenanting, delivering, and restoring. From the Flood to the Exodus, and from the Judges to the coming of Christ, each act of divine intervention reveals His steadfast commitment to redeem a wayward people. This chapter traces that long journey home—how, through signs, covenants, and deliverers, God continually beckons humanity back into relationship with Himself.

One of the earliest and most profound examples of this pursuit is found in the account of Noah and the Flood. During a time when **"The Lord saw how great the wickedness of the human race had become on the earth, and that every inclination of the thoughts of the human heart was only evil all the time"** (Genesis 6:5), God, in His righteousness, brought judgment upon the world. Yet, His justice was accompanied by grace. Noah found favor in God's eyes, and through him, a remnant was preserved, symbolizing a new beginning and the continuation of God's redemptive plan.

After the flood, God established a covenant with Abraham, choosing him to be the father of a nation through which the entire world would be blessed. This covenant was grounded not in human merit but in divine promise: "**I will make you into a great nation, and I will bless you; I will make your name great, and you will be a blessing**" (Genesis 12:2). This promise served as a cornerstone of God's redemptive mission, foreshadowing the ultimate reconciliation to come through Jesus Christ, a descendant of Abraham.

The theme of liberation and redemption is further exemplified in the Exodus, where God delivered the Israelites from slavery in Egypt. Through mighty acts of power, He demonstrated His faithfulness, leading them to freedom and establishing them as a nation under His divine rule. As Moses reminded them: "**The Lord will fight for you; you need only to be still**" (Exodus 14:14). This miraculous deliverance represented not just physical liberation but also a call to spiritual renewal—an invitation to trust and obey the One who had set them free. Despite these acts of grace, Israel repeatedly fell into cycles of disobedience, particularly during the period of the Judges. Each time the people turned away from God, they faced oppression. Yet, in His mercy, He raised up deliverers to restore them. This pattern of rebellion and redemption is encapsulated in Judges 2:18: "**Whenever the Lord raised up a judge for them, he was with the judge and saved them out of the hands of their enemies as long as the judge lived; for the Lord relented because of their groaning under those who oppressed and afflicted them.**" Even in their waywardness, God never abandoned His people but continually sought to bring them back to Himself.

> **These historical events are not merely ancient stories; they profoundly illustrate God's enduring love and faithfulness.**

These historical events are not merely ancient stories; they profoundly illustrate God's enduring love and faithfulness. They foreshadow the ultimate act of reconciliation—the coming of Jesus Christ. As Paul writes, "**But God demonstrates his own love for us in this: While we were still sinners, Christ died for us**" (Romans 5:8). Every covenant, every act of deliverance, and every divine intervention pointed toward the cross, where the chasm between humanity and God was finally bridged.

Even now, God's invitation to reconciliation remains open. Through faith in Christ, believers become partakers in the new covenant, experiencing a restoration that surpasses all previous acts of redemption. "**For if, while we were God's enemies, we were** reconciled to him through the death of his Son, how much more, having been reconciled, shall we be saved through his life!" (Romans 5:10). This promise affirms that God's pursuit of humanity is not a distant historical reality but an ever-present call for each individual to return to Him.

Thus, the story of redemption continues. From Noah to Abraham, from Moses to the Judges, from the prophets to Christ—each chapter in the biblical narrative testifies to the unfailing love of God. His desire has always been, and remains, to bring His people back to Himself, offering not only forgiveness but a renewed and everlasting relationship with the Divine.

THE FLOOD

In the context of human corruption and wickedness, the Flood serves as a stark reminder of the consequences of sin—a divine reckoning for a world that had completely turned away from its Creator. Genesis 6:5 vividly illustrates the severity of human depravity: **"The Lord saw how great the wickedness of the human race had become on the earth, and that every inclination of the thoughts of the human heart was only evil all the time."** This profound moral decay grieved God's heart and prompted the decision to cleanse the earth. Yet, even amid divine judgment, a thread of mercy runs through the narrative, highlighting God's unwavering commitment to redemption.

Amidst the overwhelming tide of destruction, Noah emerges as a beacon of hope: **"But Noah found favor in the eyes of the Lord"** (Genesis 6:8). He was not chosen for his perfection but for his faithfulness and obedience to God. In a world engulfed by violence and corruption, Noah walked in righteousness, trusting in the promises of the Almighty. Through him, God preserved a remnant, ensuring that humanity's story would not conclude in judgment but would continue with the hope of renewal and reconciliation.

God's instructions to Noah to build an ark were more than a means of survival; they represented divine providence—a tangible expression of grace amid wrath. Noah's obedience is underscored in Genesis 6:22: **"Noah did everything just as God commanded him."** His faith in following God's command, despite the apparent impossibility of the task, exemplifies the power of trust in divine wisdom. The ark became a vessel of salvation, not only for Noah and his family but also for the preservation of creation itself.

As the floodwaters rose, engulfing the earth and sweeping away its wickedness, the ark became a powerful symbol of God's ability to preserve and redeem those who trust in Him. While judgment fell upon the world due to rampant sin, Noah and his family were lifted above the destruction, demonstrating how faith and obedience lead to salvation. The ark not only provided physical refuge but also foreshadowed Christ as the ultimate means of deliverance— just as Noah and his family were saved through the ark, so too are believers saved through faith in Jesus Christ, our spiritual ark (1 Peter 3:20-21).

Once the waters receded, God's mercy took center stage, heralding a new beginning. The covenant He established with Noah and all of creation was an act of divine grace, illustrating that His ultimate plan was not destruction, but restoration. The significance of the rainbow in Genesis 9:13 is profound: "**I have set my rainbow in the clouds, and it will be the sign of the covenant between me and the earth.**"

This promise marked not just the end of the flood, but the beginning of a new era of grace, in which God vowed never to destroy the earth by water again. The rainbow became an everlasting symbol of God's faithfulness, showing that His mercy ultimately triumphs over judgment. It serves as a reminder of divine patience, as expressed in 2 Peter 3:9: "**The Lord is not slow in keeping his promise, as some understand slowness. Instead, he is patient with you, not wanting anyone to perish, but everyone to come to repentance.**"

An intriguing aspect of the rainbow's appearance after the flood is the possibility that it was the first time rain had ever fallen on the earth. Prior to the flood, Genesis 2:5-6 suggests that rain had not yet occurred, as the earth was watered by an underground aquifer system: "Now no shrub had yet appeared on the earth and no plant had yet sprung up, for the Lord God had not sent rain on the earth and there was no one to work the ground, but streams came up from the earth and watered the whole surface of the ground."

If rain was indeed absent before the flood, there would have been no natural mechanism for rainbows to form, as a rainbow is created by light refracting through water droplets in the atmosphere. This implies that when God declared the rainbow as the sign of His covenant, He was introducing a newly revealed natural phenomenon to establish an everlasting bond of trust with future generations.

Beyond serving as a reminder of God's mercy after judgment, the rainbow holds deeper theological significance throughout Scripture. In Ezekiel 1:28, the prophet describes a vision of God's throne, stating, **"Like the appearance of a rainbow in the clouds on a rainy day, so was the radiance around him."** Here, the rainbow reflects God's majesty and divine presence, emphasizing that His mercy is integral to His very nature. Similarly, in Revelation 4:3, John sees a vision of heaven where **"The one who sat there had the appearance of jasper and ruby. A rainbow that shone like an emerald encircled the throne."** This imagery illustrates that the rainbow is not merely a temporary sign but a continuous reflection of God's covenant-keeping nature, surrounding His presence and reminding creation of His unwavering faithfulness. The appearance of the rainbow in the sky after a storm symbolizes the pattern of salvation history—judgment occurs, but redemption follows. The ultimate fulfillment of God's covenant faithfulness is found in Christ, who offers not just temporary deliverance but eternal restoration.

The rainbow transcends being a natural spectacle; it is a divine declaration and a visual representation of God's mercy and unchanging faithfulness. When Noah and his family emerged from the ark, they stepped into a new creation, marked by God's renewed commitment to His people. The first appearance of the rainbow was not simply a result of rain and light, but a divinely orchestrated sign intended to remind future generations that God's mercy triumphs over judgment. Ultimately, the rainbow points to Christ, who fulfills the greatest covenant of all—one that provides not just earthly preservation but eternal salvation. Every time believers see a rainbow, they are reminded of God's faithfulness, that His grace surpasses judgment, and that through Jesus, they are invited into an everlasting covenant of redemption.

> **Ultimately, the rainbow points to Christ, who fulfills the greatest covenant of all... eternal salvation.**

The Flood narrative presents a unique and profound perspective that challenges many conventional beliefs. One common objection is that a global flood could not have submerged the entire earth, particularly given the towering heights of modern mountains like Mount Everest, which stands at 29,032 feet. Skeptics argue that there wouldn't be enough water to cover such elevations, but this viewpoint overlooks several key considerations. A particularly intriguing verse in Genesis 10:25 sheds light on the post-Flood world. It states, "**Two sons were born to Eber: One was named Peleg, because in his time the earth was divided; his brother was named Joktan.**" Peleg, Noah's great-great-great-great-grandson, was born hundreds of years after the Flood. The phrase "in his time the earth was divided" raises an important question: How was the earth divided? Some interpreters suggest this refers to the division of languages following the Tower of Babel event, when God confused human speech and scattered people across the earth (Genesis 11:7-9). However, another possibility is that this verse refers to a geological division—a physical separation of landmasses rather than merely a linguistic or cultural division.

If this interpretation holds true, Peleg's lifetime may have coincided with a significant geological event—a period of continental drift or tectonic shifts that reshaped the earth's surface. A close examination of a modern globe reveals a striking correlation between the shapes of the continents, suggesting they could fit together like pieces of a puzzle. This observation supports the theory of plate tectonics, which suggests that the earth's landmasses were once a single supercontinent—commonly referred to as Pangaea— that later drifted apart due to geological forces. If Peleg's era indeed marked the physical division of the earth, it profoundly alters our understanding of the pre-Flood topography. Prior to such tectonic shifts, high mountains likely did not exceed a thousand feet, making it more plausible that the entire earth could have been submerged during the Flood. The towering mountain ranges we see today— including the Himalayas, Rockies, and Andes—formed later due to catastrophic plate movements that pushed rock layers upward through continental collisions. This process, known as orogeny, unfolded over centuries, shaping the modern landscape long after the Floodwaters had receded.

This perspective aligns with Genesis 7:19-20, which states, "**They rose greatly on the earth, and all the high mountains under the entire heavens were covered. The waters rose and covered the**

mountains to a depth of more than fifteen cubits." If the earth's terrain before the Flood was much lower and less rugged than today, this description becomes far more plausible. The floodwaters would not have needed to reach extreme altitudes, as the land itself may have been at a significantly lower elevation prior to the catastrophic shifts that followed.

Another intriguing element of this narrative is that Peleg is an ancestor of Abraham, through whom God would later establish another divine covenant. This connection highlights a central theme in Scripture—God's sovereign orchestration of history. From the Flood to the division of the earth and ultimately to Abraham's calling, each event unfolds according to God's perfect plan. Every stage in biblical history interconnects, leading toward the ultimate covenant through Christ, in whom all nations would be blessed (Galatians 3:8). Therefore, when considering the geological and theological implications of Peleg's time and the Flood, it becomes clear that God's design is flawless. The challenges raised by skeptics— such as the supposed impossibility of a global flood covering modern mountain ranges—are not obstacles when viewed through the lens of the earth's shifting geological history. The Flood was not only a judgment on sin but also a transformative event that reshaped the world, setting the stage for God's ongoing plan of redemption. His hand has guided history from the very beginning, ensuring the fulfillment of His purposes to perfection. This detail underscores God's sovereignty and foreknowledge. From the beginning, He knew that the laws of nature He designed would eventually serve as a visible symbol of His promise. The rainbow is not simply an aesthetic phenomenon; it is a divinely intended sign. The involvement of Noah's relative and the potential for division in the world after the flood remind humanity that, although sin once led to judgment, God's heart is always inclined toward redemption. He utilizes all of His created powers to fulfill His will.

The story of Noah and the Flood is more than a historical account; it profoundly foreshadows redemption. Just as the ark provided a means of escape from destruction, Jesus Christ serves as the ultimate ark of salvation. Through Him, humanity is rescued from the floodwaters of sin and granted new life. In 1 Peter 3:20-21, Peter draws a direct connection between Noah's deliverance and the salvation found in Christ, stating, **"In it only a few people, eight in all, were saved through water, and this water symbolizes baptism that now saves you also—not the removal of dirt from the body but the pledge of a clear conscience toward God. It saves you by the resurrection of Jesus Christ."** Thus, the Flood narrative acts as both a warning and a promise—a warning about the devastating consequences of sin and a promise of God's unwavering desire to redeem. Noah's story testifies to the power of faith, the grace of divine preservation, and the hope of new beginnings. Even amidst judgment, God's mercy shines through, inviting all to enter His covenant of salvation, where destruction gives way to renewal, reconciliation, and eternal life in Christ.

The story of Noah and the Flood is one of the most profound narratives in Scripture, embodying both divine judgment and redemption. It reveals the depth of human corruption, the righteousness of God's justice, and the enduring thread of mercy woven throughout the biblical story. More than just an ancient account, the Flood serves as a theological framework for understanding God's dealings with sin and grace, echoing through various historical and cultural traditions. Throughout history, many cultures have recorded flood narratives that bear striking similarities to the biblical account. In the Epic of Gilgamesh, an ancient Mesopotamian text from the early second millennium BC, the gods send a great flood to destroy humanity. However, one man, Utnapishtim, is warned and builds a boat to survive. A similar flood myth is found in the Atrahasis Epic, which also describes how the gods, frustrated by human disobedience, unleash a catastrophic deluge.

While these accounts share thematic elements with the biblical story, the Genesis Flood narrative is distinct in its theological message. Unlike pagan flood myths that often portray divine beings acting capriciously or in anger without moral justification, the biblical account presents a God who acts with both justice and mercy. The sin of humanity prompts divine judgment, yet God's desire for renewal remains central to the story. Archaeological and geological studies indicate that ancient Mesopotamian civilizations may have experienced significant flooding, particularly in the Tigris-Euphrates valley, which could have influenced these narratives. Scholars continue to debate whether the biblical flood was a global event or a massive regional occurrence, but the spiritual and theological truths conveyed in Genesis 6-9 transcend historical specifics.

One of the most striking aspects of the Flood story is its portrayal of human depravity. Genesis 6:5 describes the world before the Flood: "**The Lord saw how great the wickedness of the human race had become on the earth, and that every inclination of the thoughts of the human heart was only evil all the time.**" This verse indicates that sin was not simply a series of isolated wrongdoings but had become a systemic, all-consuming force corrupting the entire human race. This idea aligns with the theological doctrine of total depravity, which teaches that sin affects every aspect of human nature—thoughts, desires, and actions. Humanity had reached a point where moral corruption was irreversible without divine intervention. This theme is echoed in the New Testament, where Romans 3:23 states, "**For all have sinned and fall short of the glory of God.**"

God's decision to send the Flood serves as a profound testament to His righteous judgment against sin. The widespread wickedness of humanity grieved God's heart (Genesis 6:5–6), and in His holiness, He could not allow evil to continue unchecked. The Flood was not an impulsive act of wrath but a deliberate act of divine justice—a cleansing force that eradicated the moral corruption engulfing creation. As Paul affirms in Romans 1:18, "**The wrath of God is being revealed from heaven against all the godlessness and wickedness of people, who suppress the truth by their wickedness.**" This divine judgment of the Flood is echoed throughout the biblical narrative, illustrating that God's justice is a consistent and essential aspect of His character.

> **God's decision to send the Flood serves as a profound testament to His righteous judgment against sin.**

However, judgment is never God's final word. Throughout Scripture, His justice is always tempered by mercy. Amid the waters of destruction, grace flows quietly yet powerfully. Noah is introduced in Genesis 6:9 as "**a righteous man, blameless among the people of his time,**" a man who "**walked faithfully with God.**" He finds favor in God's eyes—not because of inherent perfection, but due to his faith and obedience. His willingness to obey God's command to build an ark, despite its apparent absurdity, underscores his trust in divine instruction (Hebrews 11:7).

The ark symbolizes both divine mercy and redemptive provision. It preserves Noah and his family from the deluge, foreshadowing the salvation offered through Jesus Christ. Just as Noah was saved by entering the ark, believers find salvation through their relationship with Christ. This typology is explicitly referenced in 1 Peter 3:20–21, which states: **"In it only a few people, eight in all, were saved through water, and this water symbolizes baptism that now saves you also—not the removal of dirt from the body but the pledge of a clear conscience toward God."** Baptism, like the ark, becomes a sign of deliverance—a transition from death to life, judgment to grace.

Early Church Fathers such as Tertullian and Augustine interpreted the Flood typologically, viewing the ark as a symbol of the Church. Augustine, in *City of God*, wrote that "the ark, which was constructed in the shape of a man lying on his back, prefigured the body of Christ." The ark's dimensions and structure symbolized the incarnate Christ—fully man and fully God—whose body is the Church. The waters of judgment surrounding the ark were not the end, but the means through which new life was secured.

Similarly, the Didache and early baptismal liturgies drew connections between Noah's deliverance and the waters of baptism, reinforcing the idea that judgment and mercy often coexist in God's redemptive plans. In this theological framework, baptism becomes not only a rite of purification but a dramatic re-enactment of salvation history—transitioning from judgment into new covenant life.

After the Flood, God establishes a covenant, reaffirming His commitment to creation. Genesis 9:13 records God's words: **"I have set my rainbow in the clouds, and it will be the sign of the covenant between me and the earth."** The rainbow as discussed earlier, serves not merely as a token of peace but as a divine oath—a visible reassurance that God chooses restoration over destruction. Historically, covenants in the ancient Near East were binding legal agreements often sealed with signs. The rainbow becomes such a sign: a visual expression of God's mercy and relational faithfulness.

The theological implications of the Flood extend beyond Noah's time. The narrative is not merely about judgment and survival; it serves as a prophetic shadow of the Gospel. Just as the ark carried Noah safely through the waters of destruction, Christ carries believers safely through the judgment of sin. The ark was made of wood and sealed with pitch; the cross was made of wood and sealed with blood. Both are instruments of divine rescue. This redemptive arc culminates in John 3:16: **"For God so loved the world that he gave his one and only Son, that whoever believes in him shall not perish but have eternal life."**

After the Flood, when Noah and his family stepped onto a cleansed and renewed earth, God introduced a significant shift in how humanity would sustain itself. Prior to this moment, humanity's diet was primarily plant-based, in line with the original directive given to Adam in Genesis 1:29, where God said, **"I give you every seed-bearing plant on the face of the whole earth and every tree that has fruit with seed in it. They will be yours for food."** However, following the Flood, God expanded this provision, allowing humanity to consume animal flesh as part of their diet. This pivotal change is recorded in Genesis 9:3, where God states, **"Everything that lives and moves about will be food for you. Just as I gave you the green plants, I now give you everything."** This transition signifies not only a practical adaptation to the post-Flood world but also a profound theological shift in God's relationship with humanity and creation. The world had experienced catastrophic changes, and in this new era, humanity was given a greater role in dominion over the earth. The phrase **"just as I gave you the green plants"** suggests a parallel between the original provision for food in Eden and the expanded permission granted after the Flood, indicating that humanity was entering a new phase of existence—one that required a broader range of resources to sustain life and promote flourishing.

This development raises several important considerations. Firstly, it suggests that the earth's ecological conditions may have changed dramatically after the Flood, potentially rendering plant-based sustenance alone insufficient for human survival. If the pre-Flood world had a vastly different climate, ecosystem, and atmospheric conditions, the shift to an omnivorous diet—incorporating both animal and plant sources—might have been a necessary adaptation.

Some scientists and biblical scholars speculate that prior to the Flood, the earth may have experienced a more temperate and stable environment, possibly characterized by a denser atmosphere or an increased water canopy that protected life and supported greater longevity. However, the Flood's impact on topography, climate, and atmospheric conditions likely necessitated a greater reliance on animal protein as a vital means of sustaining human strength and health.

Secondly, this shift underscores a deepening of humanity's responsibility over creation. While the original command in Eden granted dominion over animals (Genesis 1:28), this new directive emphasizes stewardship with greater ethical implications. Although mankind was permitted to eat animals, this was not a license for reckless destruction of life. The following verse, Genesis 9:4, establishes a moral boundary: "**But you must not eat meat that has its lifeblood still in it.**" This prohibition against consuming blood highlights the sacredness of life, reinforcing the idea that while humanity could partake of creation for sustenance, life itself remained under God's sovereign authority. Additionally, this expansion of the human diet can be seen as a precursor to later biblical themes concerning sacrifice and atonement. Blood, as a symbol of life and covenant, plays a central role throughout the Old Testament sacrificial system and ultimately in the sacrifice of Christ. The restriction on consuming blood while allowing the eating of meat foreshadows the eventual understanding of blood as the means of atonement, culminating in Leviticus 17:11, which states, "**For the life of a creature is in the blood, and I have given it to you to make atonement for yourselves on the altar; it is the blood that makes atonement for one's life.**" This theme finds its fulfillment in Jesus Christ, whose blood was shed for the forgiveness of sins (Hebrews 9:22).

Beyond practical and theological considerations, this divine provision after the Flood symbolizes God's abundant re-creation. Just as He had provided for Adam and Eve in the original creation, He now equipped Noah and his descendants to thrive in the renewed world. This was not merely about survival but about flourishing, as humanity was granted the full bounty of creation to support their growth and expansion. In this way, God's grace was evident—not only in sparing Noah's family but also in ensuring their prosperity in a transformed world.

Ultimately, this moment in Genesis 9 marks a turning point in redemptive history, reinforcing themes of God's sovereignty, human responsibility, and divine provision. While the judgment of the Flood eradicated corruption, God's restorative work continued, allowing humanity to rebuild, multiply, and enjoy the earth's abundance under His ongoing care. His plan was perfectly orchestrated, guiding humanity toward a future of both physical and spiritual renewal.

COVENANT WITH ABRAHAM

In the aftermath of the Flood, as humanity began to repopulate and spread across the land, God's redemptive plan assumed a new and significant form. Instead of executing another act of global judgment, He initiated a promise of restoration—one that would shape the course of biblical history and extend beyond a single nation to all the peoples of the earth. This promise took the form of a covenant with Abraham, a man chosen not for his perfection or status, but for his faith and obedience. In Genesis 12:1–3, God calls Abraham (then Abram) to leave his homeland of Ur of the Chaldeans, an advanced Mesopotamian city known for its wealth, culture, and religious idolatry. Abraham's calling represented a radical departure from the polytheistic traditions of his time, demanding an extraordinary level of trust in the one true God.

The promise God made to Abraham in Genesis 12:2-3 was profound: **"I will make you into a great nation, and I will bless you; I will make your name great, and you will be a blessing... and all peoples on earth will be blessed through you."** This covenant marked a significant shift in the relationship between God and humanity. While the Flood addressed sin through destruction and cleansing, God chose to engage through relationship, promise, and purpose. The Flood reset humanity, but the Abrahamic covenant established a new, chosen people—a nation set apart to reflect God's righteousness and truth to the world. Through Abraham's descendants, God aimed to raise up a people who would embody His divine laws, serve as a light to the nations, and ultimately prepare the way for the coming of the Messiah.

> **The Flood reset humanity, but the Abrahamic covenant established a new, chosen people...**

Historically, Abraham's journey from Ur to Canaan parallels the movements of Semitic tribes in the early second millennium BC. Archaeological evidence indicates that Ur was a thriving city-state in the Sumerian civilization, rich in culture, trade, and religious practice. Yet, despite the city's prosperity, Abraham was called to leave this stability and embark on an uncertain journey to an unknown land. This calling was countercultural, as ancient societies were deeply connected to ancestral lands and familial traditions. Leaving one's homeland meant not just a physical transition but a complete reorientation of identity and purpose, requiring unwavering faith.

The Abrahamic covenant held both personal and universal significance. On a personal level, it assured Abraham of descendants, land, and a lasting legacy—a remarkable promise for a man advanced in age and childless. Universally, the covenant extended beyond Abraham's immediate family, pointing to a future reconciliation between God and all humanity. The phrase "**all peoples on earth will be blessed through you**" (Genesis 12:3) was not merely poetic; it was a prophetic revelation, foreshadowing the coming of Jesus Christ, who would be born through Abraham's lineage and bring salvation to all.

As the biblical narrative unfolds, God reaffirms and expands the covenant at key moments. In Genesis 15, He seals the promise through a sacred ritual, instructing Abraham to prepare a sacrifice. Afterward, God Himself passes between the pieces in a divine act of commitment. This ceremonial act reflects ancient Near Eastern treaty practices, where two parties would walk between severed animal pieces, signifying that if either party broke the covenant, they would suffer a similar fate. However, only God moves between the pieces, emphasizing that this is an unconditional covenant based on His faithfulness rather than human effort. Later, in Genesis 17, God institutes circumcision as a sign of the covenant, reinforcing Abraham's role in a set-apart nation that would uphold God's laws. Abraham's faith in these promises, despite his advanced age and Sarah's barrenness, becomes a defining characteristic of biblical faith. Romans 4:3 highlights this by stating, "**Abraham believed God, and it was credited to him as righteousness.**" His trust in God's promises serves as a model for all future believers, illustrating that righteousness is achieved not through works but through faith in God's redemptive plan.

The Abrahamic covenant acts as a bridge between judgment and grace. While the Flood demonstrated the collective consequences of sin, Abraham's covenant points to the universal offer of salvation through Christ. It reveals a fundamental truth: God's solution to human rebellion is not abandonment but an invitation into a covenant relationship, divine promise, and redemptive purpose. This covenant is not a temporary agreement; it lays the foundation for all subsequent covenants—from Moses at Sinai, where Israel receives the Law, to David's promise of an eternal king, and to the new covenant in Christ's blood, through which all nations would be reconciled to God.

By choosing, God decides to work through human history, real people, unfolding generations, and providential guidance to restore His relationship with creation. The echoes of the Flood—corruption, judgment, and mercy—find resolution in this covenant. Where the Flood wiped the slate clean, the Abrahamic covenant begins to write a new story, ultimately culminating at the cross, where the blessing promised to all nations is fulfilled through Jesus Christ. Thus, Abraham becomes not just the father of a nation but the father of faith, and through his lineage, God's plan of reconciliation continues to this day.

THE EXODUS

In the crucible of Egyptian bondage, the Israelites endured generations of harsh slavery and oppression, their cries for deliverance rising from profound suffering. Exodus 2:23–25 captures the moment their plea reached heaven: **"The Israelites groaned in their slavery and cried out, and their cry for help because of their slavery went up to God. God heard their groaning and remembered his covenant with Abraham, Isaac, and Jacob. So God looked on the Israelites and was concerned about them."** This passage sets the stage for the defining event in biblical history: the Exodus, an act of divine intervention that would become the cornerstone of Israel's national identity and theological understanding.

The enslavement of the Israelites in Egypt from a historical point of view, corresponds with the New Kingdom period

(1550–1070 BC), particularly during the reigns of pharaohs known for extensive building projects that likely required a massive labor force, including Semitic slaves. Although the exact timing and identity of the Pharaoh during the Exodus are debated among scholars, archaeological and textual records, such as the "Expulsion of the Hyksos" and the presence of Semitic peoples in the Nile Delta (especially in Avaris), provide a plausible backdrop for the Israelites' presence in Egypt. Additionally, ancient Egyptian texts like the Ipuwer Papyrus describe a period of chaos and calamity that some believe resembles the biblical plagues, though these connections remain speculative.

The Exodus narrative reveals not only God's power to liberate but also His faithfulness to the covenant made with the patriarchs. By raising up Moses, a reluctant leader with a background in Pharaoh's household, God worked through human weakness to fulfill His divine purpose. Through ten dramatic plagues, He brought Egypt to its knees, demonstrating His supremacy over the Egyptian gods and exposing the futility of their power. Each plague systematically dismantled Egypt's spiritual, agricultural, and economic stability, culminating in the death of the firstborn—a final act that struck at the heart of Pharaoh's authority and ultimately led to Israel's release.

The parting of the Red Sea and the crossing on dry ground were not merely miraculous events; they represented acts of universal re-creation, reflecting the language and imagery of Genesis 1, where God brought order out of chaos. Just as He separated the waters during creation, He now separates them again to lead His people into new life and freedom. The Israelites' journey from slavery to freedom serves as a living parable of God's desire to rescue, renew, and reconcile. Exodus from Egypt becomes a defining symbol throughout Scripture, continually referenced by prophets, psalmists, and even Jesus Himself. It serves as the lens through which we understand God's power, mercy, and covenant faithfulness. Deuteronomy 7:8 emphasizes: **"It was because the Lord loved you and kept the oath he swore to your ancestors that he brought you out with a mighty hand and redeemed you from the land of slavery."** This event transcends mere liberation from political oppression; it signifies the restoration of a relationship with

God, who desires to dwell among His people and guide them to the Promised Land.

In later Jewish tradition, the Exodus is commemorated annually through Passover, a sacred observance where the story of deliverance from Egypt is retold as the defining narrative of Jewish identity. This observance goes beyond a mere remembrance of physical liberation; it serves as a spiritual reenactment that affirms God's covenant faithfulness across generations.

In Christian theology, the Exodus is not just an ancient event—it represents a foundational typology that foreshadows ultimate deliverance through Jesus Christ. The Passover lamb, whose blood protected the Israelites from the angel of death (Exodus 12:13), becomes a powerful symbol of Christ, the Lamb of God, whose sacrificial death secures eternal salvation for believers (John 1:29; 1 Corinthians 5:7). Just as Israel was freed from Pharaoh's oppressive rule, Christ delivers humanity from the greater bondage of sin and death.

The Apostle Paul makes direct connections between the Exodus and the Christian journey of salvation. In 1 Corinthians 10:1–4, he reflects on Israel's passage through the Red Sea as a form of baptism and describes their spiritual sustenance as foreshadowing Christ. The Exodus serves as a living parable—a journey from slavery to freedom, from despair to hope, and from death to life—mirroring the spiritual transformation made possible through the Gospel.

Early Church Fathers such as Origen and Ambrose viewed the Exodus as symbolic of the Christian pilgrimage through life. Origen described the crossing of the Red Sea as the believer's baptismal moment—leaving behind the old life of sin and beginning the journey toward the Promised Land, which symbolizes the kingdom of God. Ambrose emphasized that Egypt represents the "old man," while Canaan symbolizes new life in Christ.

Thus, the Exodus is more than a historical event; it is a divine drama of redemption that transcends time. It reveals the character of a God who hears the cries of the oppressed, intervenes with power, and leads with mercy. It anticipates the fuller redemption revealed in

Thus, the Exodus is more than a historical event; it is a divine drama of redemption that transcends time.

Christ, in whom the final and greater Exodus is accomplished, not just for one nation, but for all who believe.

The cries from Egypt, met by the mighty hand of God, affirm that no oppression—whether physical, spiritual, or emotional—is beyond His reach. His desire is always to lead His people from bondage into blessing, from darkness into light, and from death into everlasting life. The Exodus, therefore, directs us to the Cross, and through the Cross, to the greater deliverance yet to come; when Christ returns to bring His people into their eternal Promised Land.

JUDGES

The period of the Judges represents one of the most volatile and complex eras in Israel's history, characterized by national fragmentation, spiritual decline, and cycles of rebellion and deliverance. After the death of Joshua, who had successfully led the Israelites in their conquest of the Promised Land, the spiritual legacy he left quickly faded. As Judges 2:10 laments, "**After that whole generation had been gathered to their ancestors, another generation grew up who knew neither the Lord nor what he had done for Israel.**" This spiritual amnesia set the stage for centuries of disobedience and disorder, during which the people repeatedly turned away from God and adopted the moral and religious practices of surrounding nations.

The book of Judges outlines a recurring pattern often referred to as the "sin cycle": apostasy (Israel sins), oppression (God allows them to be conquered), supplication (the people cry out), and deliverance (God raises up a judge). This cycle reveals not only political instability but also a profound theological crisis: a people chosen by God failing to live as a holy nation, forgetting their covenant identity, and conforming to pagan cultures. The closing verse of the book encapsulates the core issue in Judges 21:25, "**In those days Israel had no king; everyone did as they saw fit.**" This was not merely a lack of human leadership—it represented a rejection of God's kingship.

The Judges period spans roughly from 1200 to 1050 BC, coinciding with what scholars identify as the Late Bronze Age collapse and the onset of Iron Age I. This era was marked by widespread upheaval across the ancient Near East, as major empires like the Hittites, Mycenaeans, and the Egyptian New Kingdom experienced decline. This destabilization created a power vacuum in Canaan, allowing emerging groups such as the Israelites to settle and assert territorial claims. Archaeological evidence from sites like Hazor, Debir, and Shiloh supports the existence of small, agrarian-based highland settlements during this period, many of which align with the biblical depiction of Israelite tribal life.

Without centralized leadership or a standing army, Israel operated as a loose confederation of tribes, governed by charismatic leaders known as "judges" rather than kings or dynasties. These judges were not legal arbiters in the modern sense; instead, they were spirit-empowered deliverers chosen by God to address specific threats and crises. Each judge's story is unique but collectively highlights the unexpected nature of God's choices. Deborah, a prophetess and military strategist, led Israel to victory against Canaanite oppression. Gideon, despite his fears and humble origins, triumphed over the Midianites with just 300 men. Jephthah, the son of a prostitute, rose from rejection to national leadership. Samson, despite his immense strength and personal weaknesses, fought against the Philistines as his life fell apart. These narratives illustrate a central theological theme: God works through broken vessels to fulfill His sovereign purposes.

This period of the Judges emphasizes both God's justice and mercy. He remains faithful in punishing sin, allowing Israel to face the consequences of their rebellion. However, He is equally faithful in responding when they repent. Judges 2:18 offers profound insight: **"Whenever the Lord raised up a judge for them, he was with the judge and saved them out of the hands of their enemies... For the Lord relented because of their groaning under those who oppressed and afflicted them."** Here, God's relenting is not a sign of weakness but of compassion, highlighting His ongoing desire to draw His people back to Himself.

This era also sets the stage for Israel's longing for a human king, which appears in 1 Samuel. The judges' increasing inability to provide lasting peace and moral leadership prompts the people to demand a king "like all the other nations" (1 Samuel 8:5). Though this request is understandable, it reveals a deeper misunderstanding of Israel's identity as a nation set apart under God's direct rule. Their plea, ultimately granted, foreshadows both the promise and the challenges of monarchy in Israel's future.

From a messianic and theological perspective, the Judges can be understood as a type or foreshadowing of Jesus Christ, the ultimate Deliverer. Each judge served as a temporary and flawed savior, highlighting the need for a perfect, eternal Judge and King. Where they provided only fleeting peace, Christ offers lasting reconciliation. While they delivered the Israelites from foreign enemies, Christ delivers humanity from sin and death. Their imperfections underscore the necessity of a greater hope, fulfilled in the new covenant established through the cross.

Despite the darkness and moral decay of the Judges era, the overarching message remains one of hope and redemption. God did not abandon His people to their sin. Instead, He continually acted in grace, sending deliverers, reminding them of His covenant, and preserving His purposes even amidst chaos. The Judges serve as both warnings and signs—warnings of the consequences when God's people forsake His ways, and signs of His unfailing mercy. They ultimately point to a future time when God would send not just a judge, but the King of kings, who would establish justice, righteousness, and an everlasting peace. Thus, the period of the Judges is more than a historical interlude; it is a theological reflection of humanity's tendency toward rebellion, the consequences of spiritual forgetfulness, and the relentless mercy of God, who continues to raise up deliverers to call His people back to Himself.

So, what can we conclude from these events, which together form a vast tapestry of human history? Every thread—every event, every covenant, every divine intervention—has been woven with purpose by the hand of God, each strand leading toward a singular redemptive aim: the reconciliation of humanity with its Creator. From the earliest moments of Scripture, when sin first entered the world through Adam and Eve's disobedience, the narrative has been shaped by God's relentless pursuit of restoration. Though humanity has continually wandered, falling into cycles of rebellion, idolatry, and brokenness, God's love remains unshaken—a covenantal love that refuses to abandon His creation.

Throughout the biblical narrative, the theme of reconciliation resonates repeatedly. From the ark that lifted Noah above the floodwaters to the covenant God made with Abraham, from Moses' deliverance during the Exodus to the prophets' continual calls

Throughout the biblical narrative, the theme of reconciliation resonates repeatedly.

for repentance, God's intention has always been clear: to draw His people back to Himself. These events were not isolated acts of divine intervention but rather deliberate movements within a grand symphony of grace. Even in moments of judgment, mercy was present, and even in exile, there was a promise of return.

The prophets, while often tasked with conveying difficult truths, also brought messages of profound hope. For example, Isaiah spoke of a coming Servant who would bear the sins of many and restore what had been broken. Jeremiah foretold a new covenant, not inscribed on stone tablets but written on human hearts. Through such promises, the light of redemption grew ever brighter, illuminating the path into the New Testament era.

In the fullness of time, this divine purpose culminated in the person of Jesus Christ, who embodies God's love and fulfills every promise. Through His life, death, and resurrection, Jesus became the bridge between a holy God and sinful humanity. 2 Corinthians 5:18-19 powerfully encapsulates this truth: "**All this is from God, who reconciled us to himself through Christ and gave us the ministry of reconciliation: that God was reconciling the world to himself in Christ, not counting people's sins against them.**" Here, the essence of the divine plan is revealed—not condemnation, but communion; not wrath, but restoration. This ministry of reconciliation continues today, as the story of redemption unfolds in our present and future. The Holy Spirit draws hearts toward repentance, illuminating the path back to God. The church, as the body of Christ, is called to be a living testament to this grace, bearing witness to the truth that no one is beyond God's reach, that forgiveness is possible, and that restoration is real. Although the world still experiences suffering and the effects of sin, the promise of redemption stands strong. It serves as a beacon of hope, illuminating the darkness and calling every weary soul and prodigal heart to return to their Creator, who loves them.

Ultimately, every moment in this divine narrative, from Genesis to Revelation, reveals a single truth: God desires not to be distant, but to dwell with His people once again, to walk alongside them as He did in the beginning, and to bring them fully and forever into His presence.

In this grand story, humanity is not left adrift. Instead, we are invited to take our place in the unfolding tale of grace, to respond to the call of reconciliation, and to walk the path that leads back to the heart of God, where healing, peace, and eternal communion await.

CHAPTER
6

The Prophetic Influence of God on Humanity

The prophets were divinely called and continually inspired individuals who profoundly influenced nations, kings, and everyday people. There are five major prophets and twelve minor prophets whose words are recorded in the Old and New Testaments. In a fallen world desperate for direction, these prophets boldly proclaimed the Holy Word of God, even in the face of potential death. God's calling of these individuals demonstrates that He never lost contact with His creation, using them to gradually draw the fallen world back to Him. The prophetic tradition serves as one of the clearest means by which God connects with humanity, especially during times of spiritual drift and moral collapse. More than mere historical figures or religious reformers, the prophets were divinely chosen vessels through whom God spoke directly to a world in urgent need of correction, clarity, and restoration. Their voices were not mere echoes of human wisdom, but reflections of God's desire to reconcile humanity to Himself—a sacred bridge through which heaven reached into earth to stir the hearts of men and women.

From the earliest moments of Israel's formation as a nation, God raised up prophets to call His people back to faithfulness. This prophetic tradition emerged not during times of comfort or peace, but amidst political turmoil, social corruption, and spiritual decline. These messengers did not come from royal courts or priestly orders; they often arose from obscurity as ordinary men and women burdened by the word of the Lord. As Jeremiah 1:5 recounts, God told the prophet, **"Before I formed you in the womb I knew you, before you were born I set you apart; I appointed you as a prophet to the nations."** This calling underscores that prophecy was always God's initiative—a divine response to humanity's rebellion and an act of grace intended to lead His people back into covenant. The prophetic voice often stood in opposition to kings, priests, and cultural norms. These figures were spiritual outliers, national consciences, and bold proclaimers of divine truth. Amos, a shepherd-turned-prophet, was sent to the northern kingdom of Israel to confront systemic injustice during a time of material prosperity and religious decay. In Amos 5:11–12, he declared, **"You levy a straw tax on the poor and impose a tax on their grain... you oppress the innocent and take bribes and deprive the poor of justice in the courts."** His words were not merely critiques—they were God's own indictment against a nation that had forsaken righteousness and mercy.

Similarly, Micah denounced corrupt leadership and religious hypocrisy, encapsulating the prophetic call with a timeless truth in Micah 6:8: **"He has shown you, O mortal, what is good. And what does the Lord require of you? To act justly and to love mercy and to walk humbly with your God"**. This passage serves as a moral compass for all generations, anchoring God's people to His eternal standards.

...The prophets also offered hope and restoration. They were not solely messengers of judgment, but also heralds of grace.

Despite the depth of their warnings, the prophets also offered hope and restoration. They were not solely messengers of judgment, but also heralds of grace. Jeremiah, often known for his laments, conveyed the Lord's deep compassion in Jeremiah 3:14: **"Return, faithless people," declares the Lord, "for I am your husband. I will choose you... and bring you to Zion."** Though often rejected and persecuted, as shown in Jeremiah 20:9, **"His word is in my heart like a fire... I am weary of holding it in; indeed, I cannot"**; the prophets continued to speak, understanding their words were God's pursuit of reconciliation with His people.

Moreover, prophets served as countercultural witnesses, refusing to be swayed by political power or national agendas. Isaiah 31:1 warns, **"Woe to those who go down to Egypt for help... but do not look to** the Holy One of Israel or seek help from the Lord." The prophets reminded the people that true strength lay not in alliances or military power, but in covenantal faithfulness to God.

Prophetic figures extend beyond Israel, reflecting humanity's universal longing to hear from the divine and receive guidance that surpasses human limitations. While various traditions have their own expressions of prophecy, it is in biblical revelation that the prophetic voice reaches its fullest expression, culminating in the arrival of Jesus Christ—the ultimate Prophet, Priest, and King. As foretold in Deuteronomy 18:18 and confirmed in Acts 3:22, Christ is the prophet like Moses, yet greater, for He is the Word made flesh. He not only proclaimed the truth but also embodied it, revealing the Father and inviting all into His kingdom.

Jesus' life and ministry fulfilled and expanded the prophetic tradition, offering calls to repentance alongside the means of redemption and reconciliation through His death and resurrection. His message encapsulated the fullness of prophetic hope, as Mark 1:15 states: "**The kingdom of God has come near. Repent and believe the good news!**" Today, the prophetic voice continues—not through new Scripture, but through the Holy Spirit, who empowers the Church to bear witness to truth, justice, and righteousness. The Church is now entrusted with a prophetic mission, as Paul writes in 1 Corinthians 14:3: "**But the one who prophesies speaks to people for their strengthening, encouraging, and comfort.**" Thus, God's prophetic influence is far more than a historical footnote; it is a living, active force in the story of redemption. Through the prophets, God reached into the chaos of human history to reconnect with His creation, calling people not only to repentance but also to restoration, covenant, and ultimately to Himself. Their words continue to resonate through time, urging every generation to return to God, embrace His truth, and walk in His ways. Their legacy serves as a powerful reminder that God has never ceased speaking—and He has never stopped seeking His people.

Prophets hold a unique and sacred role in the biblical narrative as conduits of divine communication. Chosen by God, they speak on His behalf and reveal His will to humanity. Unlike mere fortune-tellers or detached religious figures, prophets exist at the intersection of the divine and the human, delivering messages that embody both eternal truth and the urgency of present action. Their voices, shaped by visions, dreams, and direct revelations, serve not only to foretell future events but, more importantly, to call people to live faithfully and righteously in their time.

Throughout Scripture, the prophetic function is manifested in various ways. God often communicates with prophets through visions, as seen in Isaiah 6:1, where Isaiah witnesses the majesty of God's throne: **"In the year that King Uzziah died, I saw the Lord, high and exalted, seated on a throne; and the train of his robe filled the temple."** This vision reveals God's holiness and marks Isaiah's call to deliver His message to a rebellious people. Similarly, the prophet Daniel receives divine insight through dreams and visions about the future of kingdoms and the coming of God's eternal reign. Daniel 2:19 states, **"During the night the mystery was revealed to Daniel in a vision. Then Daniel praised the God of heaven."** In other instances, God's voice comes through direct speech, as in Jeremiah 1:5, where the Lord declares: **"Before I formed you in the womb I knew you, before you were born I set you apart; I appointed you as a prophet to the nations."** This direct commissioning highlights both the intimacy and intentionality with which God selects His messengers. Prophets are not self-appointed; they are divinely chosen, often reluctant, and frequently burdened by the weight of their calling.

The content of prophetic messages varied significantly. Some served as warnings, calling for repentance and highlighting the consequences of national sin, as demonstrated in the ministries of Ezekiel and Amos. Others offered words of hope, assuring God's people that restoration and renewal were attainable. For instance, the prophet Joel urges the people in Joel 2:32 to return to God with fasting and weeping, while also proclaiming, **"Everyone who calls on the name of the Lord will be saved."** Throughout their messages, the prophets provided spiritual clarity amid moral confusion, reminding God's people to remember His covenant and to live in obedience.

Additionally, the prophets played a vital pastoral and societal role, addressing not only personal sin but also confronting systems of injustice, religious corruption, and social oppression. The prophet Micah encapsulates the ethical essence of the prophetic tradition in Micah 6:8, *stating,* "**He has shown you, O mortal, what is good. And what does the Lord require of you? To act justly and to love mercy and to walk humbly with your God.**" In this way, the prophets acted as the moral conscience of the nation, reminding both leaders and ordinary people of the importance of adhering to God's standards.

Crucially, the prophetic office was always rooted in covenantal faithfulness. The prophets did not create new religions or ideologies; rather, they called people back to the truths already revealed through Moses and the Torah. Their role was to mediate between God and His people, similar to Moses himself, who is regarded as the archetype of all prophets. Deuteronomy 18:18 anticipates a future prophet like Moses, declaring, "**I will raise up for them a prophet like you from among their fellow Israelites, and I will put my words in his mouth. He will tell them everything I command him.**" This prophecy ultimately points to Jesus Christ, the final and complete revelation of God to humanity.

In the New Testament, the prophetic role is both fulfilled and transformed through Christ, who is not only a prophet but also the Word made flesh. Hebrews 1:1-2 highlights this transition: "**In the past God spoke to our ancestors through the prophets at many times and in various ways, but in these last days he has spoken to us by his Son...**" Christ embodies and completes the prophetic mission, not merely by speaking God's word but by being God's Word, providing guidance, redemption, and reconciliation. Even after Christ's ascension, the prophetic gift persists. Through the Holy Spirit, God continues to speak, guide, and convict those He calls, offering the Church clarity and courage as it proclaims the gospel in a complex and often hostile world. As 1 Corinthians 14:3 states, "**the one who prophesies speaks to people for their strengthening, encouraging and comfort.**"

> **In the New Testament, the prophetic role is both fulfilled and transformed through Christ, who is not only a prophet but also the Word made flesh.**

Prophets are not relics of a bygone era; they are vital instruments in God's unfolding redemptive plan. Throughout biblical history, they acted as divine representatives, speaking not by their own authority but through the will and inspiration of the Holy Spirit. In times of national confusion, they brought clarity; in moments of collective error, they offered correction; and in seasons of despair, they proclaimed hope. Whether through dreams, visions, signs, or the persistent voice of conviction, the prophetic word has consistently aimed to realign the people of God with His will. The role of the prophet was never merely to predict future events but to call people to faithful living—to repentance, righteousness, and renewed covenant loyalty. Their messages pierced through cultural compromise and moral drift, continually pointing back to God's holiness, justice, and mercy.

As we reflect on the enduring influence of the prophetic voice, we are naturally led to consider what it means to live rightly before God. The prophets did not simply announce divine truth; they demanded a response. Their words were inseparable from moral and ethical exhortation, urging individuals and nations alike to pursue justice, love mercy, and walk humbly with God (Micah 6:8). Thus, the prophetic ministry opens the door to our next focus: moral guidance—how God, through both His revealed Word and Spirit, continues to instruct His people on how to live.

MORAL GUIDANCE

At the core of the prophetic mission is a deep and unwavering commitment to moral and ethical integrity—a divine call for people, especially leaders and nations, to return to God's standards of righteousness, justice, and compassion. The prophets were not mere forecasters of future events; they were bold voices of conscience, raised to confront a world that often drifts into complacency, corruption, and cruelty. Their messages were urgent and at times unsettling, aimed at exposing sin, challenging injustice, and inspiring societal transformation.

A defining characteristic of prophetic ministry is the willingness to hold the powerful accountable, even at great personal cost. The prophet Amos, for instance, vehemently condemned the exploitation of the poor by the wealthy elites in Israel. In Amos 5:11-12, he declares: **"You levy a straw tax on the poor and impose a tax on their grain. Therefore, though you have built stone mansions, you will not live in them... For I know how many are your offenses and how great your sins."** Amos denounces those who trample the needy while enriching themselves, exposing a system where economic injustice and religious hypocrisy coexist. His message emphasizes that true worship of God cannot be separated from how we treat society's vulnerable members.

Similarly, Isaiah addresses the disconnect between religious rituals and ethical behavior. God, speaking through Isaiah, states in Isaiah 1:13, 17: **"Stop bringing meaningless offerings! Your incense is detestable to me... Learn to do right; seek justice. Defend the oppressed. Take up the cause of the fatherless; plead the case of the widow."** Here, the prophet reveals God's disdain for hollow rituals that lack justice and mercy. True devotion, Isaiah insists, is demonstrated by defending the defenseless and standing with the marginalized. The prophets also consistently call for repentance and personal accountability. The prophet Micah famously summarizes God's ethical expectations into three powerful imperatives in Micah 6:8: **"He has shown you, O mortal, what is good. And what does the Lord require of you? To act justly and to love mercy and to walk humbly with your God."** This verse encapsulates the prophetic mission—not only to condemn wrongdoing but to guide individuals and nations toward a way of life that reflects God's character. The call to justice is not abstract; it is profoundly relational, originating from a heart aligned with God's compassion and holiness.

Prophetic ministry is not solely confrontational; it also brings a message of hope, healing, and restoration, particularly for the broken and forgotten. Prophets provide comfort to the afflicted, assuring them that God sees their suffering and will act on their behalf. In Jeremiah 29:11, God promises His people: **"For I know the plans I have for you... Plans to prosper you and not to harm you, plans to give you hope and a future."** Even after delivering a message of judgment, Jeremiah ultimately conveys a redemptive message—God disciplines not to destroy, but to restore His people to a covenant relationship.

Jesus embraced the prophetic mantle, echoing and fulfilling the calls of the prophets before Him. In His inaugural sermon, He declared in Luke 4:18, **"The Spirit of the Lord is on me, because he has anointed me to proclaim good news to the poor... To set the oppressed free,"** quoting Isaiah 61. Christ's ministry was deeply rooted in the prophetic tradition of challenging religious leaders, confronting injustice, and embracing the outcast. His life exemplified the righteousness and compassion that the prophets proclaimed, demonstrating that the prophetic call is not merely about rebuke, but about reconciling a broken world to God's justice and love.

Ultimately, the prophetic voice in Scripture calls every generation to engage in honest self-examination. It reminds us that God is not indifferent to injustice or silent in the face of suffering. He speaks—through the prophets, through Christ, and through His Spirit—urging us to live in a manner that honors the dignity of every person and reflects His kingdom on earth. The call is clear: turn from selfishness, walk in righteousness, and extend mercy to those in need. By doing so, we carry forward the legacy of these prophets, not only as hearers of the Word but as active participants in God's ongoing mission of justice, mercy, and redemption.

SOCIAL JUSTICE

The influence of the prophets in Scripture extends well beyond individual behavior or personal piety; it penetrates deeply into the social, economic, and political structures of society. These men and women of God were not only concerned with inner devotion but also with how that devotion was reflected in the treatment of others, especially the poor, the oppressed, and the marginalized. The prophetic voice acted as a divine conscience, courageously addressing unjust systems and corrupt leadership, and calling entire nations to accountability.

Throughout the Old Testament, prophets advocated for justice not merely as a legal concept, but as a reflection of God's own character. Isaiah 58:6 exemplifies this clearly. In this passage, God confronts a people who engage in fasting and religious rituals while turning a blind eye to injustice: **Is not this the kind of fasting I have chosen: to loose the chains of injustice and untie the cords of the yoke, to set the oppressed free and break every yoke?**". The verse continues by urging acts of compassion, such as sharing food with the hungry, sheltering the homeless, and clothing the naked. For the prophets, genuine spirituality was inseparable from social action. Righteousness was not only vertical (toward God) but also horizontal (toward others).

Amos, another compelling prophetic voice, delivered sharp rebukes against the exploitation of the poor and the corruption of justice in the courts. Addressing a society that had become comfortable and wealthy at the expense of the vulnerable, he proclaimed in Amos 5:24: **"Let justice roll on like a river, righteousness like a never-failing stream!"**. Amos exposed a false **God despises** religiosity that concealed systemic greed and **worship** oppression. His words resonate through time, **disconnected from** reminding us that God despises worship **ethical living and** disconnected from ethical living and demands **demands justice...** justice that flows freely and abundantly, not as a trickle but as a flood.

Jeremiah 22:15–16 similarly challenges kings and leaders who misuse their power and neglect the vulnerable. Through Jeremiah, God rebukes King Jehoiakim for constructing an extravagant palace without ensuring justice: **"Does it make you a king to have more and more cedar? Did not your father have food and drink? He did what was right and just, so all went well with him. He defended the cause of the poor and needy, and so all went well. Is that not what it means to know me?"** In this powerful statement, God equates knowing Him with defending the poor and acting justly, emphasizing that a genuine relationship with God necessitates social righteousness.

The prophets also condemned national pride and political alliances that disregarded God's commands. When Israel and Judah relied on military strength or alliances with pagan nations rather than trusting in God, the prophets called them back to faithfulness. For instance, Hosea 12:6 warns Israel against trusting Egypt and Assyria: **"But you must return to your God; maintain love and justice, and wait for your God always."** Their messages clarified that true security lies not in power or politics, but in obedience to God's covenant.

Moreover, the prophets envisioned a world transformed by justice and peace, often referred to as eschatological hope. Micah 4:1–4 depicts a future where nations flow to the mountain of the Lord, swords are turned into plowshares, and war ceases. **"Everyone will sit under their own vine and under their own fig tree, and no one will make them afraid."** This prophetic vision goes beyond mere critique; it offers hope for a restored and just society, rooted in God's rule and characterized by peace, security, and dignity for all.

In the New Testament, Jesus continues and fulfills the prophetic tradition by addressing both personal sin and social injustice. In His inaugural sermon in Luke 4:18–19, quoting Isaiah, He declares: "**The Spirit of the Lord is on me, because he has anointed me to proclaim good news to the poor... to set the oppressed free, to proclaim the year of the Lord's favor.**" Jesus' ministry directly engages with the suffering of the poor, the marginalized, the sick, and the sinner, demonstrating that the kingdom of God is not an abstract concept but a reality that confronts injustice and heals brokenness.

Eventually, the prophetic call for social and political righteousness is rooted in the belief that every person reflects the image of God and, as such, deserves dignity, fairness, and compassion. The prophets remind us that God cares deeply about the structures that govern human society. He is concerned with how power is wielded, how the vulnerable are treated, and how justice is upheld. Their voices continue to challenge us to create communities where righteousness serves as the foundation, justice is the standard, and compassion is a daily practice.

In every generation, the prophetic witness calls people of faith not only to pursue personal holiness but also to actively engage in the world. This call compels us to live as agents of justice, peace, and truth in a world that desperately needs to hear the quality of God's heart.

SPIRITUAL RENEWAL

At the heart of the prophetic message is an urgent and unwavering call for spiritual renewal and repentance. The prophets refused to let God's people succumb to complacency, idolatry, or empty rituals. They were entrusted with a sacred mission: to awaken the slumbering soul, challenge hardened hearts, and rekindle a fervent desire for God's truth and righteousness. Their voices, often heard in the wilderness of moral decay and spiritual decline, sought to guide individuals and entire nations back into a right relationship with their Creator.

Throughout Scripture, the prophetic call to repentance is both direct and compassionate. The prophet Joel powerfully urges the people of Judah to turn from sin with genuine inward transformation rather than mere outward displays. In Joel 2:12-13, he proclaims, "**Even now,**" declares the Lord, "**return to me with all your heart, with fasting and weeping and mourning. Rend your heart and not your garments. Return to the Lord your God, for he is gracious and compassionate, slow to anger and abounding in love.**" This passage encapsulates the essence of prophetic urgency. Repentance is not simply about appearances or ritualistic responses; it involves a deep, heartfelt return to God, acknowledging sin while longing for His mercy. The call to "rend your heart" invites the listener to be honest with God, to feel the weight of disobedience, and to return to the One who is always ready to forgive.

The prophet Ezekiel issues a powerful call for spiritual renewal during a time of exile and judgment. Speaking on behalf of God, he declares in Ezekiel 18:30–32: "**Repent! Turn away from all your offenses; then sin will not be your downfall. Rid yourselves of all the offenses you have committed, and get a new heart and a new spirit... For I take no pleasure in the death of anyone, declares the Sovereign Lord. Repent and live!**" Here, repentance transcends mere regret; it is the pathway to life. God's plea stems not from wrath but from love. His intention is not to punish, but to restore. The promise of a "new heart and a new spirit" foreshadows the transformative power of God's grace, which renews the inner being and empowers believers to live in holiness.

The prophets address spiritual apathy, which leads to a gradual distancing from God characterized by indifference and neglect. Although the people maintained their religious rituals, their hearts were distant from God. Malachi, writing after the exile, mourns the people's lukewarm worship, stating in Malachi 1:10: "**Oh, that one of you would shut the temple doors, so that you would not light useless fires on my altar! I am not pleased with you,**" says the Lord Almighty, "**and I will accept no offering from your hands.**"

These words reveal God's desire for genuine devotion rather than empty rituals. He seeks worship that arises from lives surrendered to His will. The prophetic message pierces through pretense, exposing the divide between outward piety and inward reality. This call to renewal is a recurring theme in the Old Testament prophets and continues in the New Testament, particularly in the ministry of John the Baptist. He prepared the way for Jesus by preaching a message of repentance, as captured in Matthew 3:2: **"Repent, for the kingdom of heaven has come near."** John echoed the prophetic tradition and pointed to the Messiah's arrival, who would baptize not just with water but with the Holy Spirit and fire. In Jesus, the call to repentance finds its ultimate fulfillment. His ministry began with the same urgent call in Mark 1:15: **"The time has come... The kingdom of God has come near. Repent and believe the good news!"** Jesus not only called people to repentance—He made it possible, offering grace, forgiveness, and a new way of life through His death and resurrection.

> **Jesus not only called people to repentance—He made it possible, offering grace, forgiveness, and a new way of life through His death and resurrection.**

The prophetic call, once proclaimed from mountaintops and temple courts, now resonates through the gospel itself, inviting all who hear to lay down their sin and embrace new life in Christ.

In every generation, the prophetic message continues to challenge indifference, confront sin, and inspire transformation. It serves as a divine wake-up call, urging us to reject compromise and pursue God wholeheartedly. In a world often numb to truth and distracted, the voice of the prophet still calls out—not to condemn, but to spark a deeper hunger for righteousness, a renewed passion for holiness, and a restored intimacy with the living God.

HOPE AND PROMISE

Though the messages of the prophets often conveyed warning and judgment, they were always infused with hope. Embedded within their solemn calls to repentance and vivid pronouncements of impending consequences is a consistent thread of divine promise—a forward-looking assurance that God is not finished with His people and that His purposes will ultimately lead to redemption, restoration, and peace. The prophets not only held Israel accountable for its failures but also presented a vision of what could be achieved if the people returned to God. Their words carried the weight of divine justice alongside the warmth of divine mercy. The prophets frequently pointed to the future fulfillment of God's covenantal promises, including the coming of a Messiah, the restoration of a scattered people, and the establishment of an eternal kingdom. These promises were not vague or wishful; they were firmly rooted in God's faithfulness and offered with certainty due to His character.

For instance, Isaiah prophesied during a period of significant national turmoil and moral decay. Yet, in the midst of judgment, he offers a radiant promise of hope in Isaiah 9:6: **"For to us a child is born, to us a son is given, and the government will be on his shoulders. And he will be called Wonderful Counselor, Mighty God, Everlasting Father, Prince of Peace."** This prophecy not only foretells the birth of the Messiah but also speaks of a future kingdom governed by divine wisdom and peace. It points forward to Jesus Christ, whose birth, life, and eventual reign would bring salvation not only to Israel but to all nations.

Similarly, the prophet Jeremiah, often referred to as the "weeping prophet" for his laments over Jerusalem's downfall, was entrusted with messages of future restoration. In Jeremiah 29:11, God assures His exiled people: **"For I know the plans I have for you... Plans to prosper you and not to harm you, plans to give you hope and a future."** This assurance was given not during a time of peace but amid exile and despair—a reminder that even when all seems lost, God's plan is still unfolding.

Jeremiah spoke of a new covenant, one that would not be inscribed on stone tablets but written on human hearts. He proclaims in Jeremiah 31:33, **"This is the covenant I will make with the people of Israel... I will put my law in their minds and write it on their hearts. I will be their God, and they will be my people."** This prophetic message anticipated the coming of the Holy Spirit through Christ, who would transform hearts and restore the relationship between God and humanity in a deeper, more intimate way. Similarly, Ezekiel, witnessing the destruction of Jerusalem, received visions of hope. Through him, God promised in Ezekiel 36:26, **"I will give you a new heart and put a new spirit in you... I will remove from you your heart of stone and give you a heart of flesh."** This reflects a restoration that only God can achieve—a complete renewal of the inner life that leads not merely to outward obedience but to genuine spiritual rebirth.

The prophet Micah, in Micah 4:1–4, envisioned universal peace and divine rule: **"In the last days... The mountain of the Lord's temple will be established... Nation will not take up sword against nation, nor will they train for war anymore. Everyone will sit under their own vine and under their own fig tree, and no one will make them afraid."** This eschatological vision points to a time when God's kingdom will be fully realized, characterized by peace, justice, and security—a world restored under the rule of a righteous King.

In the New Testament, the fulfillment of these prophetic hopes is found in Jesus Christ. The Gospel writers frequently highlight how Jesus' life realized what the prophets had foretold. Matthew 1:22–23 states, **"All this took place to fulfill what the Lord had said through the prophet: 'The virgin will conceive and give birth to a son, and they will call him Immanuel'** (which means 'God with us')."

The ultimate hope of the prophets extends beyond national restoration to encompass the redemption of all humanity through the coming of the Messiah. In Christ, the kingdom of God has begun, and while it has not yet been fully realized, His return assures the complete fulfillment of every prophetic vision. Therefore, the prophetic voice conveys not despair but expectant hope. It calls people to repentance and encourages belief in the goodness of God's future, assuring them that even in the darkest moments, God is still at work—still speaking, still redeeming. Empowered by divine vision, the prophets inspire hearts to persevere, fostering faith and trust. They urge each generation to look beyond present troubles and focus on the faithful God who keeps His promises.

God's prophetic influence on humanity is a profound and enduring force—multifaceted, dynamic, and divinely orchestrated to guide, correct, inspire, and restore. From ancient times to the present, the prophetic voice has served not only as a record of divine communication but also as a living call to align human life with the will of a righteous and compassionate God. Through the prophets, God has expressed not only His commands but also His deep longing for relationship, His sorrow over injustice, and His desire for the restoration of all creation.

The influence of the prophets is intricately woven throughout Scripture, revealing God's heart across different eras like a golden thread. Their legacy encompasses divine communication, exemplified in God's charge to Jeremiah in Jeremiah 1:8–9: **"Do not be afraid of them, for I am with you and will rescue you," declares the Lord. Then the Lord reached out his hand and touched my mouth and said to me, "I have put my words in your mouth."** The prophet speaks not from personal insight, but with the authority and presence of God, delivering messages that cut through deception to reveal eternal truths. Additionally, prophets serve as moral guides, ardently advocating for holiness in both private and public life. The call to justice and ethical living is encapsulated in Micah 6:8: **"He has shown you, O mortal, what is good. And what does the Lord require of you? To act justly, to love mercy, and to walk humbly with your God."** This is not merely a theoretical concept; it is a divine mandate, a way of life rooted in God's character and essential for a society to thrive in righteousness. Their messages have boldly confronted social injustice and oppression, as Isaiah 1:17 exhorts: **"Learn to do right; seek justice. Defend the oppressed. Take up the cause of the fatherless; plead the case of the widow."** The prophets were not satisfied with mere moral reform; they called for a complete restructuring of society in accordance with God's justice and mercy. Their voices carried divine authority that challenged kings, exposed corruption, and amplified the voices of the marginalized.

> **The prophets were not satisfied with mere moral reform; they called for a complete restructuring of society...**

Equally vital was the prophet's call for spiritual renewal. Time and again, they urged God's people to abandon their idolatry, ritualism, and spiritual apathy, returning with contrite hearts. In Ezekiel 18:30–31, God pleads through the prophet: **"Repent! Turn away from all your offenses; then sin will not be your downfall... Get a new heart and a new spirit. Why will you die, people of Israel?"** This is not the cry of an angry ruler, but the sorrow of a Father longing to restore His children. Through such calls, the prophets reignited the flickering flame of devotion, inviting people back into a covenant relationship with the God who loves them.

Above all, the prophetic message is infused with hope. Even while addressing sin and predicting judgment, the prophets anticipated a future of redemption—a time when justice would flow like rivers, the Messiah would reign in peace, and hearts of stone would transform into hearts of flesh. Isaiah 11:9 captures this vision: **"They will neither harm nor destroy on all my holy mountain, for the earth will be filled with the knowledge of the Lord as the waters cover the sea."** This eschatological hope— partially realized through Christ and awaiting complete fulfillment at His return; serves as the prophetic foundation of Christian faith and perseverance.

Thus, the legacy of the prophets lives on, not only through their words but also through the enduring impact of their witness to faith, truth, and righteousness. Their messages remain timeless, urging each generation to seek God's will, advocate for justice, and trust in His promises. They address the human condition with both clarity and compassion, reminding us that God is not distant but actively engaged in human history, calling His people to be lights in the darkness, reflections of His holiness, and participants in His redemptive plan.

As we reflect on the prophetic tradition, we are called anew by the ancient words of Zechariah 1:3: **"Return to me,"** declares the Lord Almighty, **"and I will return to you."** This is not merely a historical summons; it is a living invitation that transcends generations. To respond with faith means recognizing the prophets not only as historical figures but as vessels of divine urgency—an urgency that resonates in our lives today. Their messages urge us toward repentance, covenant fidelity, justice, mercy, and, above all, a renewed closeness with the God who is both holy and near.

However, the prophetic word does not conclude with exile, judgment, or longing. Instead, it points toward a deeper hope and a more complete restoration than Israel could have envisioned. This hope is realized not through law, temple, or ritual, but through a person—Jesus Christ, the promised Redeemer—in whom every prophetic promise of God is fulfilled (2 Corinthians 1:20). The long-awaited Messiah is not just another prophet; He embodies the very essence of the message proclaimed by the prophets. In Him, God's redemptive plan takes on flesh, offering not only forgiveness but also transformation, reconciliation, and eternal life.

With this understanding, we now turn to the heart of the gospel— God's perfect redemptive plan through Christ—where shadows become substance, and the hope of the prophets finds its glorious fulfillment in the cross and resurrection of Jesus.

CHAPTER

7

God's Perfect Redemptive Plan Through Christ:
Did Jesus Have to Die?

God's perfect redemptive plan through Christ unfolds as a breathtaking narrative, characterized by grace, intention, and divine wisdom. It is not an afterthought or a reaction to humanity's failure, but a meticulously designed purpose that spans from eternity past to the present and future. This redemptive story expresses God's desire to restore His creation, ultimately fulfilled through Jesus Christ's life, death, and resurrection. This redemptive story reveals God's unwavering desire to restore and reconcile His creation, expressed most clearly and powerfully through the life, death, and resurrection of Jesus Christ.

At the core of this plan is the sacrificial death of Jesus. His crucifixion was not merely an ancient tragedy or a symbolic gesture; it was a pivotal moment in human history, fulfilling centuries of prophetic expectation and divine promise. On the cross, God's justice and mercy converged perfectly. Jesus bore the full weight of sin—not His own, but ours—so that we might be forgiven and restored. As Paul writes in Romans 5:8, "**But God demonstrates his own love for us in this: While we were still sinners, Christ died for us.**" This act represents the ultimate expression of divine love, with Christ giving His life for a broken and undeserving world.

In Christian theology, the Old Testament sacrificial system is seen as a foreshadowing of the ultimate sacrifice made by Jesus Christ. The New Testament presents Jesus in John 1:29 as "**the Lamb** of God, who takes away the sin of the world," connecting His death to the Passover sacrifice and the various sin offerings of the Old Covenant. Hebrews 9:12-14 highlights that Christ, unlike the Levitical priests who repeatedly offered sacrifices, entered the heavenly sanctuary: "**He did not enter by means of the blood of goats and calves; but he entered the Most Holy Place once for all by his own blood, thus obtaining eternal redemption.** [13] **The blood of goats and bulls and the ashes of a heifer sprinkled on those who are ceremonially unclean sanctify them so that they are outwardly clean.** [14] **How much more, then, will the blood of Christ, who through the eternal Spirit offered himself unblemished to God, cleanse our consciences from acts that lead to death,** [h] **so that we may serve the living God!**" It is this offering of His own blood that secures eternal redemption, marking a significant theological transformation. While the sacrifices of the Old Testament required continual repetition, Christ's sacrifice is final and complete. Hebrews 10:10 states, "We have been made holy through the sacrifice of the body of Jesus Christ once for all."

> **While the sacrifices of the Old Testament required continual repetition, Christ's sacrifice is final and complete.**

This fulfillment eliminated the need for further animal offerings. The tearing of the Temple veil at Christ's death (Matthew 27:51) symbolizes this transition, removing the separation between God and humanity and granting direct access to God through Jesus.

Although Christians no longer offer animal sacrifices, the concept of sacrifice remains central in various forms of worship and theology, with different Christian traditions interpreting this practice in unique ways. In Protestant Christianity, there is a strong emphasis on Christ's sacrifice as fully accomplished on the cross. Protestants typically reject the idea of the Eucharist as a repeated or ongoing sacrifice, viewing Communion instead as a memorial of Christ's death, in accordance with His command, "**Do this in remembrance of me.**" The sacrificial element is understood in a spiritual context, whereby believers participate in Christ's sacrifice by faith, receiving its benefits without re-offering it in a ritualistic manner.

While Protestants do not participate in ritualistic sacrifices, the New Testament outlines spiritual sacrifices that all believers are called to offer. Hebrews 13:15 encourages us to "**continually offer** to God a sacrifice of praise—the fruit of lips that openly profess his name." Similarly, Romans 12:1 urges believers to "**offer your bodies as a living sacrifice, holy and pleasing to God—this is your true and proper worship.**" These passages indicate that, under the New Covenant, sacrifice is no longer linked to animals or material offerings but instead involves a life dedicated to God through worship, service, and obedience. Although the Old Testament sacrificial system ended with Christ's coming, its theological principles still shape Christian worship and devotion. Concepts such as substitutionary atonement, the importance of holiness and obedience, and the call for sacrificial living remain vital in Christian thought.

Independent Christians, particularly those associated with non-denominational churches, emphasize personal faith, a direct relationship with God, and biblical authority over ecclesiastical traditions when approaching biblical teachings. Their understanding of the Old Testament sacrificial system and its fulfillment in Christ reflects a commitment to scriptural interpretation, simplicity in worship, and a focus on practical expressions of faith.

Non-denominational Christians typically view the Old Testament sacrifices as foreshadowing Christ's ultimate sacrifice. Independent churches emphasize the sufficiency of Christ's atoning work, often rejecting any idea of an ongoing sacrificial presence in worship. They highlight Christ's completed work on the cross, interpreting His declaration, "**It is finished**" in John 19:30, as marking the end of the sacrificial system and the beginning of direct access to God for believers.

Unlike ritualistic traditions such as Catholicism and Orthodoxy, non-denominational Christians do not view worship as a re-sacrificial act, even in symbolic or sacramental terms. The Lord's Supper, while regularly observed, is primarily seen as a commemorative ordinance rather than a means of grace or sacrificial participation. The emphasis lies on remembering Christ's work, examining one's heart, and reinforcing faith through a personal encounter with God. Scriptures highlighted in their faith focus on renewal instead of a mystical sacrificial event. This stands in contrast to traditions that incorporate sacrificial elements into their communion practices. Non-denominational Christians typically stress the spiritual priesthood of all believers (1 Peter 2:9), negating the need for human mediators or a priestly role between the believer and God. The doctrine of direct access to God through Christ is central to their worship and theology.

While rejecting ritual sacrifice, independent Christians minimize ritualistic elements, emphasizing the concept of spiritual sacrifices. Unlike the Old Testament system of external offerings, non-denominational theology promotes an internalized and personal approach to sacrificial living. Living in obedience and moral integrity is viewed as an act of worship. They prioritize service and evangelism, considering sharing the Gospel and serving others as spiritual offerings to God. Stewardship through financial giving and encouragement is framed as cheerful and voluntary, aligning with 2 Corinthians 9:7: **"God loves a cheerful giver."** Lastly, worship is understood as a heartfelt offering of praise, music, and communal engagement, all regarded as genuine sacrifices from the heart, fulfilling Hebrews 13:15: **"Let us continually offer to God a sacrifice of praise."** This theology of everyday sacrifice ensures that faith is practical and lived out rather than confined to religious rituals. Worship is often spontaneous and spirit-led, focusing on gratitude and personal transformation rather than structured ritualistic sacrifice.

Independent churches typically reject hierarchical or institutional mediators between God and humanity, believing that Christ alone fulfills that role. This belief is rooted in 1 Timothy 2:5, which states, **"For there is one God and one mediator between God and mankind, the man Christ Jesus."** As a result, non-denominational Christians avoid concepts like priestly ordination in a sacrificial context, relics, and consecrated sacramental elements. While they minimize ritualistic practices, they emphasize sacrificial living, which is expressed through prayer, fasting, outreach, discipleship, and personal obedience to God's will. Many in independent churches stress the importance of missions and community service, viewing these actions as a modern fulfillment of Christ's call to self-denial and service (Mark 8:34).

In non-denominational Christianity, the Old Testament sacrificial system is seen as fulfilled in Christ, with worship understood as a direct, unmediated experience with God. There is no ongoing notion of ritual sacrifice; instead, the focus is on spiritual sacrifice, demonstrated through personal holiness and acts of service that foster genuine worship. Independent Christians express their faith by offering themselves in obedience, rather than participating in ritualistic reenactments of the sacrificial system. This fosters a personal relationship with God, making the believer's life an ongoing expression of love and devotion to Christ. However, the story does not end at the cross. The resurrection of Jesus powerfully confirms that His sacrifice was accepted and that sin and death have been defeated. As Paul affirms in 1 Corinthians 15:17, **"If Christ has not been raised, your faith is futile; you are still in your sins."** Because He has been raised, we now live in hope, secure in the power of His resurrection and the promise of eternal life.

This redemptive work goes beyond individual salvation; it is universal in its scope. Colossians 1:19–20 states, **"For God was pleased to have all his fullness dwell in him, and through him to reconcile to himself all things, whether things on earth or things in heaven, by making peace through his blood, shed on the cross."** God's redemptive plan is not solely about rescuing people; it encompasses the restoration of all creation, healing what was broken, and renewing what was lost. In Christ, we encounter the full heart of God: a God who loves without limit, a Savior who willingly lays down His life, and a Spirit who works within us to make us new. The story of redemption is at the heart of Scripture, inviting every person to emerge from darkness into light, to exchange guilt for grace, and to embrace the eternal purposes of a faithful, redeeming God.

> God's redemptive plan is not solely about rescuing people; it encompasses the restoration of all creation...

In the grand tapestry of God's redemptive work, the death of Jesus Christ is not a tragic twist of fate, but rather the central and foundational cornerstone—a deliberate, sovereign act ordained by God before the foundations of the world. The crucifixion of Jesus is far from a mere historical incident or an unjust execution; it is the culmination of God's eternal plan to redeem fallen humanity and reconcile creation to Himself through the atoning sacrifice of His Son.

From the very beginning of Scripture, the shadow of the cross is evident. In Genesis 3:15, following the fall of Adam and Eve, God pronounces judgment on the serpent, declaring, **"I will put enmity** between you and the woman, and between your offspring and hers; he will crush your head, and you will strike his heel." This is widely recognized by theologians as the protoevangelium—the first gospel promise—that a descendant of the woman would ultimately defeat the powers of evil, even though He Himself would suffer in the process. This prophetic thread runs through every book of Scripture, gradually revealing the contours of God's redemptive plan.

The prophetic anticipation of a suffering Savior is vividly expressed in the writings of Isaiah, particularly in the famous passage of Isaiah 53. Here, the "Suffering Servant" is described as one who is **"pierced for our transgressions"** and **"crushed for our iniquities"** (Isaiah 53:5). Isaiah further states, **"The Lord has laid on him the iniquity of us all"** (Isaiah 53:6) and **"it was the Lord's will to crush him and cause him to suffer"** (Isaiah 53:10). These verses provide profound theological insight: the suffering and death of the Messiah were part of God's will—not because He delights in pain, but because only such a sacrifice could fully atone for the depth of human sin.

The New Testament affirms that Jesus understood His mission in these very terms. In John 10:17–18, He declares, **"The reason my Father loves me is that I lay down my life—only to take it up again. No one takes it from me, but I lay it down of my own accord."** This voluntary surrender underscores the intentionality of the cross; it was not imposed on Him. He accepted it willingly out of obedience to the Father and love for humanity.

The apostle Paul elaborates on the theological significance of Christ's death with remarkable clarity in his letters. In Romans 3:25–26, he writes, **"God presented Christ as a sacrifice of atonement, through the shedding of his blood—to be received by faith. He did this to demonstrate his righteousness... So as to be just and the one who justifies those who have faith in Jesus."** Here, Paul illustrates how the death of Christ satisfies both God's justice and mercy. Sin demands judgment, but through Christ, that judgment is placed on a willing substitute, enabling the guilty to be declared righteous.

In Galatians 3:13, Paul links Jesus' death to the curse of the law: **"Christ redeemed us from the curse of the law by becoming a curse for us, for it is written: 'Cursed is everyone who is hung on a pole.'"** This citation from Deuteronomy 21:23 emphasizes that Jesus took on the full burden of covenantal judgment, freeing us from condemnation. Similarly, 2 Corinthians 5:21 states, "**God made him who had no sin to be sin for us, so that in him we might become the righteousness of God.**" This illustrates the great exchange of the gospel: Christ bears our sin and grants us His righteousness.

The crucifixion of Jesus, occurring during Passover—a festival rich in symbolism—holds significant historical meaning. The Passover lamb, whose blood protected the Israelites from judgment in Egypt (Exodus 12), serves as a powerful type of Christ, whom John the Baptist refers to in John 1:29 as "**the Lamb of God, who takes away the sin of the world.**" This is further clarified in 1 Corinthians 5:7: "**For Christ, our Passover lamb, has been sacrificed.**" The manner of Jesus' death on a Roman cross is also significant. Crucifixion was a brutal and shameful form of execution reserved for the worst criminals. Yet, in this profound humiliation, the fullness of divine love is revealed. As Philippians 2:8 states, "**He humbled himself by becoming obedient to death—even death on a cross!**" The cross, once a symbol of shame, transforms into a symbol of victory and salvation.

The imagery of Jesus as the superior sacrifice is prominently featured in the Epistle to the Hebrews. No other book in the New Testament addresses this theme as thoroughly, particularly in relation to the Jewish sacrificial system. Written during a time of significant theological tension—likely in the latter half of the first century, before the destruction of the Jerusalem Temple in AD 70—Hebrews speaks to a Jewish-Christian audience grappling with Christ's role in the context of the Mosaic covenant. These believers faced the temptation to revert to the familiar rituals of the past, seeking comfort in the visible practices of temple worship and animal sacrifice.

In response, the author of Hebrews makes a profound theological declaration: the old covenant's sacrificial system was merely a shadow, a preparatory symbol of something greater that has now been fulfilled in Jesus Christ. The book draws numerous parallels between Jesus and the high priest, notably stating that Jesus did enter by "blood of goats" but "once for all" which brought about eternal redemption.

> ...The old covenant's sacrificial system was merely a shadow, a preparatory symbol of something greater that has now been fulfilled in Jesus Christ.

Furthermore, Christ's sacrifice fulfills the Levitical system established in the Mosaic Law. The sacrificial system pointed forward to this ultimate offering, which would perfect forever those being made holy (Hebrews 10:14). In Hebrews, Jesus emerges as the definitive solution to the problem of human atonement, a conclusion drawn not only from His unique nature but also from the superiority of His role, priesthood, and once-for-all sacrifice.

The author emphasizes that, unlike the frail, sinful, and temporary priests of the old covenant, Jesus is the great and eternal High Priest. Hebrews 7:26–27 states, "**Such a high priest truly meets our need— one who is holy, blameless, pure, set apart from sinners, exalted above the heavens. Unlike the other high priests, he does not need to offer sacrifices day after day... He sacrificed for their sins once for all when he offered himself.**" In contrast to the repeated sacrifices of the Levitical system, Jesus' offering is final and complete.

Under the old covenant, the sacrificial system relied on the blood of bulls and goats, which Hebrews 10:4 reminds us could never take away sins. While these rituals were symbolic and pointed to something greater, they lacked the power to fully cleanse the human conscience. Hebrews 9:13–14 explains that while animal blood could not purify the body, only the blood of Christ can cleanse the inner person—from "**acts that lead to death, so that we may serve the living God.**" Jesus' atonement is effective because of His sinless nature. As stated in Hebrews 4:15, He was tempted in every way as we are, yet without sin. This makes Him the only appropriate substitute for bearing the penalty of human guilt. Being both fully divine and fully human, He can represent humanity before God and offer a sacrifice of infinite value—satisfying divine justice while extending divine mercy.

Moreover, Jesus' priesthood is eternal. Hebrews 7:24–25 affirms, "**Because Jesus lives forever, he has a permanent priesthood. Therefore he is able to save completely those who come to God through him, because he always lives to intercede for them.**" His intercession on our behalf is not temporary or limited; it is ongoing and effective, rooted in His unchanging nature. Most compellingly, Hebrews teaches that Jesus inaugurated a new covenant—not written on stone but in hearts. Hebrews 8:6 explains that Jesus is the mediator of a better covenant, established on better promises. His sacrifice did not merely cover sin temporarily; it removed its stain forever for those who believe.

Hebrews presents Jesus as the sole answer to humanity's need for atonement, uniquely fulfilling every requirement: a perfect priest, a spotless sacrifice, an eternal mediator, and a Savior whose death and resurrection offer not only forgiveness but also access to God and the promise of eternal life. All other systems and sacrifices are mere shadows; Christ is the substance. Therefore, as Hebrews 10:19–22 urges, **"Therefore, brothers and sisters, since we have confidence to enter the Most Holy Place by the blood of Jesus, by a new and living way opened for us through the curtain, that is, his body, and since we have a great priest over the house of God, let us draw near to God with a sincere heart and with the full assurance that faith brings."** We can now approach God with confidence, not through rituals or earthly priests, but through the new and living way that Jesus opened by His torn flesh.

Consequently, the death of Jesus is not merely central to Christian doctrine; it is the fulcrum upon which all redemptive history pivots. It fulfills the law, satisfies divine justice, completes the prophetic vision, and initiates the new covenant. It bridges the chasm between a holy God and sinful humanity, opening the path for reconciliation, healing, and eternal life. As Peter declared in Acts 2:23 to the early church: **"This man was handed over to you by God's deliberate plan and foreknowledge; and you, with the help of wicked men, put him to death by nailing him to the cross."** This statement encapsulates the paradox of the cross—it was an act of human evil, yet also the expression of God's sovereign goodness and love.

Ultimately, the cross of Christ is not just an event in history; it is the centerpiece of eternity, where the justice of God and the mercy of God converge, and where the love of God is poured out without measure. Through it, God's redemptive plan is not only revealed but fulfilled, making a way for all who believe to be restored to Him forever.

The author further deepens this understanding by drawing a striking parallel: **"Just as people are destined to die once, and after that to face judgment, so Christ was sacrificed once to take away the sins of many..."** (Hebrews 9:27–28). Human destiny—death and judgment—is contrasted with Christ's destiny: to die for the sins of others and to return, not to suffer again, but to bring salvation. This comparison reveals a sobering yet hopeful eschatological truth: while the final judgment is inevitable, for those in Christ, it holds no fear. His return will not be for wrath, but for fulfillment—the complete realization of our salvation.

To fully understand the necessity of Christ's death, one must grasp the profound biblical concept of atonement—the act through which sinful humanity is reconciled to a holy God. Atonement serves as the divine means of repairing the broken relationship between God and humanity, a rupture caused by sin. Central to this doctrine is the understanding that sin incurs guilt and demands justice, with reconciliation achievable only through the shedding of blood—an idea deeply rooted in Old Testament theology and fulfilled in the sacrificial death of Jesus Christ.

From the earliest moments of Scripture, the seriousness of sin and the need for atonement are evident. In Genesis 3:21, after Adam and Eve disobey God, their newfound shame is addressed not with immediate condemnation but with divine provision. God clothes them in garments made from animal skin, symbolizing the first shedding of blood to cover human guilt—a foreshadowing of what was to come.

The old covenant is not merely obsolete; it was preparatory. Its sacrifices were never intended to endure... Now that He has come, nothing else is needed.

Thus, Hebrews chapter 9 particularly challenges any belief system that places access to God in the hands of human ritual or merit. The old covenant is not merely obsolete; it was preparatory. Its sacrifices were never intended to endure; they pointed to the One who would come. Now that He has come, nothing else is needed. This undermines legalism and human striving, exalting Christ as the sole means of redemption.

Hebrews inspires us with a powerful promise: "**He will appear a second time... to bring salvation to those who are waiting for Him**" (Hebrews 9:28). This statement goes beyond doctrine; it invites us to live in expectation. Our Christian journey is shaped not only by remembering what Christ has done but also by anticipating what He will do. The return of Christ is framed not as a source of fear, but as a beacon of hope—His coming signifies the fulfillment of our salvation, the moment when faith gives way to sight and all things are made new. In this forward-looking perspective, believers are called to embrace readiness, holiness, and unwavering hope, confident that the One who came in humility will return in glory.

The Christian life is not passive nostalgia for what Christ has done; it is active hope in what He will do. Believers are called to wait eagerly, not fearfully. This eager anticipation transforms our daily walk, infusing it with purpose, purity, and perseverance. We do not serve a distant memory of sacrifice; we await a living, reigning Savior who will return to make all things new.

As God's covenant with Israel developed, the system of animal sacrifices was established under the Law of Moses, particularly outlined in the book of Leviticus. This system centered on the Day of Atonement (*Yom Kippur*), described in Leviticus 16, during which the high priest would offer sacrifices on behalf of the people and enter the Holy of Holies to atone for the nation's sins. This sacred ritual involved the blood of a goat and a bull, representing both the substitutionary nature of the sacrifice and the need for cleansing. Leviticus 17:11 provides the theological foundation for this system: **"For the life of a creature is in the blood, and I have given it to you to make atonement for yourselves on the altar; it is the blood that makes atonement for one's life."**

However, even within the Old Testament framework, it was clear that these sacrifices were limited and temporary. They were symbolic, intended to point forward to a greater reality. In Psalm 51:16, the psalmist declares, **"You do not delight in sacrifice, or I would bring it; you do not take pleasure in burnt offerings,"** emphasizing that external rituals cannot replace a repentant heart. This tension is thoroughly addressed in the book of Hebrews, which serves as a theological bridge between the old covenant and the new. It clearly states that the blood of animals could never fully remove sin, as Hebrews 10:4 explains: **"It is impossible for the blood of bulls and goats to take away sins."** These offerings had to be repeated year after year and failed to cleanse the conscience or transform the heart. Instead, they served as a shadow, pointing to the true and final sacrifice—Jesus Christ.

In the New Testament, Jesus is identified in John 1:29 as "**the Lamb of God, who takes away the sin of the world.**" This title directly connects to the Passover, during which a spotless lamb was slain and its blood applied to the doorposts, sparing Israel from judgment (Exodus 12). Paul affirms this typology in 1 Corinthians 5:7, stating: "**Christ, our Passover lamb, has been sacrificed.**" Unlike the animals of the old covenant, Jesus was perfect and sinless, the only one qualified to stand in humanity's place. 2 Corinthians 5:21 reinforces the substitutionary nature of His death: "**God made him who had no sin to be sin for us, so that in him we might become the righteousness of God.**" Through His death, Jesus bore the full weight of divine justice, absorbing the penalty that sin deserved.

His atonement was not only perfect; it was final. The author of Hebrews explains in Hebrews 10:12-14: "**But when this priest had offered for all time one sacrifice for sins, he sat down at the right hand of God... For by one sacrifice he has made perfect forever those who are being made holy**". No more sacrifices are needed. Christ's offering on the cross fulfilled the entire sacrificial system. It was not a symbolic gesture but a real transaction, effecting forgiveness, purification, and reconciliation.

Moreover, Christ's atoning work was not only substitutionary but also transformational. Through faith in Him, believers are not merely declared righteous; they are made new. As Romans 3:25–26 states: "**God presented Christ as a sacrifice of atonement, through the shedding of his blood—to be received by faith... So as to be just and the one who justifies those who have faith in Jesus.**" This means that God remained just by addressing sin while simultaneously extending grace, justifying the ungodly through faith.

The early church recognized the atonement as the core of the gospel. Church fathers like Athanasius and Anselm grappled with the significance of what Christ achieved. Anselm's "satisfaction theory" highlighted that only a divine being could fully address the offense against God's holiness. In contrast, figures like Irenaeus spoke of "recapitulation," where Christ, the new Adam, retraced humanity's steps and reversed the fall through His obedience, even unto death.

Therefore, the death of Jesus is not merely a religious doctrine; it is the divine solution to humanity's greatest problem: sin. Atonement through Christ's blood is the means by which forgiveness is granted, justice is satisfied, and communion with God is restored. It fulfills the expectations of the old covenant **...The death of Jesus is not merely a religious doctrine; it is the divine solution to humanity's greatest problem: sin.** and establishes a new covenant of grace, sealed by His blood and inscribed on human hearts. This truth forms the cornerstone of Christian faith and hope. As Romans 5:9 states, **"Since we have now been justified by his blood, how much more shall we be saved from God's wrath through him!"** Through the cross, God created a path where there was none; offering mercy without compromising His holiness and securing eternal redemption for all who believe.

The death of Jesus, while central and profound in the Christian faith, was never intended to be the final chapter. Instead, it served as the gateway to victory, marking the beginning of a new and glorious era in redemptive history. Though the cross symbolizes the defeat of sin and the completion of atonement, it is the resurrection of Jesus that boldly proclaims victory to the world with power and finality. Through the resurrection, Jesus triumphed over death, broke the chains of the grave, and shattered the grip of sin and the powers of darkness.

The crucifixion of Jesus is one of the most well-documented events of antiquity, supported by both the canonical Gospels and early non-Christian sources. It took place under Roman rule in Judea during the prefecture of Pontius Pilate, typically dated to around AD 30–33, most likely during the Jewish festival of Passover in Jerusalem.

Crucifixion was a Roman execution method reserved primarily for slaves, insurrectionists, and the most despised criminals. This brutal and humiliating punishment was intended to deter rebellion and uphold Roman authority. The Jewish historian Josephus, along with Roman writers such as Tacitus and Suetonius, confirms Rome's widespread use of crucifixion. Tacitus, in his *Annals* (written around AD 116), specifically mentions Jesus' execution under Pilate during Emperor Tiberius's reign, corroborating the Gospel accounts from a Roman perspective.

The Gospels recount that Jesus was arrested by Jewish religious authorities and charged with blasphemy for claiming divine authority. However, since the Jewish leaders lacked the power to impose capital punishment under Roman law, they brought Jesus before Roman governor Pontius Pilate. The charge presented to Pilate was political: Jesus was accused of claiming to be "King of the Jews," a direct challenge to Caesar's authority.

Although Pilate was initially reluctant and unconvinced of Jesus' guilt, he ultimately succumbed to public pressure and ordered the crucifixion to prevent unrest. Roman soldiers mocked Jesus by placing a crown of thorns on His head and dressing Him in a purple robe, beating Him before forcing Him to carry His cross—most likely the crossbeam (Latin *patibulum*)—to Golgotha, a hill outside Jerusalem's city walls.

The execution followed typical Roman customs. Jesus was likely nailed through His wrists and ankles to the wooden structure, and an inscription reading "Jesus of Nazareth, King of the Jews" (*INRI*) was placed above His head to indicate the official charge against Him. The crucifixion was conducted in front of onlookers, with two criminals crucified alongside Him—one on His right and one on His left.

Understanding the historical context enhances our grasp of this event. The Sanhedrin, the Jewish ruling council, viewed Jesus as a dangerous reformer who threatened both religious tradition and social order. Meanwhile, Roman authorities were wary of any messianic movements that could spark rebellion, particularly during the volatile Passover season when Jerusalem was filled with pilgrims and nationalistic fervor.

Crucifixion was agonizingly slow, with victims often lingering for hours or even days. Death typically resulted from a combination of blood loss, dehydration, asphyxiation, and shock. The Gospels report that Jesus died relatively quickly, after approximately six hours on the cross. A Roman soldier pierced His side to confirm His death—consistent with Roman practice of hastening death before sundown, as Jewish law forbade leaving bodies exposed overnight (Deuteronomy 21:23).

Jesus' body was given to Joseph of Arimathea, a member of the Jewish council who had not consented to the condemnation. Along with Nicodemus, he buried Jesus in a new tomb carved out of rock, fulfilling prophetic expectations (Isaiah 53:9).

The Roman Empire employed crucifixion to assert its authority and crush any hints of resistance. When Jesus was crucified, both His followers and enemies believed the story had ended. His disciples fled in fear and despair, while His accusers thought justice had been served. However, in a divine reversal that defied all human expectations, Jesus rose from the dead on the third day, validating His identity, confirming His message, and initiating the new creation foretold throughout Scripture.

The resurrection is the cornerstone of the Christian faith. The apostle Paul clearly states in 1 Corinthians 15:17: "**If Christ has not been raised, your faith is futile; you are still in your sins.**" Without the resurrection, the cross would merely represent a tragic martyrdom, and sin would continue to dominate humanity. However, because Christ rose, the cross becomes a testament to the triumph of divine love, and the tomb symbolizes hope and new life.

Jesus' words in John 11:25 beautifully express this reality: "**I am the resurrection and the life. The one who believes in me will live, even though they die.**" Spoken before He raised Lazarus from the dead, this statement offered comfort to Martha and Mary while also making a profound theological claim. Jesus is not just the one who brings resurrection; He is resurrection itself, the very source of eternal life for all who believe in Him.

> He is resurrection itself, the very source of eternal life for all who believe in Him.

The resurrection serves as a validation of Jesus' divine sonship and messianic mission. Romans 1:4 states that He was "**appointed the Son of God in power by his resurrection from the dead: Jesus Christ our Lord.**" His resurrection confirmed all His claims and actions, demonstrating that death could not hold the Author of life (Acts 2:24). Furthermore, Jesus' resurrection is the firstfruits of a greater harvest—the resurrection of all believers. 1 Corinthians 15:20–22 declares: "**Instead we should write to them, telling them to abstain from food polluted by idols, from sexual immorality, from the meat of strangled animals and from blood. 21 For the law of Moses has been preached in every city from the earliest times and is read in the synagogues on every Sabbath.**" Just as Adam's sin brought death to all, Jesus' resurrection brings life to everyone united with

Him by faith. This life is not merely symbolic but entails bodily resurrection and full restoration in the age to come. This future hope lies at the heart of Christian eschatology—the belief that one day, Christ will return, and those who belong to Him will be raised to eternal glory.

Philippians 3:20–21 affirms: **"But our citizenship is in heaven. And we eagerly await a Savior from there, the Lord Jesus Christ, who... Will transform our lowly bodies so that they will be like his glorious body."** The same power that raised Jesus from the grave is at work in believers, assuring them that their ultimate fate is not death, but resurrection.

The resurrection also signifies Christ's victory over the powers of darkness. Colossians 2:15 declares: **"And having disarmed the powers and authorities, he made a public spectacle of them, triumphing over them by the cross."** Although the cross seemed to represent defeat, it was actually the means by which Jesus overthrew Satan's dominion. The empty tomb stands as evidence of that cosmic triumph.

Historical accounts of the risen Jesus appearing to the disciples (Luke 24, John 20–21, Acts 1) not only restored their faith but transformed them into bold witnesses who spread the gospel worldwide. The resurrection ignited the church and empowered its mission—because the One who died is alive again, reigning forevermore.

The resurrection is much more than an event to remember; it is a reality to live by. It assures us that sin no longer has the final word, suffering is not in vain, and death is not the end. As Paul writes in Romans 6:4: **"We were therefore buried with him through baptism into death in order that, just as Christ was raised from the dead... We too may live a new life."** In Christ's resurrection, the new creation has begun.

For believers, this means eternal life is not just a future hope but a present reality—a life characterized by freedom, power, and unshakeable joy, secured by the One who conquered the grave and reigns forever as King. Indeed, the death of Jesus was not the end; it marked a turning point in a larger narrative of redemption, renewal, and resurrection. Through Him, we are invited to share in

His victory and to anticipate the day when we will experience the fullness of redemption in His eternal kingdom.

From the foundation of the world, God foresaw humanity's fall and prepared a way for reconciliation—a path that inevitably led to the cross. Throughout Scripture, we witness the unfolding of this redemptive plan. The Old Testament sacrificial system, established under the Mosaic covenant, pointed to the necessity of atonement through the shedding of blood. Leviticus 17:11 states, "**For the life of a creature is in the blood, and I have given it to you to make atonement for yourselves on the altar; it is the blood that makes atonement for one's life.**" While these animal sacrifices were ordained by God, they were temporary and symbolic, unable to fully remove sin (Hebrews 10:4). They served as a shadow of the ultimate sacrifice to come—…the Lamb of God who takes away the sin of the world! (John 1:29).

The crucifixion of Jesus was not merely the tragic end of a well-meaning teacher; it was the fulfillment of divine prophecy and purpose. As Peter declared to the crowd at Pentecost in Acts 2:23, "**This man was handed over to you by God's deliberate plan and foreknowledge.**" Jesus Himself affirmed this in John 10:18, stating, "**No one takes it from me, but I lay it down of my own accord.**" His death was a deliberate and intentional act, motivated by obedience to the Father and love for the world (Philippians 2:8; Romans 5:8).

Through His sacrificial death, Jesus achieved what no other offering could: He atoned for sin, secured forgiveness, and reconciled humanity to God. Paul explains in 2 Corinthians 5:21 that: "**God made him who had no sin to be sin for us, so that in him we might become the righteousness of God.**" This is the essence of the gospel—the great exchange in which Christ bore the penalty we deserved, allowing us to receive the righteousness we could never earn.

Moreover, His death was not the end; it paved the way for victory. Colossians 2:15 reveals that through the cross, Jesus "**disarmed the powers and authorities, he made a public spectacle of them, triumphing over them by the cross.**" Additionally, Hebrews 2:14 reminds us that through His death, He "**destroyed him who holds the power of death—that is, the devil.**" In dying, Jesus conquered death, broke its hold on humanity, and opened the door to eternal life.

This triumph is not only judicial but profoundly relational. Christ's death made it possible for sinners to be adopted as sons and daughters of God. Ephesians 1:7 states, **"In him we have redemption through his blood, the forgiveness of sins, in accordance with the riches of God's grace."** Because of His death, believers are no longer estranged from God but are brought near (Ephesians 2:13), and they are no longer under condemnation but declared righteous (Romans 8:1).

When believers reflect on the death of Christ, they are not just remembering a historical event; they are witnessing the clearest revelation of God's character. On the cross, we observe the fullness of divine love and justice. As 1 John 4:10 declares, **"This is love: not that we loved God, but that he loved us and sent his Son as an atoning sacrifice for our sins."** The cross represents the intersection where divine justice is satisfied and divine mercy flows abundantly.

> **...Christ's death calls for a response. It invites faith, repentance, and a life transformed by grace.**

Ultimately, Christ's death calls for a response. It invites faith, repentance, and a life transformed by grace. As Jesus stated in John 11:25–26, **"I am the resurrection and the life. The one who believes in me will live, even though they die; and whoever lives by believing in me will never die."** This is the promise of salvation—a gift extended to all who believe, made possible through the once-for-all sacrifice of the Son of God.

In this profound act, God demonstrates that no cost is too great for the redemption of His people. The cross offers a clear glimpse into the heart of God—a heart filled with compassion, abundant in mercy, and triumphant in love. For those who trust in Christ, His death marks not a mournful end, but a glorious beginning— ushering in forgiveness, freedom, and eternal fellowship with God.

The death of Jesus Christ is the foundation of God's perfect redemptive plan for humanity. Through His sacrificial death, Jesus atoned for sin, secured forgiveness, and achieved an irreversible victory over death and darkness. As Scripture states, **"He was pierced for our transgressions... And by His wounds we are healed"** (Isaiah 53:5). His crucifixion was not a tragic accident in history but the fulfillment of a divine purpose—a plan established before the foundation of the world (1 Peter 1:19–20).

At Calvary, divine justice and mercy converged in perfect harmony. Christ bore the punishment we deserved, allowing us to receive the righteousness we could never earn. His declaration, **"It is finished"** (John 19:30), marked the completion of a once-for-all atonement that opened the way for every believer to be reconciled to God. His atoning work. As believers contemplate the profound significance of Christ's death, they are drawn into the essence of the Gospel: God's love is not distant or abstract but made tangible and accessible through Jesus. His sacrifice reveals the depths of divine compassion and the heights of divine hope—a gift freely offered to all who believe.

However, this message of redemption was never intended to remain confined to Jerusalem or the early church. With the resurrection power that confirmed His victory, Jesus commissioned His followers to spread the good news to the ends of the earth. The next chapter in God's unfolding redemptive story begins with the Apostolic mission, where once-fearful disciples became bold witnesses, proclaiming salvation in Christ to both Jew and Gentile, and laying the foundation for a global Church rooted in resurrection hope and empowered by the Holy Spirit.

Beyond its historical significance, the crucifixion serves as the theological cornerstone of the Christian faith. While Romans viewed it as a sign of disgrace and Jews regarded it as a curse, Christians proclaim it as the means of redemption. As the Apostle Paul wrote, **"We preach Christ crucified, a stumbling block to Jews and foolishness to Gentiles"** (1 Corinthians 1:23).

In this paradox, the humiliating death of an innocent man, Christianity discovers its message of divine love, justice, and victory over sin and death. Historically brutal yet theologically redemptive, the crucifixion of Jesus stands at the intersection of human cruelty and divine mercy.

The cross, once a Roman instrument of terror, has become the symbol of hope, forgiveness, and eternal life. It is through the cross that God reconciles a broken world to Himself, establishes a new covenant, and invites all people—regardless of background, nation, or past—to receive His grace. Through Jesus Christ, the sacrificial system is fulfilled, the veil is torn, and the invitation to enter God's presence is extended to all who believe.

As we reflect on the completed work of Christ, we are reminded that redemption is not merely a theological construct—it is a lived reality. The death and resurrection of Jesus shape every aspect of Christian identity, calling believers to walk in the light of grace, to live sacrificially in response to divine love, and to await with eager expectation the glorious return of the risen Lord.

In this chapter, we have seen how God's perfect redemptive plan through Christ was foretold in prophecy, fulfilled in history, affirmed in theology, and realized in the hearts of believers. This plan—anchored in divine wisdom and driven by unrelenting love—offers the only true hope for humanity. It is finished. It is victorious. And it is eternal.

CHAPTER

8

The Apostolic Mission to Spread the Gospel;
The Gentiles Find Redemption

The Apostolic mission to spread the Gospel represents a transformative chapter in Christian history. More than just a religious campaign or institutional effort, it was a revolutionary spiritual movement ignited by the risen Christ and sustained by divine power. Rooted in Jesus' life, death, and resurrection, this mission began not with military might or political influence but with a group of ordinary men who had walked with Jesus, witnessed His miracles, heard His teachings, and encountered Him alive after the crucifixion.

The charge that initiated this movement came directly from Jesus after His resurrection, known as the Great Commission. In Matthew 28:19–20, He instructed His disciples: "**Therefore go and make disciples of all nations, baptizing them in the name of the Father and of the Son and of the Holy Spirit, and teaching them to obey everything I have commanded you. And surely I am with you always, to the very end of the age.**" This was not merely an encouraging farewell; it was a command infused with divine authority and eternal significance.

Given to the remaining eleven disciples after Judas Iscariot's death, this commission established the blueprint for the Church's mission and identity. It was revolutionary in scope, calling for the disciples to make disciples of all nations, regardless of race, class, culture, or geography. Until this point, the focus of God's covenant people had primarily been on Israel. Now, through Jesus, the covenant would be extended universally, fulfilling prophecies that anticipated the inclusion of the Gentiles, as stated in Isaiah 49:6: "**I will also make you a light for the Gentiles, that my salvation may reach to the ends of the earth.**"

This apostolic charge laid the foundation for the global Church. This apostolic charge laid the foundation for the global Church. Empowered by the Holy Spirit at Pentecost (Acts 2:1–4), the disciples began to proclaim the Gospel with boldness and clarity. Their message centered on the risen Christ—His identity as the Son of God, His atoning death for sin, and His triumphant resurrection. The early chapters of Acts illustrate how the Gospel began to spread, first in Jerusalem, then to Judea and Samaria, and eventually to the ends of the earth (Acts 1:8)

The Great Commission affirmed that salvation is available to all people, marking a radical expansion of God's redemptive plan—no longer confined to a single ethnic group or geographic region. The Apostles were tasked not only with proclaiming the message but also with baptizing new believers into the covenant community and teaching them to become disciples who would walk in obedience to Jesus. Their mission required sacrifice and suffering, and most Apostles paid for their faithfulness with their lives, enduring persecution, imprisonment, exile, and martyrdom. Nevertheless, they pressed on with deep conviction, empowered by the assurance that Christ was with them always—guiding, strengthening, and sustaining their witness.

Historically, this apostolic movement outlasted empires and reshaped civilizations, giving rise to churches across Asia Minor, North Africa, and Europe. Within a few centuries, Christianity spread throughout the Roman world and beyond, not through force, but via transformed lives and relentless proclamation.

Today, the Great Commission continues to define the Church's mission, calling each generation of believers to participate in God's work of making disciples, teaching His truth, and extending His kingdom. The Apostles ignited the flame, but the Church is tasked with keeping it alive. Their legacy compels the Church to remain faithful and globally minded, always remembering the words of Jesus: "**Surely I am with you always, to the very end of the age.**"

While it is often said that there were twelve disciples, in reality, there were fourteen named Apostles. Paul, a towering figure in the missionary expansion of the Church, joined the original Twelve, which included Judas Iscariot and Matthias, who became his replacement. Together, they laid the essential foundation for Christianity's global reach, with each Apostle contributing uniquely to the spread of the Gospel. Given Paul's pivotal role in the writing of the New Testament, I will discuss his ministry separately.

PETER

Originally named Simon, Peter was one of the first disciples called by Jesus and quickly became a prominent figure among the Twelve. Jesus renamed him "Peter," which means "rock," indicating the foundational role he would play in establishing the Church. In Matthew 16:18, Jesus stated: "**And I tell you that you are Peter, and on this rock I will build my church, and the gates of Hades will not overcome it.**" This declaration foreshadowed Peter's future leadership, not only among the disciples but also in the broader expansion of the Christian faith.

Peter's transformation from a impulsive fisherman to a bold apostolic leader is one of the most striking character arcs in Scripture. Although he famously denied Jesus three times during the crucifixion events (Luke 22:54–62), he was lovingly restored in a post-resurrection encounter, where Jesus commissioned him three times with the command, "Feed my sheep" (John 21:15–17). This moment of restoration marked the beginning of Peter's courageous public ministry.

His defining moment arrived on the Day of Pentecost. Filled with the Holy Spirit, Peter delivered the first apostolic sermon to a diverse crowd in Jerusalem, leading to the baptism of about 3,000 people (Acts 2:41). From this point, Peter played a central role in shaping the early Church.

Importantly, Peter's ministry extended beyond Jewish audiences. In a vision from God (Acts 10), he learned that the Gospel was not confined by ethnicity or ritual purity. This culminated in his groundbreaking encounter with the Gentile centurion Cornelius, after which Peter proclaimed, "**God does not show favoritism but accepts from every nation the one who fears him and does what**

is right" (Acts 10:34–35). This event marked the Church's formal outreach to the Gentiles and fulfilled the inclusive vision of the Great Commission (Matthew 28:19).

Tradition holds that Peter ministered in several cities, including Antioch, before eventually arriving in Rome. Early Christian sources such as Irenaeus and Eusebius indicate that Peter was martyred there under Emperor Nero around AD 64–67, with the common belief being that he was crucified upside down, considering himself unworthy to die in the same manner as Christ.

The significance of Peter's role has been interpreted differently across Christian traditions. Roman Catholic theology asserts that Peter was the first Bishop of Rome and the first Pope, citing Matthew 16:18–19 and John 21:15–17 as scriptural support for his unique authority. This perspective is encapsulated in the doctrine of Petrine Primacy, which maintains that Peter's leadership was passed down through apostolic succession to his episcopal successors—the popes.

Church Fathers such as Irenaeus (Against Heresies, c. AD 180) claimed that Peter and Paul founded the Church in Rome, and Eusebius, in his *Ecclesiastical History*, affirmed Peter's martyrdom there. These historical attestations have reinforced the Catholic claim of an unbroken succession from Peter to the contemporary papacy.

However, the New Testament does not explicitly identify Peter as the Bishop of Rome nor does it use the title "Pope." The ecclesial structure of the early Church was interconnected, with local bishops exercising regional authority. The concept of papal supremacy and infallibility, as defined at the First Vatican Council in 1870, developed gradually over centuries. Bishops like Callistus I and Leo I (Leo the Great) expanded the theological foundation of papal authority, drawing heavily from Peter's role and Jesus' words in Matthew 16.

The Eastern Orthodox Church honors Peter's leadership but interprets his role as a primacy of honor rather than jurisdiction. They affirm that the apostolic foundation of the Church is collectively shared among all apostles (Ephesians 2:20), with Christ Himself as the sole head (Colossians 1:18). Protestants, particularly following the Reformation, reject the notion of the papacy entirely, advocating for sola scriptura and the priesthood of all believers. Many Protestant theologians interpret the "rock" in Matthew 16 not as Peter himself, but as his confession of faith in Christ.

Despite differing views on Peter's ecclesiastical role, his impact on Christian theology and history is undeniable. He was a witness to Christ's life, death, and resurrection; a preacher of the Gospel; a bridge between Jewish and Gentile believers; and ultimately, a martyr for the faith. His epistles—1 and 2 Peter—provide timeless counsel for believers enduring hardship, urging them toward holiness, humility, and hope.

> **...Peter's ecclesiastical role, his impact on Christian theology and history is undeniable.**

Peter's legacy challenges every Christian to consider how God uses flawed yet willing individuals to advance His kingdom. Whether viewed through Catholic, Orthodox, or Protestant lenses, Peter's life remains a powerful testament to the grace of God, the authority of Christ, and the enduring mission of the Church.

JAMES THE GREATER (SON OF ZEBEDEE)

James, the son of Zebedee and brother of John, occupies a notable position in the early history of the Church, not only as a member of Jesus' inner circle of disciples but also as the first of the Twelve Apostles to be martyred for his faith. His life and death exemplify both the fervor of early Christian witness and the significant cost often associated with proclaiming the Gospel in a hostile environment.

James is first introduced in the Gospels as one of the fishermen whom Jesus called to follow Him while they were mending their nets by the Sea of Galilee (Matthew 4:21–22). Alongside Peter and John, James formed part of Jesus' closest circle. He witnessed several significant moments in Jesus' ministry, including the raising of Jairus's daughter (Mark 5:37), the Transfiguration (Matthew 17:1), and Jesus' agony in Gethsemane (Mark 14:33). This close proximity to Christ during pivotal events highlights the trust and intimacy James shared with Him.

James' prominent role among the apostles makes the account of his martyrdom in Acts 12:1–2 particularly sobering: "**It was about** this time that King Herod arrested some who belonged to the church, intending to persecute them. He had James, the brother of John, put to death with the sword." This brief but significant passage is the only record of apostolic martyrdom in the New Testament. James' execution by Herod Agrippa I, who ruled Judea from A.D. 41 to 44, occurred amid escalating tensions between Jewish authorities and the growing Christian community. Herod's actions were politically motivated, aimed at appeasing Jewish leaders who perceived the Christian movement as a threat. The phrase "put to death with the sword" likely refers to beheading, a swift yet brutal method of execution.

While the New Testament provides limited details about James' missionary activities before his death, early Christian tradition, particularly from Iberian sources, suggests that he traveled westward to the Iberian Peninsula (modern-day Spain) to spread the Gospel. Although this claim lacks direct biblical evidence, it has had a lasting cultural and religious impact. The Cathedral of Santiago de Compostela in Spain is one of the most important pilgrimage sites in Christendom, believed by many to be the final resting place of the Apostle James.

James' martyrdom exemplifies the suffering that accompanies faithfulness to Christ's commission. James' martyrdom exemplifies the suffering that accompanies faithfulness to Christ's commission. His death fulfilled Jesus' earlier prediction in Mark 10:38–39, when James and John asked to sit at Jesus' right and left in glory. Jesus responded, **"Can you drink the cup I drink or be baptized with the baptism I am baptized with?"** When they affirmed that they could, Jesus foretold, **"You will drink the cup I drink and be baptized with the baptism I am baptized with,"** alluding to the suffering and martyrdom they would endure for His sake.

James' early martyrdom serves as a sobering reminder that proclaiming the Gospel often requires the ultimate sacrifice. His death marks a turning point in the narrative of Acts, shifting from a time of relative growth and favor to one of increasing persecution. This foreshadows the trials faced by many early Christians and apostles, highlighting the conflict between the kingdom of God and worldly powers. James symbolizes apostolic courage and commitment. Although he did not live to witness the Church's expansion into Gentile territories or Paul's missionary journeys, his witness and sacrifice were foundational. His willingness to die for Christ set the stage for others to preach boldly, knowing that even death could not hinder God's redemptive purposes.

James' life exemplifies the close discipleship, faithful service, and profound cost of following Jesus. His death reminds us that the mission of the Church was born not only through preaching and miracles but also through blood and sacrifice. As stated in Revelation 12:11: "**They triumphed over him by the blood of the Lamb and by the word of their testimony; they did not love their lives so much as to shrink from death.**" James' martyrdom serves as a testament to the unwavering faith that continues to inspire believers across generations.

JOHN (BROTHER OF JAMES)

John, the son of Zebedee and brother of James, was one of the original Twelve Apostles and a key member of Jesus' inner circle, alongside Peter and James. Renowned for his close relationship with Jesus, John played a vital role in the early Church, contributing both pastorally and theologically. His writings have profoundly influenced Christian doctrine, particularly regarding the identity of Christ, the nature of love, and the assurance of eternal life.

John's intimacy with Jesus is evident throughout the Gospels. He is often referred to as "**the disciple whom Jesus loved**" (John 13:23), a title that reflects not arrogance but a deep awareness of Christ's love. This relationship was further illustrated at the crucifixion when Jesus, seeing His mother at the foot of the cross, entrusted her to John's care. In John 19:26–27, we read: "**When Jesus saw his mother there, and the disciple whom he loved standing nearby, he said to her, 'Woman, here is your son,' and to the disciple, 'Here is your mother.' From that time on, this disciple took her into his home.**" This moment highlights both the trust Jesus placed in John and John's faithful devotion to Jesus' family and mission.

John's ministry eventually led him to Ephesus, a significant city in the Roman Empire and a strategic center for the early Christian Church. From there, he offered leadership and theological guidance, particularly to the surrounding churches in Asia Minor. According

...John served as a spiritual elder and teacher ... Known for his emphasis on love, truth, and fidelity to Christ. to early Church tradition, John served as a spiritual elder and teacher in Ephesus well into old age, known for his emphasis on love, truth, and fidelity to Christ.

Traditionally, John is credited with writing five books of the New Testament: the Gospel of John, 1, 2, and 3 John, and the Book of Revelation. Each of these writings exhibits profound theological depth, especially in affirming Jesus as the incarnate Son of God. The Gospel of John begins with a powerful declaration of Jesus' divine nature: **"In the beginning was the Word, and the Word was with God, and the Word was God"** (John 1:1). It continues in John 1:14, stating: **"The Word became flesh and made his dwelling among us. We have seen his glory..."** These verses underscore the incarnation—a cornerstone of Christian theology—asserting that God entered human history in the person of Jesus Christ. John's epistles emphasize the importance of truth and love, cautioning against false teachings and encouraging believers to stay grounded in the love of Christ. 1 John 4:7–8 encapsulates this message: **"Dear friends, let us love one another, for love comes from God... Whoever does not love does not know God, because God is love."** His writings possess a pastoral tone, advocating for unity, righteousness, and a steadfast faith rooted in the identity of Jesus.

John's exile to the island of Patmos, as recorded in Revelation 1:9, occurred during a period of persecution under Roman rule, likely under Emperor Domitian (AD 81–96). While in exile, he received a series of visions that constitute the apocalyptic Book of Revelation, filled with rich symbolism and hope. He describes himself as a "brother and companion in the suffering and kingdom and patient endurance that are ours in Jesus" (Revelation 1:9), demonstrating his solidarity with persecuted believers.

The Book of Revelation offers a universal perspective on Christ's ultimate victory, judgment, and the promise of a new heaven and new earth. John's vision of the glorified Christ (Revelation 1:12–18) and the triumphant declaration in Revelation 1:18: **"I am the Living One; I was dead, and now look, I am alive for ever and ever!"**— reflect the hope that sustained the early Church during times of great suffering. I will explore Revelation in more detail in a later chapter and also recommend my other book, *Miracles, Signs, Symbols, and Judgment – God's Plan for the End Times*, available at most bookstores.

Unlike most of the other apostles, John is believed to have died a natural death, likely in Ephesus. His life was marked by suffering, exile, and tireless service, which distinguishes him historically. Nevertheless, his faithfulness to the end embodies the same sacrificial commitment seen in his fellow apostles.

John's impact on Christian theology and the early Church is monumental. Through his writings and ministry, he shaped the Church's understanding of Jesus as fully God, fully human, Savior, and Lord. His enduring message of truth, love, and eternal life continues to strengthen the faith of believers worldwide. John's legacy urges the Church to remain faithful to Christ, to walk in love, and to hope for the ultimate redemption revealed in the Lamb who is worthy to reign forever.

ANDREW

Andrew, Peter's brother, often occupies an underappreciated place among the Twelve Apostles. While he does not feature as prominently in the New Testament narrative as his brother, Andrew's role in the early Church is characterized by quiet faithfulness, evangelistic zeal, and missionary courage. His life exemplifies a disciple who seeks not recognition but the glory of Christ and the spread of His Gospel.

The Gospels introduce Andrew as a disciple of John the Baptist before he began following Jesus. In John 1:40–41, we read: **"Andrew, Simon Peter's brother, was one of the two who heard what John had said and who had followed Jesus. The first thing Andrew did was to find his brother Simon and tell him, 'We have found the Messiah' (that is, the Christ)."** This passage underscores Andrew's evangelistic heart; he was the first to recognize Jesus as the Messiah and promptly brought his brother Peter to Him. In this way, Andrew played a pivotal role in introducing one of the Church's greatest leaders to Christ. Although Andrew appears only a few times in the Gospel accounts, each mention reveals a consistent pattern: he brings people to Jesus. In John 6:8–9, it is Andrew who brings the boy with five loaves and two fish to Jesus before the feeding of

> **...Andrew again facilitates the connection... he served as a bridge between others and Christ...**

the five thousand. Later, in John 12:20–22, when some Greeks seek an audience with Jesus, Andrew again facilitates the connection. These brief instances provide insight into his character—he served as a bridge between others and Christ, always eager to lead people into the Lord's presence.

After the resurrection and ascension of Jesus, Andrew took part in the mission to carry the Gospel to the nations, fulfilling the command of the Great Commission (Matthew 28:19–20). While the Book of Acts focuses more on Peter, Paul, and a few others, early Church tradition holds that Andrew took the message of Christ to regions largely untouched by the Gospel.

Sources such as Eusebius, the 4th-century Church historian, suggest that Andrew preached in Scythia, a term used in antiquity to describe a region that includes parts of what is now Ukraine, southern Russia, and Kazakhstan. He is also believed to have ministered in Asia Minor (modern-day Turkey) and Greece, establishing churches and proclaiming Christ to both Jews and Gentiles.

Andrew's missionary work led him to Patras, a city in western Greece, where he is believed to have been martyred under Roman rule. According to tradition, he was crucified on an X-shaped cross, now commonly known as "St. Andrew's Cross," because he felt unworthy to die in the same manner as Jesus. Although this account is not found in Scripture, it is supported by early Christian writings and is widely accepted in Church history.

Andrew's life embodies humble service, deep personal faith, and obedience to Christ's call, even unto death. He represents the often unseen yet crucial work of evangelism—reaching out to individuals, building relationships, and guiding them toward Jesus. His ministry serves as a reminder to the Church that powerful impact often begins with simple, faithful acts, such as introducing a brother to Christ.

Venerated in various Christian traditions, Andrew is considered the patron saint of Scotland, Russia, and Greece, reflecting the geographic spread of his missionary efforts. The saltire cross on the Scottish flag is believed to symbolize the shape of Andrew's crucifixion cross. His legacy is honored not only in history and liturgy but also in the lives of those who, like him, quietly and faithfully bring others to Jesus.

Throughout his ministry, Andrew's story exemplifies faithful discipleship and missionary courage. Although he was overshadowed by more prominent apostles like Peter and Paul, his example shines brightly as a model for those seeking to serve Christ by leading others to Him. His words to Peter— **"We have found the Messiah"** (John 1:41)—continue to resonate as the heart cry of every evangelist and missionary. Andrew's life challenges the Church today to embody that same passion: to find Christ, to follow Him, and to make Him known to the ends of the earth.

PHILIP

Philip the Apostle, one of the original Twelve disciples chosen by Jesus, is a significant figure in the Gospel accounts, though not as prominent as apostles like Peter or John. Nevertheless, the insights Scripture provides into his life, along with early Church traditions, portray him as a faithful, inquisitive, and devoted servant of Christ who made meaningful contributions to the foundation of the Church and the spread of the Gospel.

Philip is first introduced in the Gospel of John as a resident of Bethsaida, the same town as Andrew and Peter (John 1:44). His initial encounter with Jesus is notable for its immediacy. In John 1:43, we read: **"The next day Jesus decided to leave for Galilee. Finding Philip, he said to him, 'Follow me.'"** Philip's response to Jesus reflects not only personal obedience but also a zeal for evangelism. He quickly seeks out Nathanael and proclaims in John 1:45: **"We have found the one Moses wrote about in the Law, and about whom the prophets also wrote—Jesus of Nazareth, the son of Joseph."** This early action highlights a defining characteristic of Philip: a desire to lead others to the Messiah, even in the face of skepticism, as evidenced by Nathanael's reaction to "Nazareth."

> ...Philip: a desire to lead others to the Messiah, even in the face of skepticism...

Philip reappears during the feeding of the five thousand when Jesus tests him by asking where to buy bread for the crowd. Philip responds in John 6:7: **"It would take more than half a year's wages to buy enough bread for each one to have a bite!"** Although his practical mindset seems limited in vision, it sets the stage for one of Jesus' most famous miracles, reinforcing the theme that human limitations can be overcome by divine provision.

Another significant moment occurs in John 12:20–22, when some Greeks request to see Jesus. They approach Philip first, possibly due to his Greek name or his openness. Philip then brings this request to Andrew, and together they approach Jesus. This brief exchange underscores Philip's role as a bridge between the growing multicultural interest in Jesus and the Jewish disciples, suggesting the universal scope of the Gospel message.

Finally, at the Last Supper, Philip speaks up again. In John 14:8, he asks, **"Lord, show us the Father and that will be enough for us."** Jesus responds with a powerful affirmation of His divinity in John 14:9: **"Don't you know me, Philip, even after I have been among you such a long time? Anyone who has seen me has seen the Father..."** Here, Philip's inquiry paves the way for one of the clearest declarations in the Gospels regarding the unity between Jesus and the Father, emphasizing the theological truth of the incarnation—that in Christ, God is fully revealed.

Philip's interactions with Jesus often lead to significant teachings and miracles. He is portrayed as having a sincere heart, a curious mind, and a growing faith. His questions and responses facilitate deeper revelations about Jesus' identity and mission. Philip embodies the journey of a believer—transitioning from initial faith and evangelism, through moments of doubt and limited understanding, to being used by God as a conduit for others. He exemplifies the theme of a disciple as a witness: not perfect, but increasingly trustworthy in guiding others toward Jesus.

The New Testament does not provide detailed information about Philip's ministry following Jesus' resurrection. However, Church tradition shares various accounts of his missionary work. Early sources suggest that Philip preached the Gospel in regions such as Phrygia (modern-day Turkey), Syria, and possibly Greece.

Tradition holds that Philip was martyred in Hierapolis, a city in Phrygia, where he boldly continued to proclaim the Gospel in a pagan culture. One account claims he was crucified upside down, while another suggests he was stoned or hung upside down by iron hooks in his ankles until he died. Although these details vary, the common theme is that Philip remained faithful to his calling until death, becoming a witness in both life and martyrdom.

There is often confusion between Philip the Apostle and Philip the Evangelist (or Deacon) mentioned in Acts 6 and Acts 8, particularly since both were prominent early witnesses. However, tradition and the biblical record clearly differentiate the two.

While Philip the Apostle may not have received as much attention as some of his peers, his life and witness hold great significance. From his enthusiastic proclamation to Nathanael to his involvement in key Gospel events, Philip exemplifies faithful discipleship characterized by curiosity, courage, and a passion for evangelism. His legacy encourages modern believers to trust in Christ beyond human limitations, serve as bridges for others to encounter Jesus, and remain faithful even in adversity. In Philip's life, we witness the power of responding simply to Jesus' call: "Follow me."

BARTHOLOMEW (POSSIBLY NATHANAEL)

Bartholomew, one of the Twelve Apostles, remains a somewhat mysterious figure in the New Testament. He is listed among the apostles in the synoptic Gospels (Matthew 10:3, Mark 3:18, Luke 6:14) and in Acts 1:13, yet the Bible offers little narrative detail about his ministry. However, early Church tradition and historical accounts help us piece together a broader understanding of his life, missionary work, and theological legacy.

Many scholars and Church fathers associate Bartholomew with Nathanael, who appears in the Gospel of John. In John 1:45–46, Philip finds Nathanael and tells him, "**We have found the one Moses wrote about in the Law, and about whom the prophets also wrote—Jesus of Nazareth, the son of Joseph.**" Nathanael responds skeptically, "**Nazareth! Can anything good come from there?**" When Jesus meets him, He declares, "**Here truly is an Israelite in whom there is no deceit**" (v. 47). This encounter reveals Bartholomew/Nathanael as a man of honesty, depth, and spiritual discernment. When Jesus demonstrates intimate knowledge of him— "**I saw you while you were still under the fig tree before Philip called you**" (v. 48)—Nathanael makes one of the earliest confessions of Jesus' divine identity: "**Rabbi, you are the Son of God; you are the king of Israel**" (John 1:49).

This moment foreshadows the sincere and thoughtful faith that would characterize Bartholomew's later ministry. Although the Gospel of John refers to him as Nathanael, and the synoptic Gospels use the name Bartholomew, it is widely accepted that both names refer to the same individual, as "Bartholomew" is a patronymic meaning "son of Tolmai," used alongside a personal name like Nathanael.

After the resurrection of Jesus and the coming of the Holy Spirit at Pentecost, Bartholomew, like the other apostles, would have embraced the charge of the Great Commission—to **"go and make disciples of all nations"** (Matthew 28:19). While Scripture does not specify where he traveled, early Church tradition extensively recounts his missionary journeys. Historical sources suggest that Bartholomew preached the Gospel in India, where he reportedly left a copy of the Gospel of Matthew written in Hebrew. The ancient Church historian Eusebius, quoting the 2nd-century theologian Pantaenus, supports this account by stating that when Pantaenus visited India, he discovered Christians using the Gospel of Matthew that Bartholomew had brought. This missionary journey highlights the geographical reach of the apostolic witness in the first century and reflects the early Church's commitment to global evangelism.

> **...Bartholomew, like the other apostles, would have embraced the charge of the Great Commission...**

Bartholomew is also believed to have ministered in Mesopotamia, Persia, and notably, Armenia, where tradition holds that he collaborated with the apostle Jude Thaddeus to introduce Christianity to the Armenian people. This is significant because Armenia later became the first nation to adopt Christianity as its official religion in the early 4th century, and Bartholomew is honored as one of the founding apostles of the Armenian Church.

His martyrdom in Armenia is remembered vividly. According to tradition, Bartholomew was flayed alive and then beheaded for refusing to renounce his faith and cease preaching the Gospel. While the details vary across sources, there is a consensus that he endured a brutal death as a faithful witness to Christ. His martyrdom illustrates the personal cost of discipleship and testifies to the far-reaching power of the Gospel—a message worth proclaiming even unto death.

Bartholomew's life exemplifies the implications of Jesus' command to take the Gospel to **"the ends of the earth"** (Acts 1:8).

Although he is a quieter figure in Scripture, his missionary legacy speaks volumes. His journeys beyond the Roman world into eastern territories demonstrate how the Christian faith transcended cultural and geographic boundaries from the very beginning. Bartholomew's faithfulness reminds us that the expansion of the Church has always been driven by bold, Spirit-empowered witnesses who carried the message of Christ wherever they went. He may not have written an epistle or led the Jerusalem church, but his global impact, personal faith, and sacrificial death have left an enduring legacy in Christian history. His story encourages the Church to carry the Gospel to all peoples, in all places, with unwavering courage and humility—just as he did.

MATTHEW (LEVI THE TAX COLLECTOR)

Matthew, also known as Levi, is a striking example of personal transformation among the Twelve Apostles. As a tax collector, a profession despised in Jewish society due to its association with Roman oppression and corruption, he embodies the radical grace central to the Gospel message. In calling Matthew, Jesus illustrated that no one is beyond the reach of divine mercy, and the kingdom of God is open to even those deemed least likely to be included. Matthew's calling is recorded in Matthew 9:9: "**As Jesus went on from there, he saw a man named Matthew sitting at the tax collector's booth. 'Follow me,' he told him, and Matthew got up and followed him.**" This simple, immediate response underscores the power of Christ's call and Matthew's readiness to abandon a life of material security for a new path. Shortly after, Matthew hosts a dinner at his house, where Jesus shares a meal with tax collectors and sinners—a moment that shocked the religious leaders of the time and led Jesus to declare in Matthew 9:12–13: "**It is not the healthy who need a doctor, but the sick... For I have not come to call the righteous, but sinners.**"

Matthew's experience of grace and inclusion laid the groundwork for his ministry. He is traditionally credited with writing the Gospel of Matthew, a work deeply rooted in Jewish Scripture and focused on demonstrating that Jesus is the promised Messiah. His Gospel begins with a genealogy tracing Jesus' lineage through Abraham and David (Matthew 1:1–17) and consistently emphasizes how Jesus fulfilled

Old Testament prophecies (e.g., Matthew 1:22–23; 2:5–6; 8:17). This focus reflects Matthew's intention to reach a Jewish audience and affirm the continuity between the Old Covenant and the New. One of Matthew's most distinctive contributions is the preservation of Jesus' Sermon on the Mount (Matthew 5–7)—a powerful summary of kingdom ethics. Through this teaching, Matthew illustrates that the Gospel is not solely about external observance but about inner transformation—a theme profoundly shaped by his own journey from tax collector to apostle.

Beyond his authorship, Matthew's post-resurrection ministry is not extensively detailed in the New Testament, but early Church tradition offers valuable insights. Historical sources indicate that Matthew preached the Gospel in regions such as Persia, Syria, and Ethiopia, spreading Christ's message far beyond Judea. These traditions describe his missionary journeys as marked by hardship, perseverance, and bold proclamation as he brought the light of the Gospel to diverse and often hostile cultures.

Matthew's death is believed to have been martyrdom, though accounts vary regarding how and where it occurred. Some traditions suggest he was stabbed to death in Ethiopia while celebrating the Eucharist, while others indicate he met his end in Persia. Regardless of the precise details, a common thread runs through these accounts: Matthew remained faithful to his calling, even unto death. His life illustrates several key truths. First, it showcases the transforming power of grace. Once viewed as a traitor to his people, Matthew became a foundational figure in the Church and the author of a Gospel that has shaped Christian faith for centuries. Second, his writings emphasize that Jesus is the fulfillment of God's promises, bridging the gap between the Law and the Gospel. Third, his example reminds us that God often chooses the unexpected—not the religious elite or societal favorites—to carry out His mission.

Matthew stands as a testament to the redemptive power of Christ and the universal reach of the Gospel.

Matthew stands as a testament to the redemptive power of Christ and the universal reach of the Gospel. From the tax booth to the mission field, and from social outcast to Gospel author, Matthew's story invites all who feel unworthy or unlikely to hear Jesus' call:

"**Follow me.**" His life and legacy continue to resonate within the Church today, urging believers to embrace the grace of Christ and boldly proclaim His kingdom to the ends of the earth.

THOMAS (ALSO CALLED DIDYMUS)

The apostle Thomas, often remembered by the nickname "Doubting Thomas," plays a vital and deeply human role in the Gospel narrative. His journey from skepticism to bold faith is one of the most compelling personal transformations in the New Testament. While he is mentioned briefly in the Synoptic Gospels, it is in the Gospel of John that we encounter a fuller picture of his personality, struggles, and ultimately, his profound conviction.

Thomas is best known for his reaction to the news of Jesus' resurrection. When the other disciples told him they had seen the risen Lord, Thomas refused to believe without physical proof. In John 20:25, he states: "**Unless I see the nail marks in his hands and put my finger where the nails were, and put my hand into his side, I will not believe.**" While his response is often viewed negatively, it reflects a sincere desire for truth and authenticity. Thomas was not satisfied with second-hand faith; he wanted a real, personal encounter with the risen Christ.

Jesus meets Thomas in his doubt with grace. A week later, He appears again and directly invites Thomas to touch His wounds. Confronted with the living Christ, Thomas offers one of the most powerful confessions in all of Scripture: "**My Lord and my God!**" (John 20:28). This declaration is the climactic moment of John's Gospel, affirming Jesus' divinity and lordship. It illustrates that doubt, when brought to Jesus, can become a doorway to deeper faith. Jesus responds not with rebuke, but with a blessing in John 20:29: "**Because you have seen me, you have believed; blessed are those who have not seen and yet have believed.**"

After Pentecost, Thomas's life took a remarkable turn. According to early Church tradition, he became a missionary, traveling east to proclaim the Gospel. His most enduring legacy is found in India, where he is believed to have arrived around A.D. 52. There, he preached to both Jewish and Hindu communities, and his message took root. The Mar Thoma Christians of Kerala in southwestern India trace their spiritual lineage to Thomas and honor him as the founder of their church.

Accounts such as those in the Acts of Thomas (an early Christian text not included in the biblical canon) describe his evangelistic efforts, miracles, and ultimate martyrdom. While the accuracy of every detail in these writings is debated, tradition holds that Thomas was martyred in India, likely near modern-day Chennai (formerly Madras), where a mount known as St. Thomas Mount commemorates his death. He was reportedly speared to death, giving his life for the message he had once doubted.

Thomas's journey illustrates the profound reality of the resurrection's power to transform unbelief into unshakeable faith. His story demonstrates that questioning can coexist with discipleship; in fact, Jesus honors sincere inquiries that lead to seeking Him. Thomas's bold declaration, "My Lord and my God," is one of the clearest affirmations of Jesus' divine identity in the Gospels. Additionally, Thomas embodies the missional spirit of the early Church. His travels to distant lands reveal that the apostolic witness extended far beyond the Roman Empire, fulfilling Jesus' command to **"go and make disciples of all nations"** (in Matthew 28:19). His presence in India highlights the early Church's global vision and reminds us that Christianity is not solely rooted in the West but has been inherently global from the very start.

...Thomas offers a testimony of faith shaped by encounter, doubt conquered by truth, and courage born from conviction. The apostle Thomas offers a testimony of faith shaped by encounter, doubt conquered by truth, and courage born from conviction. His life serves as a reminder that Jesus meets individuals where they are, calls them to Himself, and then sends them into the world with a mission. For those who have wrestled with faith or sought evidence, Thomas stands not as a cautionary tale but as a powerful example of what it means to transition from doubt to devotion—and from fear to fearless proclamation.

JAMES THE LESS

James, the son of Alphaeus, is one of the lesser-known apostles in the New Testament. He appears among the Twelve in the synoptic Gospels and the Book of Acts (Matthew 10:3; Mark 3:18; Luke 6:15; Acts 1:13), but little else is directly recorded about his life and ministry. The title "the Less" may indicate his stature, age, or the limited scope of his public ministry compared to the more prominent James, the son of Zebedee. Nevertheless, James the Less serves as a quiet yet faithful witness to the Gospel, reminding us that God often works powerfully through those who labor in obscurity.

James the Less's limited mention in Scripture challenges modern assumptions that spiritual significance is tied to public recognition. While he is not highlighted by miracles or major speeches, his inclusion among the Twelve signifies that he was personally chosen by Jesus, trained under His leadership, and trusted with the Great Commission. Like the other apostles, James would have witnessed the resurrection of Christ, received the Holy Spirit at Pentecost, and been sent out as a bearer of the Gospel to the nations.

James the Less's limited mention in Scripture challenges modern assumptions that spiritual significance is tied to public recognition.

Church tradition helps fill in the gaps of James's post-resurrection ministry. According to early Christian sources, including Eusebius and other ecclesiastical historians, James the Less is believed to have taken the message of Christ to Egypt, particularly to Heliopolis, a major ancient city near modern-day Cairo. There, he is said to have preached the Gospel, established Christian communities, and endured persecution for his faith. His missionary efforts in North Africa, while not as widely known or documented as those of Paul or Thomas, nonetheless reflect the expanding reach of Christianity into diverse cultures and geographies.

Tradition also holds that James met a violent end. He is believed to have been martyred by stoning and clubbing, possibly in Egypt, for refusing to renounce the faith he preached. His manner of death echoes that of Stephen, the first Christian martyr, underscoring the early Church's unwavering commitment to the Gospel, even unto death. Though the Bible provides few details about James's specific actions, his life illustrates an essential theological truth: faithfulness is not measured by fame. In the body of Christ, not every servant stands on a platform, but each one plays a crucial role in advancing God's kingdom. James's story affirms Paul's teaching in 1 Corinthians 12:22: **"Those parts of the body that seem to be weaker are indispensable."** James the Less reminds us that obedience, not visibility, defines greatness in God's eyes. While his name may be mentioned only in passing in the New Testament, he lived out his calling with courage and conviction, spreading the Gospel to places others might not have reached, laying foundations for future generations of believers.

James the Less embodies the quiet strength of discipleship. His life and martyrdom reflect a legacy of humble service, unwavering faith, and unseen yet indispensable Kingdom impact. In honoring his story, we are reminded that no act of obedience is wasted, and every faithful witness contributes to the unfolding story of redemption that continues through the Church today.

THADDAEUS (ALSO CALLED JUDAS, SON OF JAMES)

Thaddaeus, also known as Jude and sometimes referred to as Lebbaeus, is another of the more obscure members of the Twelve Apostles, yet his life and legacy are deeply woven into the fabric of the early Church. He is mentioned briefly in the apostolic lists found in Matthew 10:3 and Mark 3:18, where he is identified as Thaddaeus, and in Luke 6:16 and Acts 1:13, where he is referred to as Judas son of James, likely to distinguish him from Judas Iscariot. Despite the limited information provided in Scripture, Church tradition and theological reflection offer valuable insights into his character, ministry, and enduring witness.

Thaddaeus represents the often-unseen servant—one who is called, equipped, and sent by Christ but not placed at the forefront of the biblical narrative. In John 14:22, we find his only recorded question to Jesus, which reveals a thoughtful and spiritually curious mind: **"But, Lord, why do you intend to show yourself to us and not to the world?"** Jesus answers him in the next verse, John 14:23, by emphasizing love and obedience: **"Anyone who loves me will obey my teaching. My Father will love them, and we will come to them and make our home with them."** This exchange, though brief, captures a profound truth—Thaddaeus was engaged, attentive, and eager to understand the implications of Jesus' mission. His question also reflects a missionary impulse: why should knowledge of the Messiah be limited to a few? That same impulse would drive his ministry in the years following Jesus' resurrection.

> ...Thaddaeus was engaged, attentive, and eager to understand the implications of Jesus' mission.

After Pentecost, tradition holds that Thaddaeus traveled to Syria and Mesopotamia, regions rich in ancient religious and cultural heritage. These areas, encompassing parts of modern-day Iraq, Syria, and southeastern Turkey, were vital crossroads for early Christian expansion. His mission would have involved navigating complex religious dynamics and opposition from both pagan authorities and entrenched religious systems.

According to early Church writings, including Eusebius's Ecclesiastical History, Thaddaeus (referred to as Addai in Syriac traditions) is said to have brought the Gospel to Edessa, an influential city in Mesopotamia. A well-known apocryphal story, preserved in the Doctrine of Addai, recounts that Thaddaeus was sent by the apostle Thomas or by Jesus Himself to heal King Abgar of Edessa, who had heard of Jesus' miracles. After healing the king, Thaddaeus is said to have established a Christian community in the city, making Edessa one of the earliest centers of Christian faith outside Jerusalem. Though this account is not found in canonical Scripture, it reflects the deep respect and veneration early Christians held for Thaddaeus. His evangelistic efforts in such significant cultural and religious centers suggest he played a critical role in planting the seeds of Christianity in the East—work that would bear fruit for generations to come.

Tradition also tells us that Thaddaeus continued his mission into Persia, where he boldly preached the Gospel in a predominantly Zoroastrian culture. His message, challenging the dominant religious paradigms of the time, eventually led to his martyrdom, likely by beating or being killed with arrows or a club—accounts vary. Regardless of the details, what remains consistent is that Thaddaeus, like many of his fellow apostles, gave his life for the Gospel he once asked to be revealed to the world.

His legacy, though quiet in the New Testament, resounds with the faithfulness of obedience. He may not have performed public miracles or delivered famous sermons recorded in Scripture, but his devotion reflects the truth found in Romans 10:15: "**How beautiful are the feet of those who bring good news!**" The apostle Thaddaeus stands as a symbol of unsung faithfulness. He reminds us that the Kingdom of God is built not only by those in the spotlight but also by those who serve steadfastly in obscurity, bringing the light of Christ to dark and distant places. His obedience to Jesus' commission, his ministry in challenging cultural settings, and his martyrdom for the sake of the Gospel affirm that every disciple—whether prominent or unknown—has a vital role in God's redemptive plan. Through Thaddaeus, we are invited to embrace the quiet, courageous faith that advances the mission of Christ to the ends of the earth.

SIMON THE ZEALOT

Simon the Zealot, one of the Twelve Apostles, remains a mysterious yet intriguing figure in the New Testament. Though Scripture provides little detail about his life and ministry beyond listing him among the apostles in Matthew 10:4, Mark 3:18, Luke 6:15, and Acts 1:13, the designation "Zealot" attached to his name opens a window into his past and the powerful transformation he underwent as a follower of Jesus.

The title "Zealot" likely indicates Simon's former affiliation with a radical Jewish political movement. The Zealots were nationalistic revolutionaries committed to liberating Israel from Roman rule, often through violent means. Their passion for the Law and for Jewish sovereignty sometimes erupted into rebellion, contributing to the Jewish-Roman War (A.D. 66–73). That Jesus would call someone from this extremist background into His inner circle—alongside someone like Matthew the tax collector, who had cooperated with Rome—speaks volumes about the unifying, transforming power of the Gospel. Within the community of Christ, former enemies became brothers, not through shared ideology but through faith in the Messiah.

Simon's life exemplifies how God redirects human passion. Simon's zeal, once likely aimed at political revolution, was now channeled toward the spiritual revolution of the Kingdom of God. Jesus did not erase his passion; He redeemed it. This transformation reflects the calling of all believers to present their fervor, gifts, and ambitions before God, to be shaped for His purposes. As Paul later writes in Romans 12:11: "**Never be lacking in zeal, but keep your spiritual fervor, serving the Lord.**" After the resurrection and Pentecost, Simon, like the other apostles, would have gone out into the world to fulfill the Great Commission—to "**go and make disciples of all nations**" (Matthew 28:19). Though the New Testament does not detail his missionary journeys, early Church tradition provides several accounts of his travels.

Historical sources and Christian traditions vary, but many associate Simon with evangelistic efforts in regions as diverse as Egypt, Cyrene in North Africa, Persia (modern-day Iran), Armenia, and even Britain. Some sources suggest that Simon teamed up with Thaddaeus to preach in Mesopotamia and Persia, where they faced opposition from pagan authorities. These reports indicate that Simon's ministry took him far from Jerusalem into some of the most challenging and unreached regions of the ancient world.

Traditions concerning his death are equally varied, but they all converge on one point: Simon was martyred for his faith. Some accounts claim he was sawed in half, others say he was crucified, and still others suggest he died alongside Jude in Persia, executed for refusing to worship pagan deities. Regardless of the manner, what stands clear is that Simon remained faithful to Christ unto death, bearing witness with his life to the Gospel he once might never have imagined embracing.

Simon's story, though veiled in mystery, holds deep theological and historical significance. His background as a Zealot shows that no one is beyond the reach of Christ's call—not the political extremist, not the revolutionary, not the hardened nationalist. Christ's message transcends political ideologies and national boundaries, transforming even the fiercest passions into instruments of peace, mercy, and truth. Simon the Zealot is a powerful reminder that Jesus calls people from every walk of life, including those whose past may be filled with violence or division. In Christ, Simon's fiery zeal became holy conviction, and his passion was reoriented toward eternal things. Though his life may have been largely hidden from historical record, his impact as part of the apostolic witness helped lay the foundation of the Church and fulfilled Christ's vision of a Gospel proclaimed to all nations. His legacy continues to inspire believers to passionate, unwavering commitment to the Kingdom of God—where former zealots become peacemakers and servants of the cross.

> **Simon's story... His background as a Zealot shows that no one is beyond the reach of Christ's call...**

Matthias (Chosen to Replace Judas Iscariot)

Matthias, although one of the lesser-known apostles, occupies a unique position in the early history of the Church. His selection to replace Judas Iscariot, the betrayer of Jesus, is documented in Acts 1:23–26, making him and Saul the only apostles chosen after Jesus' ascension. I will discuss Paul later. While Scripture does not provide further direct accounts of Matthias' life or ministry, the historical and theological significance of his appointment, along with later traditions about his work, serves as a profound testament to God's divine order and faithfulness to His redemptive plan.

Following the resurrection and ascension of Christ, the remaining eleven apostles gathered in Jerusalem and felt the need to restore their number to twelve. This number held symbolic importance, reflecting the twelve tribes of Israel and representing the new people of God. Peter addressed the assembly, referencing Psalm 109:8, stating: **"May another take his place of leadership"** (Acts 1:20). Two qualified candidates were proposed—Joseph called Barsabbas (also known as Justus) and Matthias—both of whom had accompanied Jesus and His followers from the time of John the Baptist until the resurrection. After prayer and the casting of lots, a method rooted in Old Testament practice for discerning God's will, Matthias was chosen. Scripture records this in Acts 1:26: **"Then they cast lots, and the lot fell to Matthias; so he was added to the eleven apostles."**

Matthias's appointment illustrates that the apostolic mission was not a human invention... Matthias's appointment illustrates that the apostolic mission was not a human invention but one initiated and sustained by divine guidance. His inclusion restores the symbolic unity of the Twelve, emphasizing that the Church's mission would continue faithfully to Jesus' design, despite Judas's betrayal. The selection process—grounded in prayer, scriptural reflection, and trust in God—highlights the early Church's reliance on divine direction during leadership transitions.

Although Matthias is not mentioned again in the canonical New Testament, early Church traditions shed light on his missionary activities. Various accounts suggest that Matthias preached the Gospel in regions such as Cappadocia, an area in modern-day central Turkey, as well as around the Caspian Sea, including places like

Colchis (present-day Georgia) and parts of Ethiopia or Armenia, depending on the tradition.

While his martyrdom is not described in Scripture, it is a recurring theme in various traditions. Some accounts suggest Matthias was stoned and then beheaded, while others propose he was crucified or met another violent end. Regardless of the details, his readiness to sacrifice his life for Christ links him with the other apostles, whose collective witness—a testimony sealed in blood and offered in love—was centered on the message they preached.

Although Matthias remains a relatively obscure figure, his story embodies the profound truth that faithfulness is not defined by fame. He serves as a reminder that God recognizes and appoints those who have quietly journeyed along the path of discipleship. Matthias followed Jesus from the beginning but was not included among the original Twelve. Nevertheless, his perseverance and faith prepared him for the moment when God called him to greater responsibility. In this way, Matthias symbolizes all believers who serve faithfully in the background, essential to the unfolding of God's plan. While Matthias's life may lack dramatic narratives or recorded miracles, his divinely guided selection, steadfast discipleship, and ultimate martyrdom exemplify the core values of apostolic ministry: obedience, endurance, and a readiness to serve. His story highlights that the Gospel advances not only through prominent voices but also through those who remain in the background—watchful, willing, and chosen by God. Through Matthias, the continuity of the Twelve was maintained, and the Church's mission progressed—rooted in unity, guided by prayer, and empowered by the Spirit.

PAUL

The apostle Paul, originally known as Saul of Tarsus, is one of the most influential and transformative figures in Christian history. His life and ministry serve as a powerful testament to God's grace to redeem, repurpose, and commission lives for His glory. Deeply rooted in the first century and rich in theological significance, Paul's work laid the foundation for the early Church and continues to resonate in Christian thought and mission today.

Paul was born in Tarsus, a city in Cilicia (modern-day Turkey), and held a unique combination of identities as both a Jew by birth and a

Roman citizen. This dual heritage would later enhance his mission. A Pharisee trained under the esteemed teacher Gamaliel (Acts 22:3), Paul was initially zealous for the Law and hostile toward the burgeoning Christian movement. He actively persecuted the early Church, approving of the stoning of Stephen, the first Christian martyr (Acts 7:58–8:1), and seeking to imprison followers of Jesus. However, his life took a radical turn on the road to Damascus. In Acts 9:4, we read how the risen Christ appeared to him in a blinding light, asking: **"Saul, Saul, why do you persecute me?"** This moment marked the beginning of his dramatic transformation—from persecutor to preacher, from enemy of the Church to its greatest evangelist. After his conversion, Saul took the name Paul and dedicated his life to proclaiming the Gospel of Jesus Christ.

Paul's conversion and calling emphasize the central Christian theme of grace. In 1 Timothy 1:15–16, he writes: **"Here is a trustworthy saying that deserves full acceptance: Christ Jesus came into the world to save sinners—of whom I am the worst. But for that very reason I was shown mercy so that in me... Christ Jesus might display his immense patience as an example for those who would believe in him and receive eternal life."** His story reassures us that no one is beyond the reach of God's mercy and highlights how God's power is made perfect in weakness. Paul's ministry was unmatched in scope and intensity. He undertook at least three major missionary journeys, as recorded in the Book of Acts, traveling throughout Asia Minor, Greece, and eventually to Rome. He established churches in cities such as Philippi, Corinth, Ephesus, Thessalonica, and Galatia, often in the face of intense opposition. Paul's preaching reached both Jews and Gentiles, breaking cultural and religious barriers to proclaim the universality of the Gospel. His theological assertion that salvation comes by grace through faith, rather than through works of the Law, was revolutionary, especially in the context of Jewish-Gentile relations in the early Church.

Paul's letters, or epistles, to various churches constitute a significant portion of the New Testament. Ranging from Romans to Philemon, these writings provide profound theological insights, pastoral care, and doctrinal clarity. In his epistle to the Romans, Paul explores the gravity of human sin alongside the grandeur of God's redemptive plan, as expressed in Romans 5:1: **"Therefore, since we**

have been justified through faith, we have peace with God through our Lord Jesus Christ." In Galatians, he passionately defends the Gospel of grace, declaring: "**It is for freedom that Christ has set us free**" (Galatians 5:1, NIV).

Throughout his ministry, Paul faced immense suffering for the Gospel. In 2 Corinthians 11:23–27, he recounts the beatings, imprisonments, shipwrecks, and near-death experiences he endured for Christ. Despite these challenges, he remained resolute, stating in Philippians 4:12–13: "**I have learned the secret of being content... I can do all this through him who gives me strength.**" According to Church tradition, Paul was ultimately imprisoned in Rome and martyred by beheading under Emperor Nero, likely around A.D. 64–67. Though his life ended in chains, his influence only grew. His writings have shaped Christian doctrine for two millennia, and his missionary legacy has inspired countless generations of evangelists, theologians, and church planters.

> Throughout his ministry, Paul faced immense suffering for the Gospel.

During his ministry, a significant conflict arose between Paul and Peter, often referred to as the Antioch incident. This event highlighted the growing tensions within the early Church regarding how Jewish and Gentile believers were to coexist under the Gospel. Paul describes this confrontation in Galatians 2:11–14, where he publicly challenges Peter in Antioch.

The crux of their disagreement centered on table fellowship—a powerful symbol of unity within the early Christian community. Peter had previously dined freely with Gentile believers, consistent with the vision God gave him in Acts 10. However, he withdrew from them when a group of Jewish Christians arrived from Jerusalem, associated with James, who adhered to Jewish customs regarding purity and separation. Fearing criticism, Peter distanced himself from the Gentile believers, inadvertently influencing others, including Barnabas, to do the same.

Paul viewed this behavior as hypocritical and damaging to the truth of the Gospel. He confronted Peter, asserting that their actions were inconsistent with the Gospel of grace, which teaches that both Jews and Gentiles are justified by faith in Christ, rather than by adhering to the law. Paul's rebuke was driven not by personal pride but by a commitment to uphold the inclusive and transformative essence of the Gospel.

This moment was not a rivalry but a critical clarification. Paul emphasized that salvation is rooted in faith in Jesus Christ, not in ethnicity or legal observance. It marked a pivotal moment in the early Church's understanding that the Gospel dismantles barriers, and that unity in Christ must surpass cultural and religious divisions. Although the encounter was intense, it ultimately contributed to a more unified and inclusive Church, dedicated to the radical message articulated in Galatians 3:28: **"There is neither Jew nor Gentile, neither slave nor free, nor is there male and female, for you are all one in Christ Jesus."**

Another potential conflict that Paul had was the difference between Grace and works as emphasized by James. The relationship between faith, grace, and works has been a significant topic of theological reflection, especially in the writings of the apostles Paul and James. At first glance, their teachings on salvation may seem contradictory. Paul, particularly in his letters to the Romans and Galatians, emphasizes that salvation is attained by grace through faith, independent of works of the law. In contrast, James highlights the importance of works as evidence of a vibrant and active faith. Rather than opposing one another, these perspectives provide a complementary and more comprehensive understanding of Christian salvation.

Paul's teachings are deeply rooted in his mission to the Gentiles and his opposition to Judaizing influences, groups that insisted on adherence to the Mosaic Law, such as circumcision, as prerequisites for salvation. In this context, Paul clearly states: **"For we maintain that a person is justified by faith apart from the works of the law"** (Romans 3:28). For Paul, grace represents the unearned favor of God, and faith is the exclusive means by which one receives salvation. He emphasizes that no human effort or observance of the law can earn righteousness before a holy God. This focus stems from his belief in the sufficiency of Christ's atoning work on the cross. Paul is concerned with the essence of salvation—how one enters into a right relationship with God.

Conversely, James writes to Jewish believers who may have misunderstood faith as mere intellectual agreement. He challenges a superficial faith that lacks evidence of transformation, asserting, "**Faith by itself, if it is not accompanied by action, is dead**" (James 2:17). For James, true faith naturally produces righteous living. He does not deny the importance of faith; rather, he insists that genuine faith must be accompanied by works. James focuses on the outcomes of salvation—what authentic belief looks like in practice.

The tension between Paul and James is best understood by recognizing that they address different issues. Paul contends with legalism—the notion that salvation can be earned. James addresses lawlessness, the belief that faith frees one from the obligation to live righteously. Paul teaches how we are saved; James teaches what saved people do.

The early Church acknowledged this harmony. Even Martin Luther, who initially struggled with James' emphasis on works, eventually recognized the epistle's value in encouraging believers to live out their faith. Augustine of Hippo similarly reconciled the two teachings, stating, "Paul said that a man is justified through faith without works of the law, but not without those works of which James speaks."

In essence, Paul and James are not adversaries but allies. Paul proclaims the grace that saves, while James illustrates the life that grace produces. Together, they present a robust theology: salvation is by grace alone, through faith alone—but the faith that genuinely saves is never alone. It is accompanied by a transformed life characterized by obedience, love, and good works, all for the glory of God.

Paul's life exemplifies redemption, transformation, and unwavering devotion. He embodies both a theologian and a practitioner, merging profound doctrinal truth with the urgency of global mission. His ministry illustrates that God can use even the most unlikely individuals to effect change—not through human strength, but through divine calling and grace. Through Paul, the Church received a lasting testament found in Romans 1:16: "**For I am not ashamed of the gospel, because it is the power of God that brings salvation to everyone who believes: first to the Jew, then to the Gentile.**"

> **Paul's life exemplifies redemption, transformation, and unwavering devotion.**

Historically, the Apostles established the foundation for what would evolve into a global movement, grounded not in political power but in spirit-empowered witness. Their obedience to the Great Commission ignited the spread of Christianity across continents, cultures, and centuries.

Their lives exemplified the core truths of the Gospel: self-sacrifice, bold proclamation, grace for sinners, and the hope of eternal life. Their ministries fulfilled Jesus' promise in Acts 1:8: **"You will be my witnesses... to the ends of the earth."** Despite facing persecution, isolation, and martyrdom, they persevered, holding onto Jesus' assurance: **"I am with you always, to the very end of the age"** (Matthew 28:20). Through their faithful obedience, the message of Christ began in Jerusalem and spread like wildfire throughout the Roman Empire and beyond. Their example calls today's Church to embody the same courage, commitment, and vision, taking the Gospel to every nation, people, and generation until Christ returns.

The Apostles did not embark on this mission in their own strength; they were empowered by the Holy Spirit at Pentecost. This transformative event turned a group of once fearful followers into bold witnesses. Jesus' promise in Acts 1:8 states: **"But you will receive power when the Holy Spirit comes on you; and you will be my witnesses in Jerusalem, and in all Judea and Samaria, and to the ends of the earth."** The Holy Spirit provided the Apostles with both courage and clarity as they ventured into dangerous and often hostile territories.

Their mission was characterized by miracles, persecution, and unwavering perseverance. Peter's sermon at Pentecost (Acts 2) led to the conversion of thousands. Paul, who once persecuted the Church, became its most devoted missionary, traveling across the Roman world to plant churches, disciple believers, and defend the truth of the Gospel. In Romans 1:16, Paul boldly declared, **"For I am not ashamed of the gospel, because it is the power of God that brings salvation to everyone who believes."** The conversion and inclusion of Gentiles into the family of God represented a transformative and often contentious development in the early Christian movement. Initially, the Gospel was preached primarily to the Jews, as the early Church emerged from Jewish tradition and expectation. However, as the message of Jesus Christ spread, it became evident that salvation through Him was not confined by ethnicity, culture, or nationality.

The Book of Acts captures several key moments that illustrate a significant shift in the early Church. One of the most pivotal events was the conversion of Cornelius, a Roman centurion, as described in Acts 10. Through a vision, God revealed to the Apostle Peter that the Gospel was meant for all people, not just the Jews. When Peter witnessed the Holy Spirit descend upon Cornelius and his household, he proclaimed in Acts 10:34–35: **"I now realize how true it is that God does not show favoritism but accepts from every nation the one who fears him and does what is right."** This moment confirmed that Gentiles could receive the Holy Spirit just as Jewish believers had, effectively dismantling the long-standing barriers between the two groups.

However, the inclusion of Gentiles faced both resistance and rejoicing. Some Jewish Christians contended that Gentiles must first convert to Judaism and adhere to the Law of Moses—especially circumcision—to be saved. This controversy reached a critical juncture at the Jerusalem Council in Acts 15, where Church leaders, including Peter and James, affirmed that salvation comes by grace through faith, not through compliance with the law. This decision officially welcomed Gentiles into the Church without requiring them to first become Jews.

The Apostle Paul emerged as the foremost missionary to the Gentiles, dedicating his life to preaching Christ in non-Jewish regions. In cities such as Antioch, Corinth, Ephesus, and Rome, Paul boldly proclaimed that the righteousness of God is available to all who believe. Through his ministry, many Gentiles came to faith, and new churches were established throughout the Roman world. This inclusion of Gentiles fulfilled God's ancient promise to bless all nations through Abraham's offspring (Genesis 12:3) and revealed the universal scope of redemption in Christ. It reaffirmed that the Gospel transcends race, language, and culture, offering good news to all people.

As Paul stated in Ephesians 2:14: **"For he himself is our peace, who has made the two groups one and has destroyed the barrier, the dividing wall of hostility."** The spread of the Gospel to the Gentiles marked the beginning of Christianity's global mission. While it sparked conflict and debate, it also showcased the depth of God's grace and the expansive reach of His kingdom, welcoming all who believe into one body united in Christ. The conversion of Gentiles stands as a powerful testament to God's inclusive love—a love that transcends boundaries and embraces people from all corners of the earth. Through faith in Jesus Christ, Gentiles were integrated into the family of God, becoming co-heirs with Jewish believers of God's promises. As the Apostle Paul eloquently expresses in Galatians 3:26-28: **"For in Christ Jesus you are all sons of God, through faith. For as many of you as were baptized into Christ have put on Christ. There is neither Jew nor Greek, there is neither slave nor free, there is no male and female, for you are all one in Christ Jesus."** The Apostolic mission also confronted the Church with complex cultural and theological challenges. The inclusion of Gentiles sparked discussions about identity, law, and grace. Yet, throughout these challenges, the message of the Gospel remained clear and steadfast: salvation is by grace through faith in Jesus Christ.

Despite facing opposition, imprisonment, and martyrdom, the Apostles remained resolute. Their unwavering commitment fulfilled Jesus' prayer in John 17:18, **"As you sent me into the world, I have sent them into the world."** They lived and died with the conviction that the world needed to hear the message of the risen Christ. This mission established the foundation for the global Church. What began with a small group of Galilean disciples evolved into a world-changing movement that spread across continents and generations. The Apostolic era serves as a powerful reminder that the Gospel is not limited by geography, culture, or time. It is, as Hebrews 4:12 describes, **"alive and active,"** continually transforming lives today.

Reflecting on the Apostolic mission reminds us that the call to share the message of Jesus Christ did not conclude with the Twelve.

Reflecting on the Apostolic mission reminds us that the call to share the message of Jesus Christ did not conclude with the Twelve. The Great Commission—to go and make disciples of all nations—extends beyond the original apostles to every believer throughout history. Their legacy urges the modern Church to live boldly, faithfully, and with a global perspective, carrying the Gospel to every corner of the world. We are empowered by the same Holy Spirit, anchored in the same unchanging truth, and invited into the same divine purpose. God's selection of the apostles—men from diverse and often unexpected backgrounds—reveals that His intimate involvement with creation did not end at the Fall and has remained steadfast throughout history. These twelve were not chosen for their prestige, power, or perfection, but for their willingness to follow, be transformed, and ultimately become vessels of God's restoring presence in a broken world. From fishermen to tax collectors, zealots to skeptics, their calling affirms that our Heavenly Father has never turned His back on humanity. Instead, He meets people where they are, redeems their stories, and weaves them into His divine plan.

The apostles' calling echoes the same voice that walked through the garden in the cool of the day, asking, "**Where are you?**" This call is not one of condemnation, but of restoration. In Christ, God was not only reconciling the world to Himself (2 Corinthians 5:19) but also commissioning others to carry that message of reconciliation forward. The apostles became a bridge—ambassadors of a Kingdom breaking into the world with the truth and powered by grace.

Their lives and witness are not relics of sacred history but living testimonies that God's redemptive work did not cease with the cross or the resurrection; it continues even now. The same God who walked with Adam, called Abraham, parted the Red Sea, and raised Christ from the dead is still drawing people back to Himself with unwavering love. The apostles' mission marked the beginning of a global and generational invitation; to return to the God who created us and still loves us, and longs to dwell with us once more.

Like the apostles, we are part of this ongoing mission. Their story is our inheritance, their calling our example. And their God—the God who seeks, saves, and sends—is still at work, restoring the broken, reclaiming the lost, and drawing all creation back into the harmony once known in the garden.

CHAPTER
9

Satan's Move to Foil God's Plan:
How Sin Interacts with Christians—
What is God's Plan to Deal with this Trend

The origin of evil is one of the most profound and complex questions in theology, encompassing the nature of God, free will, and the moral fabric of creation. Within the Christian worldview, evil is not a creation of God, who is perfectly good, holy, and just (Psalm 145:17; 1 John 1:5). Instead, it entered the world through the misuse of free will by created beings.

The first manifestation of evil is often linked to Satan's rebellion. While the Bible does not provide a comprehensive account of Satan's fall, passages such as Isaiah 14:12–15 and Ezekiel 28:12–17 are traditionally interpreted as describing a powerful angel who became prideful and sought to elevate himself above God. This pride led to his downfall, transforming him into the adversary—Satan—who opposes God's purposes and people.

Following this celestial rebellion, evil was introduced into human history through the disobedience of Adam and Eve in the Garden of Eden (Genesis 3). Tempted by the serpent, Eve and then Adam ate from the tree of the knowledge of good and evil, defying God's explicit command. This act of rebellion was the first human sin and resulted in a rift between humanity and God, introducing both moral and natural evil into the world. Sin brought spiritual death, suffering, and corruption not only to humanity but also to the created order (Romans 5:12; Romans 8:20–22).

Theologically, evil is understood not as a substance created by God, but as a corruption or distortion of the good. It arises from willful rebellion—choosing something contrary to God's will and design. While God, in His sovereignty, permits evil for a time, He does not cause it. Instead, He works through and despite evil to fulfill His purposes. As Romans 8:28 affirms: "**In all things God works for the good of those who love him, who have been called according to his purpose.**" Ultimately, the Christian faith teaches that evil will not have the final say. Through Jesus Christ, God has initiated a plan of redemption that addresses evil at its core. Christ's death and resurrection triumphed over sin, Satan, and death, and a day will come when God will completely eradicate evil, wipe away every tear, and make all things new (Revelation 21:4–5).

> **Through Jesus Christ, God has initiated a plan of redemption that addresses evil at its core.**

The origin of evil lies in the free will of created beings who chose to rebel against God's authority. While God did not create evil, He allowed for its possibility, enabling love and obedience to be freely given rather than coerced. Although evil is real and destructive, it is ultimately limited in power and time. God's goodness, justice, and love will prevail, leading to the restoration of all things.

Satan's role in this biblical narrative is intricately linked to the broader theological theme of God's redemptive plan for humanity. He is not merely a symbolic force of evil but a personal, spiritual adversary committed to opposing God's will and leading humanity into rebellion. His influence begins early in the biblical account, appearing in Genesis 3 as a cunning serpent who tempts Adam and Eve, introducing sin into a world that God had declared "very good" (Genesis 1:31). This pivotal moment marks the initial fracture between God and humanity and sets the stage for the unfolding drama of redemption.

Satan's rebellion against God predates the events in the Garden and is often associated with passages like Isaiah 14:12–15 and Ezekiel 28:12–17. Although these passages originally reference earthly kings, many Christians traditionally interpret them as symbolic of Satan's fall from heaven. His pride and desire to ascend above God resulted in his expulsion and his subsequent role as "**the accuser of our brothers and sisters**" (Revelation 12:10). From that moment on,

Satan's mission has been to deceive, divide, and destroy—countering God's truth with lies, as highlighted in John 8:44: "**He was a murderer from the beginning, not holding to the truth... For he is a liar and the father of lies.**"

In the New Testament, Satan's tactics are further revealed. He masquerades as an angel of light (2 Corinthians 11:14), sows temptation (Luke 4:1–13), and seeks to devour the faithful (1 Peter 5:8). His objective is always to disrupt God's plan, distort God's word, and discourage God's people. In the wilderness, he even tempts Jesus by offering Him the kingdoms of the world in exchange for worship—a temptation that Jesus firmly rejects by adhering to the truth of Scripture (Matthew 4:1–11). This encounter underscores Satan's persistent strategy: to present counterfeit promises in exchange for disobedience. For Christians, the reality of sin, often influenced by Satan's schemes, presents a daily spiritual battle. Paul vividly captures this internal struggle in Romans 7:19: "**For I do not do the good I want to do, but the evil I do not want to do—this I keep on doing.**" Sin is more than just moral failure; it represents a spiritual condition that disrupts fellowship with God, damages relationships, and hinders spiritual growth. While Christians are not exempt from this struggle, they are not left helpless. God's solution to sin and Satan's influence is found in the person and work of Jesus Christ. In 2 Corinthians 5:21: Paul states, "**God made him who had no sin to be sin for us, so that in him we might become the righteousness of God.**" Jesus' sacrificial death on the cross and His resurrection broke the power of sin and death, providing forgiveness, reconciliation, and the promise of eternal life. This victory is not merely judicial; it is transformational. Through faith in Christ, believers have the indwelling of the Holy Spirit and are empowered to resist sin, and called to live righteously.

Moreover, God equips His people with spiritual armor to stand firm against the devil's schemes. In Ephesians 6:11–18, Paul urges believers to "**put on the full armor of God,**" which includes truth, righteousness, faith, salvation, and the Word of God. These elements are not just metaphors; they are essential spiritual disciplines and truths that strengthen believers in their walk with Christ. With these tools, Christians can resist temptation and advance God's kingdom in a world darkened by sin.

Satan's attempts to derail God's plan through temptation, deception, and sin are real and ongoing. However, the greater truth is that God's redemptive plan through Jesus Christ has already secured the ultimate victory. While Christians continue to struggle with sin in this life, they do so not as victims but as victors in Christ, walking in grace and empowered by the Spirit. The journey may be challenging, but it is filled with hope, for **"greater is he who is in you than he who is in the world"** (1 John 4:4). As they embrace God's truth and live by His Spirit, believers become living testimonies of redemption; shining lights in the darkness and witnesses to a world in desperate need of hope.

Satan's role and influence in the lives of Christians today is a sobering yet essential aspect of the faith, rooted in both historical understanding and rich theological reflection. While he cannot ultimately thwart God's redemptive purposes, Satan's activity remains a source of temptation, deception, and spiritual warfare for believers as they navigate their faith journey.

Often referred to in Scripture as the adversary, the tempter, and the accuser, Satan operates as a cunning force opposed to God's will. In 1 Peter 5:8, the apostle warns, **"Be alert and of sober mind. Your enemy the devil prowls around like a roaring lion looking for someone to devour."** Though not omnipotent, Satan employs subtle deception, discouragement, and distortion of God's truth to undermine the spiritual lives of believers. His primary strategy is to tempt Christians into sin, weakening their fellowship with God and neutralizing their effectiveness in ministry and witness.

> ...Satan operates as a cunning force opposed to God's will.

The early Church Fathers recognized Satan's influence as a real and ongoing threat. Thinkers like Augustine and Origen emphasized the spiritual nature of Christian life, describing Satan's work as a constant battle against the soul. This perspective was not rooted in superstition, but reflected the lived reality of Christians who faced temptation, persecution, and moral conflict in their daily lives. The struggle against sin and Satan was seen as intrinsic to discipleship, demanding vigilance, humility, and reliance on God's grace.

Satan's rebellion was not a solitary act of defiance; it triggered a ripple effect in the spiritual realm, drawing with him a multitude of fallen angels—now known as demons. These beings, originally part of God's heavenly host, chose to reject their divine purpose and joined Satan's prideful revolt. Revelation 12:4 alludes to their fall, mentioning a third of the stars being swept from the sky, which many interpret as symbolic of the angels who followed Satan.

Demons operate under Satan's leadership, sharing his ultimate goal: to oppose God's will and to corrupt, deceive, and destroy humanity, which is made in God's image. While Satan can be likened to a general in rebellion, demons act as his foot soldiers, executing strategic attacks in various forms. They are spiritual entities seeking to influence human thoughts, behaviors, cultures, and institutions—spreading confusion, idolatry, bondage to sin, and separation from God. Jesus illustrated their desire to inhabit human lives in Luke 11:24–26, where unclean spirits seek rest but return to a spiritually unguarded "house."

Deceptive by nature, demons often disguise their influence through false teachings, counterfeit miracles, and worldly ideologies that distort truth. The apostle Paul warned that **"Satan himself masquerades as an angel of light"** (2 Corinthians 11:14), and his demonic servants do the same. This highlights the insidious nature of spiritual warfare, which is often subtle and enticing, aiming to lead people away from the truth and into destruction.

However, God is not absent in this struggle—He is always present, actively working to protect, deliver, and empower His people. Scripture clearly states that the authority of Jesus Christ surpasses all powers of darkness. When Christ cast out demons during His earthly ministry, He demonstrated supreme authority over them, signaling the arrival of the Kingdom of God (Luke 11:20). Believers are not defenseless; God has equipped them with the armor of God (Ephesians 6:10–18), the indwelling power of the Holy Spirit (1 John 4:4), and the authority of Christ's name (Luke 10:17–19) to withstand demonic assaults.

Although demons are real and active, they are not omnipotent, omnipresent, or omniscient. They remain subject to God's sovereignty. Their time is limited, and their defeat is assured. Colossians 2:15 proclaims that Jesus **"disarmed the powers and authorities"** and **"made a public spectacle of them, triumphing over them by the cross."** What began as a rebellion in heaven will culminate in their judgment in hell (Matthew 25:41), a fate sealed by Christ's victory.

In the midst of spiritual warfare, we are reminded that God has never relinquished control. He is not a distant observer but an engaged Deliverer. He fights on our behalf, encouraging us not to fear but to stand firm in His truth, clothed in righteousness, guarded by faith, and armed with His Word. Regardless of the darkness that encroaches, we serve the Light that darkness cannot overcome (John 1:5). Even now, as the enemy prowls, the Good Shepherd is near, guiding, protecting, and leading His people through every shadowed valley toward ultimate triumph and eternal peace.

> **In the midst of spiritual warfare, we are reminded that God has never relinquished control.**

In today's world, this struggle remains profoundly relevant. Christians are surrounded by a culture filled with distractions, false narratives, and moral relativism; tools that Satan often uses to dull spiritual awareness and entice believers into compromise. Sin manifests in countless ways: pride, lust, greed, envy, bitterness, and selfishness. These are not mere bad habits; as Scripture defines them, they are transgressions of God's moral law. Sin is not simply an action; it is a condition that permeates the human heart.

The Apostle Paul vividly expressed his inner conflict in Romans 7:19: **"For I do not do the good I want to do…"** This verse illustrates the tension between a regenerate heart, which desires to please God, and the lingering sinful nature that opposes His will. This battle manifests in the minds, emotions, and decisions of believers. Satan takes advantage of this conflict by whispering lies, convincing Christians that they are unworthy, beyond forgiveness, or incapable of change. His accusations aim to isolate and shame, leading believers into guilt rather than repentance.

However, the Christian faith does not leave believers helpless. God, in His grace, provides both forgiveness and spiritual resources to combat sin and resist the devil. James 4:7 encourages us, **"Submit yourselves, then, to God. Resist the devil, and he will flee from you."** Through prayer, Scripture, and the indwelling presence of the Holy Spirit, Christians are empowered to overcome sin's pull and stand firm against spiritual attacks.

Satan's influence in the lives of Christians today is both subtle and real. His goal is not always to shock with overt evil but to gradually erode faith and obscure truth. Nevertheless, through Christ, believers are not only forgiven but also equipped to resist him. While sin remains a persistent challenge, it does not define a believer's identity or destiny. As 1 John 4:4 reassures us, **"The one who is in you is greater than the one who is in the world."** In the face of sin and Satan's schemes, Christians can walk confidently in God's power, embrace the freedom of grace, and claim the victory that is theirs in Jesus Christ.

In response to humanity's brokenness and the pervasive power of sin, God chose not to abandon us but to offer redemption. From the earliest pages of Scripture, we witness the unfolding of a divine plan rooted in God's unchanging love and mercy. This plan culminates in the person and work of Jesus Christ, who is central to God's redemptive purpose for the world. Christ's life, death, and resurrection are not merely historical events; they are the means by which humanity is reconciled to its Creator.

Sin fractured the relationship between God and mankind, introducing death, separation, and corruption into what was once a perfect creation. The Old Testament sacrificial system, established under the Mosaic Covenant, provided a temporary solution for sin, pointing towards a greater and final atonement. In Jesus, the Lamb of God, that promise was fulfilled. As 2 Corinthians 5:21 states: **"God made him who had no sin to be sin for us, so that in him we might become the righteousness of God."** This exchange, Christ bearing the penalty of sin so that we might receive His righteousness, is the essence of the Gospel.

The early Church communicated this message with urgency and clarity. From Peter's sermon at Pentecost (Acts 2) to Paul's letters to early Christian communities, the death and resurrection of Christ were proclaimed as the pivotal moment in history—the event through which God reconciled the world to Himself. The cross became a symbol not of defeat but of divine victory, where sin was condemned, Satan was disarmed, and salvation was made available to all who believe.

Redemption is not just about forgiveness; it is also about transformation.

Redemption is not just about forgiveness; it is also about transformation. Through faith in Christ, believers are justified and empowered. The indwelling of the Holy Spirit identifies the believer as God's own and initiates a lifelong process of sanctification. The Spirit convicts of sin, comforts in weakness, and guides in truth, enabling believers to walk in newness of life. As Paul writes in Galatians 5:16: "**So I say, walk by the Spirit, and you will not gratify the desires of the flesh.**" God has not left His people defenseless in the battle against temptation and spiritual opposition. Paul presents a powerful metaphor in Ephesians 6:11–17, describing the armor of God—spiritual tools for resisting the assaults of the devil. This armor is both symbolic and practical, equipping believers to stand firm against evil forces. It begins with the belt of truth, grounding us in the unchanging reality of God's Word and securing everything else. Next is the breastplate of righteousness, which protects our hearts, not with our own goodness, but with the holiness of Christ imputed to us. We are also given the shoes of the gospel of peace, enabling us to stand firm and walk with purpose, ready to share the message of reconciliation with the world. The shield of faith is essential for deflecting the flaming arrows of doubt, fear, and accusation hurled at us by the enemy. The helmet of salvation guards our minds, providing confidence and assurance of our eternal hope in Christ. Finally, we are armed with the sword of the Spirit, the Word of God—our only offensive weapon, powerful enough to cut through deception and withstand temptation. Together, this divine armor equips believers not only to endure but to stand victoriously against spiritual opposition.

This imagery illustrates both the seriousness of the spiritual battle and the sufficiency of God's provision. Christians are called not to passivity but to active resistance—rooted not in their own strength, but in God's power. God's response to sin encompasses forgiveness through Christ's sacrifice and empowerment through His Spirit. The believer's life becomes a journey of victory and transformation, made possible by grace and sustained by truth. The cross represents the defining act of love; the resurrection signifies the dawn of hope; and the Spirit embodies the ongoing presence of God in the lives of His people. Through Christ, God's plan for redemption and restoration is not merely a past event; it is a living reality for all who believe.

I am often asked about repeated sin and whether it jeopardizes our salvation. After all, Satan has not ceased his efforts to undermine God's plan. There are compelling arguments on both sides of this discussion, so I believe it is important to present these perspectives to ensure clarity and share my personal viewpoint. While my opinion is ultimately just that—an opinion—it is vital to consider all available evidence before forming a theological conclusion.

I hold two key beliefs regarding salvation. First, salvation is positional, meaning that when one is justified by Christ, they transition from a state of being unsaved to being saved. For an individual to become unsaved, they would have to take an action that removes them from that justified position. The only scriptural reference that explicitly addresses this is found in Hebrews 6:4-6: **"It is impossible for those who have once been enlightened, who have tasted the heavenly gift, who have shared in the Holy Spirit, ⁵ who have tasted the goodness of the word of God and the powers of the coming age, ⁶ and who have fallen away, to be brought back to repentance. To their loss they are crucifying the Son of God all over again and subjecting him to public disgrace."** This passage strongly indicates that if one rejects Jesus as Lord and Savior and publicly denounces Him, they are no longer in a justified position and will lose their salvation.

Confession and repentance are essential for believers and it becomes the mechanism to maintain our righteousness before God, even as they inevitably fall short of His glory. Consequently, eternal salvation is not lost due to sinful behavior. Although sin may lead to other consequences, the loss of salvation is not among them.

Those who believe that repeated sin jeopardizes their salvation often cite various scriptural warnings about the dangers of ongoing sin. They argue that those who persist in sin without repentance may ultimately forfeit their place in God's kingdom. A key passage that addresses this concern is Hebrews 10:26-27, which states, **"If we deliberately keep on sinning after we have received the knowledge of the truth, no sacrifice for sins is left, but only a fearful expectation of judgment and of raging fire that will consume the enemies of God."** This verse highlights the seriousness of willful sin and its potential consequences. If a believer knowingly and intentionally continues to sin, it implies a rejection of Christ's sacrifice, which could lead to divine judgment.

Jesus emphasizes the importance of obedience and perseverance in faith. In Matthew 7:21, He states, **"Not everyone who says to me, 'Lord, Lord,' will enter the kingdom of heaven, but only the one who** does the will of my Father who is in heaven." This indicates that a mere verbal profession of faith is inadequate without corresponding faithful obedience to God's will. Additionally, Matthew 24:13 warns, **"But the one who stands firm to the end will be saved."** This suggests that enduring in righteousness is crucial for salvation.

Paul also addresses the risks of continuing in sin and its potential to disqualify individuals from inheriting God's kingdom. In 1 Corinthians 6:9-10, he states, **"Or do you not know that wrongdoers will not inherit the kingdom of God? Do not be deceived: Neither the sexually immoral nor idolaters nor adulterers nor men who have sex with men nor thieves nor the greedy nor drunkards nor slanderers nor swindlers will inherit the kingdom of God."** This passage explicitly warns that persistent engagement in sinful behavior can prevent individuals from entering the kingdom, reinforcing the significance of one's lifestyle and choices.

Jesus' Parable of the Unforgiving Servant in Matthew 18:32-35 illustrates that a person who has been forgiven can be condemned if they fail to extend mercy and repentance. The servant, initially pardoned for a significant debt, later refuses to forgive another, prompting his master to revoke the forgiveness and subject him to punishment. Jesus concludes with a stern warning: **"This is how my heavenly Father will treat each of you unless you forgive your brother or sister from your heart."** This indicates that forgiveness and alignment with God's character are essential for maintaining salvation.

Additionally, Romans 11:22 offers a cautionary perspective: **"Consider therefore the kindness and sternness of God: sternness to those who fell, but kindness to you, provided that you continue in his kindness. Otherwise, you also will be cut off."** This passage suggests that God's kindness is available to believers as long as they remain in faith, implying that straying from righteousness could lead to being "cut off" from His grace.

John reinforces this idea in 1 John 1:6, stating, **"If we claim to have fellowship with him and yet walk in the darkness, we lie and do not live out the truth."** This verse highlights that habitual sin is incompatible with a genuine relationship with God. Claiming fellowship with Christ while walking in darkness is self-deception, raising doubts about the authenticity of one's salvation.

Based on this information above, one might conclude that continual sin and succumbing to the temptations of Satan jeopardize salvation. However, there are other passages in Scripture that tell a different story.

While Scripture provides serious warnings about persistent wrongdoing, it also highlights the assurance of salvation for those who have faith in Christ. A key argument for eternal security is found in Ephesians 2:8-9, which states, **"For it is by grace you have been saved, through faith—and this is not from yourselves, it is the gift of God—not by works, so that no one can boast."** This passage makes it clear that salvation is solely a work of God's grace, independent of human effort. Since salvation is a gift that cannot be earned, it logically follows that it cannot be lost due to human moral failure alone. Additionally, Jesus offers further assurance in John 10:28-29, declaring, **"I give them eternal life, and they shall never perish; no one will snatch them out of my hand. My Father, who has given them to me, is greater than all; no one can snatch them out of my Father's hand."** This verse underscores the security believers have in Christ's protection. If salvation could be forfeited through repeated sin, this promise would contradict the notion of eternal life as an unbreakable gift.

> ...Salvation is solely a work of God's grace, independent of human effort.

Paul further strengthens this assurance in Romans 8:38-39, proclaiming, **"For I am convinced that neither death nor life, neither angels nor demons, neither the present nor the future, nor any powers, neither height nor depth, nor anything else in all creation, will be able to separate us from the love of God that is in Christ Jesus our Lord."** If nothing in creation can separate believers from God's love, then even sin cannot undo salvation once it has been granted.

The theological foundation for justification by faith bolsters the argument for eternal security. In Romans 5:1, Paul states, **"Therefore, since we have been justified through faith, we have peace with God through our Lord Jesus Christ."** Justification is a legal declaration that a believer is deemed righteous in God's eyes. Because this justification is based on faith rather than behavior, repeated sin does not automatically negate it. Additionally, Jesus' Parable of the Prodigal Son in Luke 15:11-32 underscores the theme of restoration rather than rejection. The wayward son, after squandering his inheritance, returns to his father and is warmly welcomed back. The father's reaction illustrates that God's grace surpasses human failure, affirming that no amount of sin disqualifies someone from returning to Him in repentance.

Furthermore, Paul openly acknowledges the ongoing struggle with sin in Romans 7:19-20, stating, "**For I do not do the good I want to do, but the evil I do not want to do—this I keep on doing. Now if I do what I do not want to do, it is no longer I who do it, but it is sin living in me that does it.**" If struggling with sin jeopardized salvation, even Paul would be at risk. However, he ultimately praises Christ for delivering him from condemnation, suggesting that salvation is secure despite human weaknesses. Finally, 2 Timothy 2:13 offers reassurance: "**If we are faithless, he remains faithful, for he cannot disown himself.**" This verse confirms that God's faithfulness to believers is not contingent upon their perfection; even in their failures, God remains steadfast in His promises.

These seemingly opposing views, while appearing contradictory at first glance, can be reconciled through a broader understanding of salvation. True salvation is transformative, as 2 Corinthians 5:17 states: "**Therefore, if anyone is in Christ, the new creation has come: The old has gone, the new is here!**" A genuine believer will demonstrate repentance and spiritual growth, reflecting the ongoing work of God in their life. Additionally, believers are called to perseverance, as Matthew 24:13 emphasizes: "**But the one who stands firm to the end will be saved,**" highlighting the importance of continued faithfulness.

God's response to sin in the lives of believers is not immediate rejection but rather discipline. Hebrews 12:6 states: "**The Lord disciplines the one he loves, and he chastens everyone he accepts as his son.**" This suggests that while sin carries consequences, God's correction aims to restore rather than condemn. In contrast, apostasy, a deliberate and willful rejection of Christ, differs from the everyday struggles with sin. Hebrews 6:4-6 warns about the seriousness of completely turning away, describing those who have been enlightened yet later reject the faith.

Genuine faith is characterized by obedience, but salvation relies not on human effort but solely on God's mercy and grace. Titus 3:5 emphasizes this truth: "**He saved us, not because of righteous things**

While faith results in a transformed life, it is ultimately God's grace that sustains and secures salvation. we had done, but because of his mercy. He saved us through the washing of rebirth and renewal by the Holy Spirit." While faith results in a transformed life, it is ultimately God's grace that sustains and secures salvation. This understanding balances divine sovereignty with human responsibility, highlighting that salvation is an act of God's mercy while also urging believers to remain steadfast in faith and obedience. Ultimately, salvation rests entirely in God's hands, and those who truly belong to Christ will demonstrate their faith through repentance and perseverance. Although sin is serious, God's grace is greater; however, grace should never be taken for granted or misused.

As flawed human beings, we must recognize the importance of prayer, where we can present our sins—repeated or otherwise—before Jesus, who bore the weight of transgression as the substitutionary sacrifice. Through His atoning work on the cross, He offers forgiveness to all humanity for all time, extending salvation to all who will receive it. In fact, Jesus speaking to Peter about forgiveness in Matthew 18:21-22 states: **"Then Peter came to Jesus and asked, "Lord, how many times shall I forgive my brother or sister who sins against me? Up to seven times?" Jesus answered, "I tell you, not seven times, but seventy-seven times."** If Jesus teaches us to forgive one another seventy-seven times, how much more is God willing to forgive us? After all, the number seven in Scripture symbolizes completeness or perfection—implying that God's forgiveness is limitless and without end. The ongoing struggle between Satan's attempts to sabotage God's purposes through sin and God's unwavering redemptive response through Jesus Christ is a central theme in Christian theology and history. From humanity's fall in the Garden of Eden, where Satan, in the form of a serpent, led Adam and Eve into disobedience (Genesis 3), sin has tainted every aspect of human life. This spiritual rebellion resulted in separation from God, death, and the corruption of God's good creation. Throughout Scripture, Satan actively opposes God's work and seeks to derail His redemptive plan by enticing people into sin and spiritual blindness.

This is not the end of the story. God's response to sin was not defeat or retreat, but grace. In His love and foreknowledge, He provided the perfect solution through Jesus Christ, the incarnate

Son of God. The life, death, and resurrection of Jesus serve as the ultimate countermeasure to Satan's schemes. As Paul writes in Romans 5:20: "**Where sin increased, grace increased all the more.**" Jesus not only bore the penalty for sin on the cross but also broke the power of sin and death, triumphing over the very forces that sought to undermine God's plan.

This redemptive work transformed the early Church, where many believers came from deeply sinful or pagan backgrounds and found new life and identity in Christ. The message of the Gospel spread rapidly, not by human power, but through the compelling witness of transformed lives. Similarly, Christians today live in the tension of being redeemed yet still vulnerable to sin's influence. While the presence of sin remains a spiritual reality, it no longer reigns over those who belong to Christ.

God does not leave His people to face this struggle alone. Through the indwelling Holy Spirit, believers are empowered to resist temptation, grow in holiness, and reflect the character of Christ. 1 John 4:4 assures us: "**The one who is in you is greater than the one who is in the world.**" God's grace provides not only forgiveness but also transformation, enabling a life of righteousness even in a fallen world.

Thus, Christians are not passive victims in this universal battle; they are active participants in God's redemptive mission. By embracing the victory of Christ, they are called to live as children of light, as Paul exhorts in Ephesians 5:8: "**For you were once darkness, but now you are light in the Lord. Live as children of light.**" This calling involves resisting evil, walking in love, and proclaiming the truth of the Gospel to a world still under the shadow of sin.

> By embracing the victory of Christ, they are called to live as children of light...

God's extraordinary measures on behalf of humanity reveal the profound depth of His love and unwavering commitment to His creation. Despite rebellion, deception, and spiritual warfare, He has not distanced Himself or abandoned the world to the enemy's schemes. From the very beginning, God has been intimately involved—calling, guiding, delivering, and redeeming. Even while Satan and his demons wage war against truth and attempt to distort the divine image within us, God remains close, actively working to restore what has been broken.

Through prophets, covenants, and ultimately through Christ, a clear pattern emerges: God does not give up on those He loves. His justice addresses the weight of sin, while His mercy provides a path to restoration. The presence of evil in the world makes His redemptive plan shine even more brightly. The spiritual battles we face remind us that we are part of a larger story—one in which God is the Author, the Defender, and the Redeemer.

This prompts a powerful question that deserves our full attention: Why would God go to such extensive lengths for us? Why would the Creator of the universe pursue fallen humanity with such relentless grace, even at the cost of His own Son? As we move into the next chapter, we will explore the heart of God's redemptive mission—a mission born not of obligation, but of boundless love.

CHAPTER
10

Why Would God Go to These Extensive Measures?

God's extraordinary measures on behalf of humanity reveal the profound depth of His love and unwavering commitment to His creation. This divine initiative is not merely an emotional response; it is a purposeful, redemptive act that flows from God's very nature. As 1 John 4:8-10 states: **"Whoever does not love does not know God, because God is love. 9 This is how God showed his love among us: He sent his one and only Son into the world that we might live through him. 10 This is love: not that we loved God, but that he loved us and sent his Son as an atoning sacrifice for our sins."** Love is intrinsic to who God is, demonstrated most clearly in His response to human rebellion—not with swift judgment, but with a long and patient pursuit of restoration. Romans 5:8 declares: **"But God demonstrates his own love for us in this: While we were still sinners, Christ died for us."** This powerful verse stands at the heart of Christian theology, capturing the radical and counterintuitive nature of God's love. Unlike human love, which is often conditional and based on merit or reciprocity, the love described here is divine—freely given, unearned, and sacrificial. Paul makes a profound statement about the character of God and the nature of grace. This declaration is part of a broader argument in Romans, where Paul explains humanity's universal need for salvation. Earlier, he emphasizes that **"all have sinned and fall**

> ...The love described here is divine—freely given, unearned, and sacrificial.

short of the glory of God" (Romans 3:23), making it clear that no one can earn righteousness through works or personal goodness. Against this backdrop of universal guilt, Romans 5:8 emerges as a beacon of hope and divine mercy: even when humanity was lost in sin, God acted decisively through Jesus Christ.

This concept of sacrificial love contrasts sharply with prevailing Greco-Roman values, which often celebrated honor, strength, and reciprocity. The gods of ancient mythologies were depicted as distant, capricious, and self-serving. In contrast, Paul presents a vision of God whose love is most clearly revealed not in power or conquest, but in the humiliating death of Jesus on a Roman cross—a punishment reserved for the worst criminals. The scandal of the cross becomes the very stage on which God's love is vividly displayed. Christ's death is not portrayed as an accident or defeat, but as a divine act of redemption. The fact that it occurred "while we were still sinners" underscores that God's love precedes our repentance. He does not wait for us to become worthy or to clean ourselves up. Instead, He meets us in our brokenness, offering reconciliation through the blood of Christ. This aligns with Paul's broader theology of grace, particularly in Ephesians 2:8–9: "**For it is by grace you have been saved, through faith—and this is not from yourselves, it is the gift of God—not by works, so that no one can boast.**" Moreover, Romans 5:8 reminds believers that God's love is not static or abstract; it is demonstrated and actively revealed in history. The Greek verb used for "demonstrates" (συνίστησιν, *sunistēsin*) suggests a continuous action, emphasizing that the cross is not just a past event but an enduring revelation of God's heart. Every time believers reflect on the crucifixion, they encounter anew the overwhelming evidence of divine love.

This verse also speaks to the Christian understanding of justification. In the very next verse, Romans 5:9, Paul writes: "**Since we have now been justified by his blood, how much more shall we be saved from God's wrath through him!**" The death of Christ not only demonstrates love; it achieves something eternally significant— securing our right standing before God. The cross becomes the intersection where divine justice and mercy meet, where sin is judged and sinners are forgiven. Romans 5:8 serves as a theological cornerstone, proclaiming that God's love is not a passive sentiment but an active sacrifice. It challenges human notions of worthiness and invites us to marvel at a God who moves toward us even when we are furthest from Him. Historically, it redefines love and power, anchoring the doctrine of salvation by grace through faith. More importantly, it offers every believer the unshakeable assurance that God's love is not based on who we are, but on who He is.

From the beginning, after Adam and Eve's disobedience in the Garden of Eden, God did not abandon His creation. Instead, He clothed them (Genesis 3:21), promised a future redeemer (Genesis 3:15), and began a long story of salvation history. Despite humanity's repeated failures—through idolatry, injustice, and indifference—God remained faithful to His covenant. The call of Abraham, the liberation of Israel from Egypt, the giving of the Law, and the establishment of the prophets and the temple were milestones in this divine pursuit, not isolated acts, but elements of a unified plan to reconcile the world to Himself.

The people of Israel often strayed from their calling, yet God's love endured. The prophets regularly reminded Israel of God's covenant faithfulness. In Hosea 11:8–9, God, speaking as a loving Father, says: **"How can I give you up, Ephraim? How can I hand you over, Israel?... My heart is changed within me; all my compassion is aroused."** This divine compassion, even in the face of betrayal, reveals a God whose mercy consistently triumphs over judgment (James 2:13). This divine love reached its fullest expression in the incarnation of Jesus Christ. As John 3:16 states: **"For God so loved the world that he gave his one and only Son, that whoever believes in him shall not perish but have eternal life."** In Christ, God took on human flesh, entered into human suffering, and bore the full weight of sin and death—not because humanity deserved it, but because love compelled Him. The cross is not merely a moment of atonement; it is a universal declaration that God will go to unimaginable lengths to restore what was lost. The resurrection further affirms that God's commitment to redemption is not temporary or symbolic, but powerful and eternal. It marks the beginning of new creation, assuring believers that restoration is not a wishful hope but a guaranteed promise.

Even now, through the work of the Holy Spirit, God continues this redemptive mission. He calls, convicts, comforts, and transforms hearts. He empowers His Church to be agents of reconciliation (2 Corinthians 5:18–20) and patiently waits for more to come to repentance, as 2 Peter 3:9 reminds us: "**The Lord is not slow in keeping his promise... Instead he is patient with you, not wanting anyone to perish, but everyone to come to repentance.**" In the grand scope of history and theology, God's persistent love for humanity defies logic. It is a love that absorbs offense, bridges impossible gaps, and offers life where there was death. In a world that often withholds forgiveness and demands merit, God's love is shockingly generous and eternally faithful. His desire is not condemnation, but communion. His goal is not retribution, but relationship. And His method, from Genesis to Revelation, is always redemption.

> ...God's love is shockingly generous and eternally faithful. His desire is not condemnation, but communion.

At the heart of God's redemptive work lies a love so profound and enduring that it surpasses human understanding. It is not love in a shallow, sentimental sense, but a deep, sacrificial love that consistently acts for the good of creation—even when met with rejection, rebellion, or indifference. This love is not merely one of God's attributes; it is foundational to His very nature. As the Apostle John boldly declares in 1 John 4:8: "**God is love.**" This divine love is evidenced from the very beginning of the biblical narrative. In Genesis 1, God created the world not out of necessity or compulsion, but from an overflow of generosity and goodness. Every act of creation was pronounced "good," culminating in the formation of humanity, made in His image and entrusted with stewardship of His world (Genesis 1:26–28). God's love was woven into the very fabric of existence, evident in the care and harmony of the original creation.

Even after humanity's fall in Genesis 3, when Adam and Eve disobeyed God's command and sin entered the world, God's love did not waver. Though justice required consequences, love ensured that hope remained. God clothed them in their shame (Genesis 3:21), promised a future redeemer (Genesis 3:15), and initiated a long, unfolding plan of redemption. This steadfast commitment in the face of betrayal illustrates that God's love is not reactive but proactive, rooted in grace.

Throughout Israel's history, God's love is repeatedly shown in His patient dealings with a people prone to idolatry and disobedience.

Through prophets like Hosea, God expresses His love as that of a faithful spouse longing for His wayward bride. In Hosea 11:1–4, God tenderly recalls how He led Israel with "cords of human kindness," emphasizing a love that disciplines but never abandons. The Psalms are filled with declarations of this faithful love, often described by the Hebrew word chesed, which conveys God's steadfast, loyal, and covenant-keeping love.

The fullness of God's love is most powerfully revealed in the incarnation of Jesus Christ. As 1 John 4:9 states, "**This is how God showed his love among us: He sent his one and only Son into the world that we might live through him.**" This is not a distant affection, but love made manifest. In Jesus, God did not simply express love; He became love in action, stepping into human flesh, experiencing our suffering, and ultimately dying in our place. The cross serves as the ultimate revelation of divine love, as articulated by Paul in Romans 5:8: "**But God demonstrates his own love for us in this: While we were still sinners, Christ died for us.**" Christ's sacrificial death was not just an atonement for sin; it was a declaration of the lengths to which God will go to redeem His people.

No divine attribute has shaped the Christian understanding of God more profoundly than His love. The early Church, even under persecution, clung to the belief that God's love had been poured out through Christ—a conviction that transformed communities and reshaped cultures. The doctrine of divine love gave rise to values such as charity, forgiveness, and humility, rooted in the understanding that love, not power, is the true expression of God's nature. Unlike human love, which can be inconsistent and conditional, God's love is unchanging. Malachi 3:6 reminds us: "**I the Lord do not change.**" His love remains constant in times of triumph and failure, faithfulness and faltering. It is a love that seeks, pursues, heals, and restores, calling the sinner home, the broken to wholeness, and the lost to life. As Romans 8:38–39 affirms: "**For I am convinced that neither death nor life... Nor anything else in all creation, will be able to separate us from the love of God that is in Christ Jesus our Lord.**"

God's love is not an abstract theological concept but a living, powerful force that defines His relationship with creation. It motivates every act of grace and underpins every promise of salvation. To know this love is to encounter the very heart of God, which is unchanging, unrelenting, and eternally redemptive. God's desire for a relationship with humanity is a central and enduring theme throughout Scripture, rooted in His very nature as a relational and loving God. From the moment of creation, humanity was not an afterthought or a mere component of the world, but the crown of God's creative work, made in His image (Genesis 1:27) and designed to live in fellowship with Him. The opening chapters of Genesis depict a deeply personal relationship between God and the first humans, Adam and Eve, who walked with Him in the garden, sharing in a divine closeness that reflects God's original intent to dwell with His creation in harmony and love.

...God's longing for communion with humanity did not wane. Even after the fall, when sin entered the world through disobedience, God's longing for communion with humanity did not wane. Although Adam and Eve were expelled from Eden, God's presence never left the narrative. The entire Old Testament serves as a testament to God's ongoing pursuit of His people. From His covenant with Abraham in Genesis 12, promising to bless all nations through his offspring, to the giving of the Law to Moses at Sinai, God continually finds ways to draw near, despite humanity's repeated rebellion. In the wilderness, God instructed the Israelites to build the tabernacle, saying in Exodus 25:8, **"Then have them make a sanctuary for me, and I will dwell among them."** Later, under Solomon, the temple became a permanent symbol of God's dwelling with His people, where sacrifices and priestly mediation allowed for a measure of restored relationship. The prophets also conveyed God's heartfelt desire to His people, calling them to repentance not out of mere obligation, but to restore their covenant intimacy with the Lord. Jeremiah 31:33 looks forward to a deeper relationship, declaring: **"I will be their God, and they will be my people."**

This divine pursuit was revolutionary. Unlike the distant deities of ancient pagan religions, who were often capricious or cruel, Yahweh is portrayed as near, personal, and deeply invested in the lives of His people. He was not satisfied with ritual compliance; He longed for hearts turned toward Him in love and trust. As Hosea 6:6 states, **"For I desire mercy, not sacrifice, and acknowledgment of God rather than burnt offerings."** This longing for relationship reaches its pinnacle in the incarnation of Jesus Christ. In Him, God did not merely send another prophet or priest; He came Himself. John 1:14 powerfully states, **"The Word became flesh and made his dwelling among us."** Jesus became the bridge between heaven and earth, between a holy God and sinful humanity. His life fully revealed the heart of God through His compassion, justice, truth, and grace. By His sacrificial death and victorious resurrection, Jesus opened the way for humanity to be fully reconciled to God, not through rituals or offerings, but through faith and grace. As 2 Corinthians 5:18 declares, **"All this is from God, who reconciled us to himself through Christ."** The relationship once severed in Eden was restored at the cross. Jesus not only atoned for sin but also offered the invitation to know God intimately as Father, Friend, and Redeemer.

This restored relationship is not one of mere obedience or servitude but of adoption and union. Believers are called children of God (John 1:12) and are indwelt by the Holy Spirit, who enables ongoing communion with the Father. In Romans 8:15, Paul writes, **"The Spirit you received brought about your adoption to sonship. And by him we cry, 'Abba, Father.'"** This closeness is not theoretical; it is deeply personal, transformative, and eternal.

God's desire for relationship is not peripheral; it is foundational to the biblical narrative and the Christian faith. From Eden to Calvary, from the temple to the indwelling Spirit, every act of divine grace reflects a God who does not withdraw but instead draws near. His love is not passive; it is pursuing. His grace is not abstract; it is incarnate in Christ. And His invitation remains unchanged: to walk with Him in restored fellowship, now and forever.

> **God's desire for relationship is not peripheral; it is foundational to the biblical narrative and the Christian faith.**

From the earliest moments of creation, God's actions have been guided by His sovereign purposes and faithful promises. Far from being spontaneous or reactionary, His redemptive plan has always unfolded according to a divine intention set in place before the foundation of the world. This illustrates God's omniscience and providence; His ability to foresee history and shape it toward His ultimate goal of reconciliation and restoration. Throughout the Old Testament, God's covenant relationship with humanity reveals a pattern of divine promise and fulfillment. In Genesis 12, God calls

Abraham and makes a covenant with him, saying in Genesis 12:2–3: **"I will make you into a great nation... And all peoples on earth will be blessed through you."** This covenant wasn't merely a personal promise to Abraham; it laid the foundation for the entire redemptive mission that would culminate in Jesus Christ. Abraham's descendants, the nation of Israel, became the people through whom God would reveal His character, His law, and ultimately, His salvation. Despite Israel's repeated failures through idolatry and disobedience, God never revoked His promises. Instead, He reaffirmed them through figures such as Moses, David, and the prophets, each serving as a signpost pointing to something greater. For instance, the Davidic covenant in 2 Samuel 7 promised a king from David's line whose throne would be established forever—a prophecy ultimately fulfilled in Jesus, the Messiah, who is called the "Son of David" (Matthew 1:1).

The prophets played a vital role in holding Israel accountable to the covenant, but they also spoke with hope about a future Redeemer. Isaiah 9:6 foretold a child who would be called **"Wonderful Counselor, Mighty God, Everlasting Father, Prince of Peace,"** while Jeremiah 31:31–34 speaks to a new covenant: **"This is the covenant I will make with the people of Israel after that time," declares the Lord. "I will put my law in their minds and write it on their hearts. I will be their God, and they will be my people."** These prophetic declarations were not isolated hopes but part of the divine script woven through centuries of Israel's history, all pointing to Jesus.

When the Apostle Paul writes in 2 Corinthians 1:20: **"For no matter how many promises God has made, they are 'Yes' in Christ,"** he makes a bold theological declaration that spans the entire arc of redemptive history. This statement is more than poetic assurance; it is a profound affirmation of Christ's central role in fulfilling God's covenantal faithfulness from Genesis to Revelation.

The people of Israel lived with the tension between promise and fulfillment. From the moment God called Abraham in Genesis 12, promising to make him into a great nation and to bless all peoples through him, the unfolding of that promise would take centuries to fully realize. The Mosaic covenant at Sinai, the Davidic covenant promising an eternal king from David's line, and the voices of the prophets who foretold a coming Messiah all pointed forward to a future fulfillment, often amid exile, suffering, and national failure. These divine promises were both deeply personal and globally significant, creating a long-standing expectation for a Savior who would deliver, restore, and reign in righteousness.

The Apostle Paul asserts that every promise, regardless of when or how it was made, ultimately finds complete fulfillment in Jesus Christ. He is not merely a step in the journey; He is the destination. Christ is the true seed of Abraham (Galatians 3:16), the greater Moses who mediates a better covenant (Hebrews 8:6), the eternal Son of David (Luke 1:32–33), and the suffering servant of Isaiah 53 who bears the sins of many. In Him, shadows become substance, and prophecies become reality.

Paul's use of the word "Yes" in verse 20 is particularly powerful, implying certainty, completion, and affirmation. While human promises often falter, God's promises are confirmed and fulfilled in Christ. In a world filled with broken covenants and disappointed hopes, Christ is the divine "Yes"—God's unwavering and faithful response to humanity's deepest needs. Paul continues in the same verse, stating, **"And so through him the 'Amen' is spoken by us to the glory of God."** This indicates that not only is Jesus the confirmation of God's promises, but believers also participate in this fulfillment by responding with faith and praise.

The resurrection of Jesus serves as the ultimate validation of this truth. His victory over sin and death demonstrates that God's plan was not thwarted by human sin or satanic schemes. Rather, it affirms that every word God has spoken, from Eden to Calvary, has been leading toward this redemptive climax. As Paul writes elsewhere, **"But when the set time had fully come, God sent his Son..."** (Galatians 4:4), indicating that Christ's arrival was not accidental, but perfectly timed according to God's sovereign plan.

> **...Every word God has spoken, from Eden to Calvary, has been leading toward this redemptive climax.**

In a broader sense, 2 Corinthians 1:20 speaks to the reliability of God Himself. Since Christ is the fulfillment of every promise, believers can live with confidence and hope, not only in what God has accomplished, but in what He will continue to do. The promise of the Holy Spirit (John 14:26), the assurance of eternal life (John 3:16), and the hope of Christ's return (Titus 2:13) are all part of the ongoing "Yes" we receive in Him. 2 Corinthians 1:20 serves as both a theological cornerstone and a spiritual anchor. It connects the promises of the Old Testament to their fulfillment in Christ, emphasizes the trustworthiness of God, and invites believers to live in the assurance that every divine word finds its "Yes" in Jesus. His life, death, and resurrection are not just historical events; they are the eternal validation that God keeps His word and that His purposes will never fail.

The early Church viewed itself as the continuation of this long-awaited fulfillment. Jewish believers recognized Jesus as the Messiah who came to establish the Kingdom of God, not through military power, but through sacrificial love. Gentile believers were grafted into this covenant story (Romans 11), illustrating that God's redemptive promise truly extends to "all nations," just as He promised Abraham.

This continuity between the Old and New Testaments, between promise and fulfillment, demonstrates that the Gospel is not a new plan, but the unfolding of God's eternal purpose. As Ephesians 1:9–10 declares: **"He made known to us the mystery of his will... To bring unity to all things in heaven and on earth under Christ."** God's actions throughout history have never been random or disconnected. Each promise, each covenant, and each prophetic vision has been a step in a grand redemptive narrative, culminating in the life and work of Jesus Christ. This continuity confirms God's faithfulness— He does not forget His promises, nor does He abandon His people. Instead, He brings His word to completion in ways that exceed human expectations, demonstrating that He is the same yesterday, today, and forever. In Christ, every divine promise is not only remembered but fulfilled with perfect faithfulness.

Ultimately, the extraordinary measures God has taken on behalf of humanity stand as the supreme revelation of His grace and mercy. Throughout history, humanity has persistently turned away from their Creator, falling into cycles of rebellion, idolatry, and injustice. Yet, instead of abandoning His creation to judgment and ruin, God chose to intervene with overwhelming compassion. This divine initiative is best understood through the lens of grace—unmerited favor freely given, not based on human worthiness, but on God's boundless love and generosity. Ephesians 2:8–9 states: **"For it is by grace you have** been saved, through faith—and this is not from yourselves, it is the gift of God—not by works, so that no one can boast." These verses encapsulate the heart of the Christian doctrine of salvation and form a cornerstone of New Testament theology. In them, the Apostle Paul dismantles any notion that salvation can be earned by human effort while simultaneously elevating the all-sufficient grace of God as the sole means of salvation.

Paul wrote this letter to the early church in Ephesus, a thriving Greco-Roman city known for its wealth, religious pluralism, and devotion to the goddess Artemis. In a culture steeped in works-based religion, where divine favor was believed to be earned through sacrifice and moral achievement, Paul's message was revolutionary. He tells believers that salvation is not a transaction or reward for good behavior; rather, it is an unmerited gift from God, made possible solely through Jesus Christ.

> ...Salvation is not a transaction or reward for good behavior; rather, it is an unmerited gift from God...

These verses address two critical concepts: grace and faith. Grace (charis in Greek) refers to the unearned favor of God. It is the divine initiative to redeem humanity despite our sinfulness. Paul emphasizes this earlier in Ephesians 2:1, stating: "As for you, you were dead in your transgressions and sins." Therefore, salvation is not the outcome of a sick person recovering or a misguided soul finding the right path; it is the miracle of the spiritually dead being made alive by God's sheer mercy. Grace is not something we deserve; it is something freely given.

Faith, on the other hand, is the means by which this grace is received. It is not a work or merit in itself, but rather trust; a surrendering of one's own efforts to rely entirely on what God has done through Christ. Even faith, Paul suggests, "is not from yourselves"; it too is part of the gift. In other words, salvation, from beginning to end, is entirely the work of God. Paul further emphasizes this by stating, "not by works, so that no one can boast." This was a crucial correction for both Jewish and Gentile believers who might be tempted to rely on the Law, moral superiority, or human achievement. In the Jewish tradition, obedience to the Law was central, while for Gentiles, virtue and civic duty were highly esteemed. But Paul levels the playing field: salvation excludes all boasting because it depends solely on God's mercy, not human merit.

As Romans 3:28 similarly affirms: **"For we maintain that a person is justified by faith apart from the works of the law."** This doctrine of salvation by grace through faith became a hallmark of the Protestant Reformation, particularly through the teachings of Martin Luther and John Calvin. They recognized in these verses a liberating truth that contrasted sharply with medieval ideas of penance and indulgences. Luther famously declared justification by faith to be "the article by which the church stands or falls." However, this passage is not only theological; it is deeply pastoral. It offers assurance. If salvation depended on human performance, it would always be uncertain and anxiety-inducing. But because it relies on God's unchanging grace, believers can rest secure in His love. This truth also fosters humility and unity. Since no one can boast, no one is superior. All stand equal at the foot of the cross, saved not by their own efforts, but by what Christ has accomplished.

Ephesians 2:8–9 presents a stunning portrait of divine generosity. It reminds us that salvation is a gift, not a wage. It was accomplished by Christ, offered by the Father, and received by faith through the Spirit. This message has resonated throughout church history as the core of the Gospel: that we are saved by grace alone, through faith alone, in Christ alone, and all glory belongs to God alone. In his epistle to the Ephesians, the Apostle Paul articulates this truth with remarkable clarity in Ephesians 2:8: **"For it is by grace you have been saved, through faith—and this is not from yourselves, it is the gift of God."** Here, Paul emphasizes that salvation is not the result of human effort or moral achievement; it is entirely a gift, a divine act rooted in God's mercy. This concept of grace stands in stark contrast to the prevailing religious mindset of the ancient world, where gods were thought to demand appeasement through ritual, performance, or sacrifice. The God of Israel, and later of the Church, revealed something entirely different: a God who initiates salvation, not because of human merit, but in spite of human failure.

This grace reaches its highest expression in the incarnation, death, and resurrection of Jesus Christ. In Him, God did not merely send a messenger; He came Himself to absorb the consequences of sin and offer new life. Romans 5:8 captures this beautifully: **"But God demonstrates his own love for us in this: While we were still sinners, Christ died for us."** Instead of demanding retribution,

God provides redemption. Through Christ's **Through Christ's** sacrificial death, the debt of sin is paid; **sacrificial death, the** through His resurrection, the power of death **debt of sin is paid...** is broken. From a theological perspective, grace is both forgiving and transformative. It restores the broken relationship between God and humanity and initiates a new way of life, empowered by the Holy Spirit. Titus 2:11–12 teaches that "**the grace of God has appeared that offers salvation to all people. It teaches us to say 'No' to ungodliness... And to live self-controlled, upright, and godly lives.**" God's grace does not leave people unchanged; it transforms hearts, renews minds, and empowers holy living.

The historical impact of this message of grace is profound. The early Church grew amidst persecution not through force but through lives transformed by grace. Former outcasts, sinners, and idolaters became witnesses to a new way of life, founded on the mercy they had received. The Church's acts of charity, inclusion, and forgiveness were radical, rooted in the belief that God's grace extends to all, regardless of status, ethnicity, or past sin.

Today, God's grace remains the hope of the world. It is offered freely to all who will receive it—not as a reward but as a gift. As John 1:16 states, "**Out of his fullness we have all received grace in place of grace already given.**" This unending grace invites humanity into a restored relationship with God, offering not only forgiveness for the past but also the promise of eternal life and purpose. Ultimately, God's actions for humanity—His patience, promises, and redemptive plan—are all wrapped in grace, revealing a God who delights not in punishment but in mercy (Micah 7:18). This is a God whose heart longs to rescue and restore. In Christ, this grace is most fully known, and through Him, the door remains open for every soul to come home to the God who gives, forgives, and transforms with limitless love.

God's decision to take extensive measures on humanity's behalf is a divine testament to His boundless love, His relentless desire for communion with His creation, the faithfulness of His eternal promises, and the incomparable richness of His grace. From the beginning of time, God has acted not out of obligation, but from a heart that longs to restore what sin has shattered. Humanity's rebellion in the Garden did not thwart God's purposes; it set in motion a redemptive plan culminating in the person and work of Jesus Christ.

God's love has been revealed progressively through covenants, prophets, and acts of deliverance, reaching its climax in the incarnation. In Jesus, God did not merely send another prophet or teacher; He gave Himself, Emmanuel, "**God with us**" (Matthew 1:23). Through Christ's life, sacrificial death, and victorious resurrection, God opened the way for sinners to be reconciled to Himself. As the Apostle Paul writes in 2 Corinthians 5:19: "**God was reconciling the world to himself in Christ, not counting people's sins against them.**" This act of reconciliation was not earned through human merit, but made possible by God's initiative, demonstrating grace in its purest form.

Through faith in Christ, individuals are not only forgiven but also made new creations (2 Corinthians 5:17). They are invited into a living, vibrant relationship with the God who once walked with humanity in the garden and now walks with them through the indwelling of the Holy Spirit. This renewed relationship fulfills God's long-standing promise in Jeremiah 31:33: "**I will be their God, and they will be my people**".

As recipients of this lavish grace, believers are called not to complacency but to a life of grateful response. This gratitude is expressed not only in emotion but through transformed living, marked by obedience, compassion, humility, and love. Romans 12:1 exhorts us to: "**Offer your bodies as a living sacrifice, holy and pleasing to God—this is your true and proper worship.**" This means reflecting God's character in the world, becoming ambassadors of reconciliation, and shining as lights in the midst of darkness. The early Church modeled this response; transformed by the Gospel, believers turned the world upside down—not through political power or coercion, but through sacrificial love and unwavering faith. They cared for the poor, forgave their enemies, and proclaimed Christ to the ends of the earth, all demonstrating evidence of lives reshaped by divine mercy. In the same way, Christians today are entrusted with this legacy. As those who have received forgiveness, salvation, and new life, they are now agents of God's redemptive work in the world. The call is clear for Christians to live in the reality of God's love, to walk in the joy of restored relationship, and to embody the hope found in Christ alone.

Ultimately, God's extensive measures were never about religion; they were about relationship. From the very beginning, His desire has been to dwell with His creation and walk in fellowship with humanity, just as He did in the garden. Through Jesus Christ, the door has been opened wide, and the invitation has been extended: come, be reconciled, be made new. In Him, we discover not just forgiveness, but restoration, identity, and eternal belonging.

> **From the very beginning, His desire has been to dwell with His creation and walk in fellowship with humanity...**

For those who accept this invitation, the only appropriate response is a life surrendered to the One who gave everything to make it possible. However, this story is not yet complete. Redemption, while secured, still awaits its full revelation. The final chapter of God's redemptive plan looks forward to a time when evil will be vanquished, justice will be perfected, and the faithful will see God face to face.

It is in this hope that we now turn to the last movement in the grand narrative of Scripture: The Final Victory—God's Plan for the End Times. Far from being a tale of fear or confusion, the end times reveal the triumph of divine justice, mercy, and love. What began in the garden and was redeemed at the cross will culminate in the glorious return of Christ and the establishment of a new heaven and a new earth.

Let us now explore this blessed hope and the theological framework that supports it.

CHAPTER
11

The Final Victory: God's Plan for the End Times
A Theological Framework for the End of Days

Before delving into God's final resolution to sin and His ultimate judgment of the world, it is crucial to establish a solid theological foundation. The events depicted in the latter chapters of Revelation are not mere isolated apocalyptic visions; they represent the culmination of a divine plan woven throughout the entire biblical narrative. To fully understand their significance, one must grasp the broader theological framework known as eschatology.

Eschatology, derived from the Greek word eschatos (meaning "last" or "final"), refers to the study of the "last things" or "end times." It encompasses not only the dramatic imagery found in Revelation—seals, trumpets, bowls, beasts, and thrones—but also the grand themes of Scripture's final act: the rapture, the tribulation, the millennial reign of Christ, and the final judgment. As Henry C. Thiessen insightfully notes in *Lectures in Systematic Theology*, biblical eschatology does not portray an ending that devolves into chaos or nothingness; rather, it points to a divinely ordained culmination—a purposeful transition from the temporal to the eternal. It reveals God's justice, restoration, and glory.

A helpful distinction exists between Personal Eschatology and General Eschatology. Personal Eschatology addresses the fate of individuals—what occurs at death, the intermediate state of the soul, and the final resurrection. In contrast, general eschatology concerns the destiny of the world itself: the return of Christ, the resurrection of the dead, the final judgment, and the establishment of a new heaven and new earth. This universal aspect dominates the book of Revelation and frames the drama of the End Times. For the purpose of this discussion, I plan to address only general eschatology.

At the heart of general eschatology is the Second Coming of Jesus Christ. This is not an abstract notion or a symbolic spiritual event; it is a literal, visible, and glorious return of the risen Lord. The New Testament affirms that Christ will return personally (John 14:3; John 21:22), unexpectedly (Matthew 24:42–44), suddenly (Matthew 24:26–28), and triumphantly (Luke 19:28–38). This event serves as the anchor of Christian hope and the cornerstone of eschatological expectation.

> **At the heart of general eschatology is the Second Coming of Jesus Christ.**

One of the most definitive passages on this subject is 1 Thessalonians 4:13–17, where the Apostle Paul offers comfort and clarity regarding the fate of believers who have died: "**Brothers and sisters, we do not want you to be uninformed about those who sleep in death, so that you do not grieve like the rest of mankind, who have no hope. For we believe that Jesus died and rose again... The Lord himself will come down from heaven, with a loud command, with the voice of the archangel and with the trumpet call of God, and the dead in Christ will rise first. After that...we who are still alive...will be caught up...to meet the Lord in the air. And so we will be with the Lord forever.**" This passage teaches both the bodily resurrection of the saints and the "catching up"—commonly referred to as the rapture—of those who are alive at His coming. Paul echoes this in Philippians 3:20–21, reminding believers that our true citizenship is in heaven, and from there we await a Savior who will transform our lowly bodies to be like His glorious body.

> **The Second Coming is not the beginning of Christ's work—it is its culmination. He comes not to suffer again, but to rule and reign.**

The apostolic witness is unanimous: Peter, James, Jude, and Paul all present the return of Christ not as a metaphor or private spiritual awakening, but as a public, bodily, and victorious re-entry of Jesus into the world He redeemed. The Second Coming is not the beginning of Christ's work—it is its culmination. He comes not to suffer again, but to rule and reign.

This eschatological expectation is central to the message of Revelation. Every judgment, vision, heavenly scene, and earthly woe ultimately points to this reality: Christ is coming again. When He returns, He will bring about the final defeat of evil, the restoration of righteousness, and the consummation of God's eternal Kingdom.

As we prepare to examine the remainder of Revelation with this understanding in place, may we do so not merely to satisfy curiosity or interpret symbols, but to be awakened to the glorious hope that animates every page: The King is returning. His justice is certain, His mercy unwavering, and His victory complete.

Despite the clarity of Scripture, various misinterpretations regarding the return of Christ have persisted throughout history. Some equate His return with the outpouring of the Holy Spirit at Pentecost or with the internal transformation that occurs at salvation. Others claim that the prophecies of Christ's coming were fulfilled in the destruction of Jerusalem in A.D. 70. However, these interpretations fall short when examined in light of Scripture written after that event. Passages such as Revelation 1:7, 3:11, 22:12, and 22:20 clearly speak of a future, visible return of Jesus Christ—a return that has not yet taken place and cannot be reduced to a historical or spiritual metaphor. These passages were written by the Apostle John more than twenty years after the fall of Jerusalem and the destruction of the temple in 70 AD.

Another common but erroneous belief is that the entire world will be converted before Christ returns. Yet Jesus Himself warned of a different trajectory: not worldwide revival, but widespread apostasy. In Luke 18:8, Jesus asks, **"When the Son of Man comes, will He find faith on the earth?"** Similarly, Paul forewarns of a great rebellion in 2 Thessalonians 2:3–12, and 1 Timothy 4:1 prophesies that many will abandon the faith in the last days. These passages indicate not a global conversion, but increasing deception and defiance against God—a spiritual climate consistent with the conditions described in Revelation.

A foundational aspect of eschatology is the distinction between Christ's coming in the air—as described in 1 Thessalonians 4:16–17—and His return to the earth. The first refers to the rapture, when

Christ comes for His Church. This event is characterized by hope, deliverance, and reward. Believers are "caught up" to meet the Lord, and the restraining presence of the Church—empowered by the Holy Spirit—is removed from the earth (2 Thessalonians 2:6–8), setting the stage for the rise of evil and the onset of tribulation.

In contrast, Christ's second coming to earth will be a dramatic and public event, marked by judgment and glory. He will return to the Mount of Olives (Zechariah 14:4; Acts 1:11), defeat the Antichrist, and bind Satan for a thousand years (Revelation 20:1–3).

Christ's second coming to earth will be a dramatic and public event...

This return initiates the Millennial Kingdom—a literal, physical reign of Christ on earth. Early church figures such as Papias and Justin Martyr affirmed this belief, historically known as Premillennialism.

The seven-year tribulation period, foretold in Daniel 9:24–27 and elaborated upon in Revelation, will be a time of unparalleled suffering. It will feature the rise of a global leader—the Antichrist—who will deceive many and lead a false religious system. The prophetic imagery in Revelation and Daniel—beasts, horns, and kings—serves as symbolic language for both political empires and spiritual deception. These symbols reflect real events and figures, rendered in apocalyptic form to unveil spiritual realities and future fulfillment.

The Millennium (Revelation 20:2–7) is not just a poetic image; it is a literal, thousand-year reign of Christ during which Satan is bound and righteousness prevails. Believers will reign with Christ, justice will flourish, and the earth will be renewed. However, even after this period of peace, Satan will be released for a short time to deceive the nations once more. His final rebellion is swiftly crushed by God, leading to the Great White Throne Judgment. At this climactic moment, all unbelievers are judged according to their deeds and cast into the lake of fire—the eternal destiny of all who reject the grace of God (Revelation 20:11–15).

This entire eschatological framework affirms God's unwavering promises and underscores critical theological distinctions—particularly between Israel and the Church. While God's covenant with Israel remains intact, the Church is not appointed to suffer His wrath (1 Thessalonians 5:9). This supports the pretribulational view: that the Church will be taken up before the tribulation begins.

Eschatology offers more than a timeline; it provides a lens through which to see the culmination of God's sovereign plan. Studying the return of Christ is not about sensational predictions or fear-based speculation; it is about preparation. Christ will return. The signs, the judgments, and the triumphs all point to this truth. Therefore, believers must remain watchful, hopeful, and faithful.

The doctrine of eschatology—the study of last things—is one of the most layered and debated subjects in Christian theology. What has been presented here is only an introductory outline, intended to offer a clear foundation. For those seeking a deeper understanding, further study is both recommended and spiritually enriching. Over the centuries, many scholars and theologians have produced valuable commentaries, expositions, and systematic theologies to help believers navigate this complex yet glorious subject. Among these resources, I humbly commend my own contribution, *Miracles, Signs, Symbols, and Judgment: God's Plan for the End Times*, which seeks to provide clarity, balance, and reverence in exploring the prophetic messages of Scripture as a commentary to the book of Revelation.

The goal of this study is to lead readers to a profound understanding: from Genesis to Revelation, Scripture reveals a God who is purposeful, merciful, and faithful in all His ways. The title of this book—It Is All About You—does not suggest that humanity is the story's focal point, but rather highlights that God's redemptive plan has always aimed at restoring His relationship with creation. He is a God who never abandons His people, even in times of judgment. His promises are certain, His justice is righteous, and His mercy endures forever.

Understanding the Book of Revelation requires both diligence and awe. Its structure is not chaotic or arbitrary; it is divinely ordered. Faithful interpretation demands humility and a desire to see Christ glorified. Revelation is not merely about future events; it centers on the One who reigns eternally, whose Kingdom will have no end, and whose presence will once again dwell with His people. This is our blessed hope.

As we begin the careful and reverent task of examining the Book of Revelation, two guiding interpretive principles must be central to our approach.

First, wherever the context supports it, the Book of Revelation should be interpreted in its plain, literal sense. This does not advocate for a rigid or simplistic reading, but rather encourages a faithful understanding of the text according to its plain meaning. Unless the language clearly indicates symbolism, metaphor, or visionary imagery, we should assume the author intends for us to take his words at face value. This principle helps prevent the interpretive excesses that arise when the entire book is treated as an allegory. Although Revelation is filled with vivid imagery, unchecked spiritualization can lead to wildly divergent interpretations, many of which are more speculative than scriptural. Taking the text literally where appropriate provides clarity and consistency.

This leads to the second guiding principle: when symbolism is employed, as it often is in apocalyptic literature, it is usually marked by qualifying language. Words like "like," "as," or "resembled" signal that a metaphor or simile is being used to point beyond the image itself to a deeper spiritual reality. For example, when John describes Jesus' face as being **like the sun shining in all its brilliance** (Revelation 1:16), he uses a simile to convey the indescribable radiance of the glorified Christ. Such figurative language does not obscure the truth but bridges the gap between earthly understanding and heavenly revelation, helping us grasp transcendent realities that cannot be fully articulated in human language.

Historically, the Church has grappled with how to interpret Revelation. In the earliest centuries, particularly during Roman persecution, believers found hope in this book—a declaration that God's justice would ultimately prevail and that the suffering of the saints would not be in vain. The beasts, judgments, and visions were not merely predictions of the future; they proclaimed God's sovereignty amid present trials.

Over time, various interpretive models emerged—historicist, preterist, futurist, and idealist—each offering distinct perspectives. Historicism views Revelation as unfolding throughout church history. Preterism sees it as largely fulfilled in the first century, particularly with the fall of Jerusalem. Idealism interprets the book as symbolic of timeless spiritual truths, while futurism (the approach taken in this study) regards most of Revelation as describing literal future events, especially concerning the end of the age. Each view has strengths and limitations, but a literal-historical approach—one aiming to understand the visions in light of their original context and in harmony with the entirety of Scripture—provides the most balanced and grounded framework.

Theologically, Revelation serves as the grand conclusion to all biblical prophecy. It ties together the promises made to Israel, the redemptive mission of the Church, and the ultimate defeat of evil. It reveals the completion of God's covenantal plan and the full manifestation of His Kingdom. Above all, it focuses on the person of Jesus Christ—not only as Savior and Redeemer but also as the righteous Judge, the conquering King, and the Lamb who reigns forever. As Revelation 19:10 states, **"the testimony of Jesus is the spirit of prophecy."** This signifies that all prophecy ultimately points to Him.

It is vital to remember that any study of eschatology that does not place Christ at the center risks missing the essence of Revelation. The book is not merely about dragons, trumpets, and bowls of wrath. It is not simply a timeline of doom. It is the unveiling (apokalypsis) of Jesus Christ. It reveals His glory, authority, and ultimate victory over every force of evil. It announces the fulfillment of God's greatest promise—to dwell again with His redeemed people (Revelation 21:3).

> Revelation...is not merely about dragons, trumpets, and bowls of wrath. It is not simply a timeline of doom. It is the unveiling of Jesus Christ.

It reminds us that the Lamb who was slain is also the Lion of Judah who will rule the nations.

As we reflect on this sweeping vision of divine triumph, we recognize that Revelation is not a detour from the biblical narrative; it is its culmination. From the garden of Eden in Genesis, where mankind first walked with God, to the garden-like New Jerusalem in Revelation, where God dwells among His people once more, Scripture tells a single, unified story: the tale of God's relentless love and pursuit of redemption. It is a story of creation, fall, covenant, and ultimately—restoration.

Thus, as we delve deeper into the pages of Revelation, let us do so not only with a desire to understand events but with a longing to encounter the One who holds history in His hands. May our study deepen our reverence, inspire our repentance, embolden our hope, and fix our eyes on Jesus—the Alpha and the Omega, who is, who was, and who is to come.

This final act of divine redemption, vividly portrayed in Revelation, completes the overarching narrative of God's unwavering faithfulness, mercy, and sovereign love. As we prepare to explore the book more closely, let us remember that the ultimate goal is not merely to decode symbolic prophecy or chart timelines. Rather, the heart of Revelation is the heart of God—a God who persistently reaches out to His creation, who warns, restores, redeems, and triumphs. He has never forgotten us, and He never will. May our journey through this prophetic text deepen our awe, increase our humility, and draw us into closer communion with the One who reigns forevermore and fulfills every promise.

Having briefly touched on the identity of Revelation's author earlier, it is now appropriate to examine this essential question more closely. The traditional and most widely accepted view in Christian history is that the author is John the Apostle, one of the original twelve disciples of Jesus. This identification is supported by internal evidence within the book, where the writer refers to himself simply as "John" (Revelation 1:1, 1:4, 1:9; 22:8)—a name that would have held authority and recognition among early Christian communities.

The context of this authorship is also significant. John is believed to have written Revelation during his exile on the island of Patmos, a small rocky island in the Aegean Sea near Ephesus. This exile likely occurred during the reign of the Roman Emperor Domitian, around A.D. 94–97. Patmos served as a place of banishment for those deemed enemies of the Roman state—political or religious dissidents. It was in this environment of isolation and persecution that John received the extraordinary visions that comprise the book. At this point, John would have been in his eighties and most likely the last surviving member of the original twelve apostles.

The early Church Fathers provide substantial support for Johannine authorship. Justin Martyr, writing around A.D. 140, affirmed that Revelation was authored by "John, one of the apostles of Christ." In his *Dialogue with Trypho*, he references John's vision of the thousand-year reign of Christ—a key eschatological theme. Other respected figures, such as Irenaeus, Clement of Alexandria, Tertullian, and Melito of Sardis (bishop of one of the seven churches mentioned in Revelation), all echo this conviction, reinforcing the historical tradition.

However, not all have agreed. In the third century, Dionysius of Alexandria raised doubts, suggesting that the stylistic differences between Revelation and the Gospel and Epistles of John implied a different author—perhaps "John the Elder." This theory was based on differences in grammar, vocabulary, and tone. Yet, as many scholars and theologians have noted, these differences can be attributed to the unique genre of apocalyptic literature, which employs heightened symbolism, and possibly to the use of a scribe. Moreover, the emotional intensity and dramatic context of Revelation may account for the distinct voice found in the text.

As theologian Thomas Adams and others have argued, inspiration by the Holy Spirit does not negate the use of human language, personality, or perspective. Rather, God works through these elements to accomplish His purpose. Thus, John's situation on Patmos, his background as an apostle, and his pastoral concern for the churches all influenced how Revelation was received and recorded.

John's unique qualifications as the last surviving apostle and a member of Jesus' inner circle, alongside Peter and James, lend significant authority to his role in conveying this expansive prophetic vision. His deep relationship with the churches of Asia Minor and his intimate walk with Christ establish him as a trustworthy voice through whom God reveals His final word of hope and judgment.

When studying Revelation, the translation of Scripture significantly influences comprehension. While the poetic resonance of the King James Version (KJV) is cherished, the complex and symbol-rich language of Revelation necessitates clarity. Therefore, I have chosen to use the New International Version (NIV) throughout this study, as it strikes a strong balance between readability and fidelity to the original texts. I also encourage readers to compare translations—such as the KJV, ESV, NASB, and others—since each provides helpful nuances that enhance one's understanding of the text.

Though scholarly debate over authorship persists in some academic circles, a robust historical and theological consensus exists: the Apostle John, a servant of Christ and a faithful witness to His glory, authored this final book of the Bible. With this foundation established, we are now ready to explore Revelation not only as prophecy but also as the concluding message of a God who has never abandoned His people—and never will. It is a message of justice and mercy, judgment and restoration, meant for every generation yearning for the return of our King.

Let us proceed with reverence and expectation, guided by the Spirit and anchored in the truth that the Lamb who was slain is also the Lion who reigns—and He is coming soon.

> **...The Lamb who was slain is also the Lion who reigns—and He is coming soon.**

While this book does not aim to serve as an exhaustive commentary on Revelation, my goal is to provide a broad and accessible overview that helps readers grasp the flow and depth of John's apocalyptic vision.

Revelation is rich in imagery, layered with symbolism, and anchored in the unshakeable promise of God's eternal plan. In the pages that follow, we will witness not only the unfolding of judgment but also the unveiling of hope, culminating in the eternal dwelling of God with His redeemed people.

For clarity, I have divided the book into twelve sections. This structure is both practical and theologically symbolic: the number twelve frequently appears in Scripture, often representing divine governance and completeness—examples include the twelve tribes of Israel, the twelve apostles, and the twelve gates of the New Jerusalem.

Here is the outline for the book of Revelation:

SECTION 1

Chapter 1 – The Vision on Patmos

John's dramatic encounter with the glorified Christ sets the stage. He receives the divine command to write what he sees and send it to the seven churches of Asia Minor.

SECTION 2

Chapters 2–3 – Letters to the Seven Churches

Chapter 2: Messages to Ephesus, Smyrna, Pergamum, and Thyatira

Chapter 3: Messages to Sardis, Philadelphia, and Laodicea

Each church receives a personal evaluation from Christ—commendation, correction, and a call to overcome.

SECTION 3

Chapters 4–6 – The Heavenly Throne Room and the Seals

Chapter 4: A door opens to heaven; John is caught up, symbolizing what many believe to be the rapture of the Church.

Chapter 5: A scroll sealed with seven seals is held by God; only the Lamb is worthy to open it.

Chapter 6: The first six seals are opened, revealing conquest, war, famine, death, and cosmic upheaval.

SECTION 4

Chapter 7 – A Pause for Mercy

Before further judgment, God seals 144,000 from the tribes of Israel. A great multitude appears before the throne, praising God for salvation.

Section 5

Chapters 8–9 – The Trumpet Judgments Begin

Chapter 8: The seventh seal is opened, ushering in the first four trumpet judgments.

Chapter 9: The fifth and sixth trumpets unleash demonic torment and a vast army of destruction.

Section 6

Chapter 10 – The Mighty Angel and the Little Scroll

John is given a small scroll to eat—sweet in his mouth but bitter in his stomach—symbolizing the dual nature of prophecy: hope for the faithful, sorrow for the rebellious.

Section 7

Chapter 11 – The Two Witnesses and the Seventh Trumpet

Two prophetic witnesses declare God's truth for 1,260 days before being slain and resurrected. The seventh trumpet sounds, signaling the kingdom of God drawing near.

Section 8

Chapters 12–14 – Spiritual Warfare and the Final Harvest

Chapter 12: A woman (Israel), a dragon (Satan), and a male child (Christ).

Chapter 13: The rise of the beast from the sea (Antichrist) and the beast from the earth (False Prophet).

Chapter 14: The Lamb and the 144,000, three angelic proclamations, and the harvest of the earth.

Section 9

Chapters 15–16 – The Bowl Judgments

Chapter 15: Seven angels are prepared with the final plagues.

Chapter 16: The seven bowls of God's wrath are poured out—devastating judgments on those who follow the beast.

SECTION 10

Chapters 17–19 – The Fall of Babylon and the Return

Chapter 17: The woman on the beast—Babylon, the great harlot—is revealed and condemned.

Chapter 18: The economic and spiritual collapse of Babylon is mourned by the nations.

Chapter 19: Heaven rejoices; Christ returns as the Rider on the white horse. The beast and the false prophet are thrown into the lake of fire.

SECTION 11

Chapter 20 – The Millennial Reign and Final Judgment

Satan is bound for 1,000 years as Christ reigns on earth. After a brief final rebellion, Satan is defeated and cast into the lake of fire. The Great White Throne Judgment follows for all unbelievers.

SECTION 11

Chapters 21–22 – The New Heaven, New Earth, and New Jerusalem

Chapter 21: The old heaven and earth pass away; God reveals the New Jerusalem, where He dwells with His people.

Chapter 22: A river of life flows from God's throne. Jesus affirms, *"I am coming soon,"* and John closes with a call to readiness and worship.

This outline helps clarify Revelation's flow and focus. While interpretations of certain elements vary across theological traditions, what remains central is this: Revelation is the revelation of Jesus Christ (Revelation 1:1). He is the Lamb, the Judge, the King, and the Bridegroom. This book was not given to frighten but to fortify the faith of believers—to remind us that history is not spiraling into chaos but moving with divine intention toward a glorious

> **Revelation is the revelation of Jesus Christ (Revelation 1:1). He is the Lamb, the Judge, the King, and the Bridegroom.**

conclusion. For all who call upon His name, eternity awaits in His presence.

Let this structure guide you—not just to study prophecy but to see Christ more clearly, worship Him more deeply, and live more faithfully until He returns.

As we begin our exploration of the twelve divisions of the Book of Revelation, we must first revisit the island of Patmos, a barren, rocky exile used by the Roman authorities. In this remote setting—cut off from the world yet fully in tune with the Spirit of God—John was caught up in a vision that would unveil the culmination of God's eternal plan.

From the very beginning, two essential truths demand our attention. The first is the divine chain of revelation outlined in Revelation 1:1: "**The revelation from Jesus Christ, which God gave him to show his servants what must soon take place. He made it known by sending his angel to his servant John.**" This verse reveals a profound theological structure: the message originates with God the Father, is given to Jesus Christ the Son, conveyed through an angelic messenger, and ultimately delivered to John, the human servant. This chain affirms the source and authority of the revelation— it is God-breathed, untainted by speculation, and meant to be understood as divine truth. Every word that follows flows from the very heart and will of God.

The second truth is found in Revelation 1:3, which tells us this is a prophecy—a special form of divine communication. It carries a unique blessing for those who read it aloud, hear it, and take it to heart: "**Blessed is the one who reads aloud the words of this prophecy, and blessed are those who hear it and take to heart what is written in it, because the time is near.**" This blessing was especially significant in the first-century Church, where copies of Scripture were rare and literacy limited. The Word was transmitted orally, often read aloud during worship gatherings. The promise of blessing at the beginning of Revelation underscores the importance of not only understanding the message but also responding to it in faith and obedience.

It is ironic that Revelation—the only book that explicitly promises a blessing to its readers—is often the most neglected, avoided due to its symbols, imagery, and judgments. Yet, as this verse reminds us, its purpose is not to confuse but to prepare, to awaken, and to assure believers of God's sovereign control over history and the future.

One of the most captivating features of Revelation chapter 1 is John's vision of the glorified Christ. In Revelation 1:13–14, we find a majestic portrait: "**And among the lampstands was someone like a son of man, dressed in a robe reaching down to his feet and with a golden sash around his chest. The hair on his head was white like wool, as white as snow, and his eyes were like blazing fire.**" The phrase "**like a son of man**" echoes the prophetic vision of Daniel 7:13–14, where one "like a son of man" comes with the clouds of heaven to receive authority and everlasting dominion. By invoking Daniel's imagery, John unmistakably identifies Jesus as the Messianic ruler, both divine and human, possessing eternal sovereignty.

The robe and golden sash signify Christ's role as the Great High Priest (cf. Hebrews 4:14–16) and King of Kings. His white hair symbolizes wisdom, purity, and timelessness, while His blazing eyes represent the penetrating gaze of divine judgment—nothing escapes His sight. This is not the meek and lowly Jesus of the Gospels; this is the exalted and glorified Christ, radiant in heavenly glory and appearing in overwhelming splendor. John's depiction likely mirrors the Transfiguration experience described in Matthew 17:2, where Jesus' face shone like the sun and His clothes became as white as light. This brilliance indicates that John sees Jesus not in weakness, but in His true and eternal glory—a glimpse of His divine nature unveiled.

Revelation is not merely a book of fear or confusion, but one of hope, majesty, and divine assurance. Every aspect of this opening vision reminds us that Revelation is not merely a book of fear or confusion, but one of hope, majesty, and divine assurance. It focuses not on wild speculation or coded timelines, but on the exalted Christ— "**the faithful witness, the firstborn from the dead, and the ruler of the kings of the earth**" (Revelation 1:5). He is the one who holds the keys of death and Hades, who walks among His churches, and who is coming again in glory.

As we journey deeper into the book, this foundational chapter sets the tone: Revelation is Christ-centered, worship-filled, and hope-saturated. It calls us not only to interpret prophecy but to behold the Lamb, trust in His sovereignty, and prepare ourselves for the day when faith becomes sight. This is not just John's vision—it is God's invitation for us to see history through heaven's eyes.

Turning our attention to the seven churches of Revelation brings us to one of the most personal and pastoral sections of the book. In Revelation 1:11, John is commanded: "**Write on a scroll what you see and send it to the seven churches: to Ephesus, Smyrna, Pergamum, Thyatira, Sardis, Philadelphia, and Laodicea.**" These were not fictional congregations, but real churches located in the Roman province of Asia, in what is now western Turkey. Their geographic arrangement forms a circular postal route, suggesting a deliberate and efficient method for delivering the scroll—evidence of both divine and practical design. The messages to these churches are recorded in chapters 2 and 3, each following a consistent literary pattern. Christ introduces Himself with a title drawn from John's initial vision in chapter 1, emphasizing an aspect of His character particularly relevant to each congregation. He then addresses their strengths, confronts their failures, calls them to repentance, and extends a promise to the one who overcomes. This structure reveals the Lord's intimate knowledge of each church's spiritual condition and His ongoing presence among them. He is not distant—He is the One who "**walks among the seven golden lampstands**" (Revelation 2:1), symbolizing His active oversight of His Church.

A noteworthy aspect of these messages is the address "**to the angel of the church in...**" The Greek word ángelos can mean "messenger," leading to two primary interpretations. Some believe these refer to literal angelic beings, spiritual guardians of each church. Others suggest that the term metaphorically refers to the leaders or pastors responsible for conveying God's word to their congregations. Regardless of interpretation, the point is clear: God holds His messengers and His churches accountable for how they respond to His revelation.

Each church reveals a distinct spiritual profile. Ephesus is commended for doctrinal orthodoxy but criticized for losing its first love (2:4). Smyrna, though materially poor, is described as spiritually rich and is exhorted to endure tribulation and suffering without fear (2:10). Pergamum is warned against compromise with pagan practices, while Thyatira is rebuked for tolerating false teaching. Sardis receives perhaps the most sobering message: they have a reputation for being alive but are spiritually dead (3:1). Philadelphia is praised for keeping Christ's word despite limited strength and is promised an open door that no one can shut (3:8). Laodicea, the final church, is infamous for being lukewarm, symbolizing indifference and self-sufficiency, which Christ finds nauseating (3:16).

The spiritual application of these messages transcends time and geography. Though addressed to first-century churches, they provide timeless insight into the condition of Christ's people across generations. Many theologians and scholars have also seen in the sequence of the churches a possible prophetic overview of Church history, with each church symbolizing a distinct era or spiritual characteristic of the Christian age. While this view is debated, the practical relevance of the letters is universally affirmed.

These letters, theologically, remind us that the Church is under the loving scrutiny of Christ. He sees with perfect clarity—unclouded by appearances or reputation. His commendations are pure, and His rebukes are just. Yet even in rebuke, there is always a path to restoration. His calls to repentance are not words of condemnation but invitations to renewal. His promises to those who overcome— eternal life, hidden manna, a white stone, a new name, authority over the nations—are stunning reminders of the inheritance awaiting the faithful.

Reflecting on these seven letters, we realize that the Church is never left without guidance or accountability. These messages serve as divine evaluations of spiritual health, providing a mirror in which churches and individual believers can examine their own condition. The risen Christ is not passive—He is the active Shepherd of His people, desiring that His Church be faithful, watchful, enduring, and pure.

Ultimately, the letters to the seven churches prepare the way for the remainder of Revelation. They illustrate that before judgment is poured out upon the earth, Christ first purifies His own household (1 Peter 4:17). They leave every reader with a solemn charge: **"Whoever has ears, let them hear what the Spirit says to the churches."** These are not merely ancient letters—they are living exhortations, meant for all who would walk with Christ in every age.

As we enter Revelation chapter 4, the tone and setting of the book shift dramatically. Up to this point, the Apostle John has been conveying messages from the risen Christ to the seven churches of Asia Minor—earthly congregations reflecting both the spiritual condition of the first-century Church and, as many believe, the stages of the Church throughout history. These messages were delivered by **"the voice like a trumpet"** that John first heard in Revelation 1:10, a voice later identified as that of Christ Himself.

Now, John sees **"a door standing open in heaven,"** and the same trumpet-like voice invites him: **"Come up here, and I will show you what must take place after this"** (Revelation 4:1). This moment marks a distinct transition in the vision—from the Church on earth to the unfolding events in heaven and beyond. The phrase "after this" (Greek: meta tauta) appears twice in the verse, signaling a clear chronological shift in the narrative. Though the exact time between these events is unknown, this marks a new prophetic section in the structure of Revelation.

For many scholars, particularly those within pretribulational and premillennial frameworks, John's invitation to "come up here" is often interpreted as a symbolic representation of the Church's rapture. Although the text does not explicitly state that the Church is raptured at this moment, the absence of the term "church" (ekklesia) in the subsequent chapters—until it reappears in Revelation 22:16, which actually refers back to the seven churches of chapters 2 and 3—is frequently seen as evidence that the Church is no longer present on earth during the tribulation judgments. This interpretation aligns with 1 Thessalonians 4:16–17, which describes the rapture as an event marked by a trumpet call and a sudden ascent to meet the Lord. The parallels in language and imagery between these passages, while not definitive, are indeed striking.

Furthermore, this transition supports the doctrine of imminence, which teaches that Christ's return for His Church could occur at any moment, without warning or prerequisites. This concept is rooted in Jesus' teachings, such as Matthew 24:36 and Luke 12:40, urging believers to maintain a constant state of spiritual readiness. The phrase "after this" emphasizes the uncertainty of timing and bolsters the belief that the Church Age will end abruptly with Christ's call to His people.

Historically, the premillennial view—asserting that Christ will return before a literal thousand-year reign—was held by early Church fathers like Irenaeus and Hippolytus. However, the pretribulational rapture gained systematic attention in the 19th century through theologians like John Nelson Darby and was later popularized by dispensational theology. This theological model presents the Church Age as a unique "parenthesis" in God's dealings with Israel. Once the Church is removed, focus shifts back to Israel and the fulfillment of end-time prophecies during the seven-year tribulation.

From a literary and theological standpoint, Revelation 4 acts as a crucial pivot. It transitions from messages of exhortation and correction directed at the Church to visions of heavenly worship, divine sovereignty and eventual judgment. The following throne room scene sets the stage for the unveiling of the sealed scroll, which contains God's decrees for the final stages of human history. The Lamb, found worthy to open the scroll (Revelation 5), becomes central as the executor of God's justice and redemption. Even for those who do not adopt a pretribulational interpretation, the transition in Revelation 4 clearly presents a heavenly perspective on the ensuing events. The judgments are not arbitrary; they emanate from God's throne and are initiated by the Lamb. The narrative shifts from the Church's witness on earth to God's direct intervention in human history.

The narrative shifts from the Church's witness on earth to God's direct intervention in human history.

Revelation 4 signifies more than a mere change of scenery; it marks a theological turning point—a shift from Christ's messages to His Church to the unfolding of God's final plan for creation. Viewed either symbolically or literally, John's upward call embodies the believer's ultimate hope: being caught up into God's presence to witness His glory and the fulfillment of His promises. It invites us to look beyond the present world and live in anticipation of the day when heaven opens once more and the King returns.

As the vision progresses into Revelation 5, the setting remains in the heavenly throne room, but the tone shifts from adoring God's majesty in chapter 4 to revealing His redemptive and judicial purposes. A dramatic moment arises as a scroll sealed with seven seals appears in the right hand of the One seated on the throne. This scroll signifies God's sovereign plan and His decrees for the consummation of history, encompassing both judgment on evil and the ultimate redemption of creation. Essentially, it serves as the divine blueprint for the end of the age.

The significance of this scroll becomes immediately evident. John weeps bitterly when **"no one in heaven or on earth or under the earth could open the scroll or even look inside"** (Revelation 5:3). This weeping represents not mere sorrow but a profound lament over the apparent absence of one worthy enough to fulfill God's plan. Humanity stands powerless, unable to break the seals of judgment or enact its own redemption.

Yet, in this moment of despair, hope emerges. One of the elders reassures John not to weep, for **"the Lion of the tribe of Judah, the Root of David"** has triumphed and is worthy to open the scroll (Revelation 5:5). However, when John looks, he sees not a lion but a Lamb, appearing as if it had been slain (v. 6). This paradox—the Lion who is a Lamb—reveals the mystery at the core of God's redemptive plan. Jesus Christ, the victorious Messiah, triumphed not through force but through sacrificial love.

The Lamb stands at the center of the throne, alive and bearing the marks of death, a powerful image that attests to His atoning work on the cross. He is described as having seven horns and seven eyes—symbols of perfect power and complete vision, representing the sevenfold Spirit of God (Isaiah 11:2). This depiction of Christ in His fullness illustrates His omnipotence, omniscience, and unity with the Spirit of God, now prepared to execute divine judgment and salvation.

In Revelation 5:7, the Lamb takes the scroll from God's hand—a breathtaking act that signifies His exclusive authority to bring God's plan to fruition. In Roman and Jewish cultures, sealed scrolls were often used for official legal documents, such as wills or property deeds, and only someone with legal authority could open such documents. In this heavenly courtroom, Jesus alone has earned that right—through His death, resurrection, and perfect obedience.

What follows is not only judicial in nature but also profoundly doxological. Heaven erupts in worship as the hosts declare, **"Worthy is the Lamb, who was slain, to receive power and wealth and wisdom and strength and honor and glory and praise!"** (Revelation 5:12). This sevenfold doxology underscores the completeness of Christ's worthiness and sets the tone for the rest of the book: whatever judgments follow stem from the hand of the One who first bore the judgment meant for us.

Thus, Revelation 5 serves as both a theological and narrative pivot. It connects the majestic vision of God's glory in chapter 4 with the terrifying judgments that commence in chapter 6. It also offers a critical reminder: what is to come is not unrestrained wrath but righteous justice, executed by the Lamb who was slain. The judgments are not cruel or arbitrary; they are the final necessary acts to eradicate sin, vindicate the saints, and usher in the eternal Kingdom of God.

This chapter also encapsulates a microcosm of the gospel. The Lamb who died is alive and reigns. The One who bore the curse now wears the crown. And the scroll—symbolic of history's destiny—is in **Christ is at the center, and all that follows flows from His victory, authority, and love.** trustworthy hands. Every development in the following chapters must be understood in light of this: Christ is at the center, and all that follows flows from His victory, authority, and love.

Beginning in Revelation chapter 6 and continuing through chapter 19, we encounter a series of escalating judgments—commonly categorized as the seven seal judgments, the seven trumpet judgments, and the seven bowl (or vial) judgments. These twenty-one divine acts of judgment, totaling 19 different plagues, collectively referred to as the wraths, depict a world plunged into chaos and suffering. Throughout this period, the earth experiences unparalleled destruction—economically, ecologically, militarily, and spiritually.

A frequently asked question about this period is, "How many people will die during the Tribulation?" While the Bible does not provide exact population figures, it offers significant clues. For illustration, let us consider a rough estimate: as of 2025, the global population is approximately eight billion people. Assuming, for argument's sake, that around two billion of these are true Christians taken in the rapture before the tribulation begins, that leaves roughly six billion on earth at the start of the judgments.

As each judgment unfolds, the death toll rises. Some judgments specify numerical fractions—such as a fourth or a third—while others indicate widespread destruction without precise figures. Nevertheless, we can reasonably approximate the attrition of the global population through these events:

SEAL JUDGMENTS (REVELATION 6)

The four horsemen of the apocalypse bring conquest, war, famine, and death. The fourth seal alone kills one-fourth of the earth's remaining population, a staggering blow. Assuming six billion remain after the rapture, approximately 1.5 billion perish, leaving around 4.5 billion. Other seals suggest further loss of life, and while not quantified, it is reasonable to assume the total is in the millions.

TRUMPET JUDGMENTS (REVELATION 8–9)

These judgments amplify God's wrath. The sixth trumpet states that a third of mankind is killed. If we estimate a population already reduced to around 3.5 billion, this means another 1.25 billion die, leaving approximately 2.5 billion survivors.

BOWL JUDGMENTS (REVELATION 16)

The final series of judgments does not always specify casualties but describes catastrophic plagues, scorching heat, complete destruction of marine life, darkness, and massive earthquakes. The seventh bowl, in particular, mentions hailstones weighing a hundred pounds and the collapse of global cities—implying significant but unspecified loss of life. A cautious estimate suggests that approximately 1 to 1.5 billion may survive by the time of Christ's return in chapter 19.

While all these numbers are speculative and symbolic, they highlight the immense devastation accompanying God's final judgment on a rebellious world. The scale of human suffering described in Revelation is unprecedented in history. Wars, natural disasters, cosmic disturbances, demonic torment, and ecological collapse contribute to these events—not as random chaos but as deliberate judgments with divine purpose: to bring justice, to call the remaining world to repentance, and to prepare the way for Christ's return. All population estimates are just that—estimates. The true toll of the seal, trumpet, and bowl

The scale of human suffering described in Revelation is unprecedented in history.

judgments is ultimately known only to God. However, starting with a global population of approximately 8 billion at the time of the rapture, and subtracting those who are taken or perish in the ensuing judgments, it can be speculated that only about 10 to 12 percent of humanity will survive to witness the final confrontation between the forces of evil and the returning Christ. Even so, 1 to 1.5 billion people is a significant number—yet no army, regardless of size, can stand against the power and authority of the King of Kings.

What is particularly striking about this progression is not only the magnitude of death and destruction but also the spiritual response of the survivors. Revelation repeatedly states that instead of repenting, many curse God (Revelation 16:9, 11, 21). This tragic detail emphasizes the hardness of heart that characterizes much of humanity during this time and underscores the justice of God's judgments.

Amid this chaos, a remnant is preserved, and a global witness continues. The 144,000 sealed servants of God (Revelation 7) and the two witnesses (Revelation 11) actively proclaim God's truth during this period. A great multitude also appears in heaven, having come out of the great tribulation (Revelation 7:14), suggesting that many will come to faith during this time—often at the cost of martyrdom.

It is important to understand that the book of Revelation does not glorify destruction; rather, it reveals a holy and merciful God who delays judgment until it is absolutely necessary, allowing time for repentance. But eventually, justice must prevail. The tribulation is a climactic period of transition when the kingdoms of this world are dismantled in preparation for the establishment of the Millennial Kingdom of Christ (Revelation 20).

While exact numbers may elude us, the message is unmistakably clear: the judgments of Revelation will bring unprecedented devastation to a world that has rejected God's offer of salvation. Yet, even amid wrath, God's mercy shines through—offering redemption to all who call upon the name of the Lord.

Much of Revelation's narrative progresses in a linear series of judgments, several chapters interrupt this flow to address other significant spiritual realities unfolding concurrently. These "parenthetical" or interlude chapters deepen the reader's understanding of what is happening in heaven and behind the scenes on earth.

Chapter 7 is one such interlude. It presents the sealing of the 144,000 servants of God—12,000 from each of the twelve tribes of Israel. These individuals are set apart and protected for a special mission during the tribulation. While the text does not explicitly state their role, they are often viewed as witnesses or evangelists during this tumultuous time. Later, in Revelation 14:3, these

12,000 from each of the twelve tribes of Israel. These individuals are set apart and protected for a special mission during the tribulation.

144,000 appear again, singing a new song before the throne. Because they are described as having been "redeemed from the earth," some believe this indicates they were martyred. Their appearance in this heavenly vision suggests they have completed their mission and now share in the worship of the Lamb. Although the discussion about the 144,000 is not central to this study, it remains a rich topic for further exploration through commentaries and scholarly works on eschatology.

Revelation 8 begins with a significant moment of silence in heaven lasting half an hour, a dramatic pause that highlights the seriousness of the forthcoming judgments. As the seventh seal is broken, silence prevails instead of immediate action—perhaps representing awe, reverence, or anticipation before divine judgment. Seven angels are given seven trumpets, while another angel presents incense at the golden altar, symbolizing the prayers of the saints ascending to God. This act of intercession connects heavenly worship with earthly events, emphasizing the importance of prayer during times of tribulation.

When the trumpets sound, cosmic and ecological judgments are unleashed. The first four trumpets impact the natural world: hail and fire devastate vegetation, a fiery mountain is cast into the sea killing marine life, a star named Wormwood poisons freshwater sources, and darkness envelops the sun, moon, and stars. These judgments mirror the plagues of Egypt and indicate God's sovereign disruption of the created order. However, they are partial—only a third of creation is affected—suggesting that mercy tempers judgment, urging humanity to repent before the final wrath is unleashed.

Chapter 9 intensifies the judgment with the fifth and sixth trumpets. The fifth trumpet reveals a fallen star from heaven, likely symbolizing a fallen angel or demonic being, who opens the abyss. From this abyss emerge locust-like creatures with terrifying features—

crowns, human faces, lion's teeth, and stinging tails. They are given the power to torment those without God's seal for five months, but not to kill. This imagery suggests intense psychological or spiritual torment, reflecting demonic oppression unleashed upon an unrepentant world.

The sixth trumpet introduces an even more devastating judgment. Four bound angels at the Euphrates are released to kill a third of mankind, leading a massive army of 200 million mounted troops. Their description is surreal and horrifying—fiery breastplates, lion-like heads, and plagues of fire, smoke, and sulfur. Despite the overwhelming judgments, the chapter ends with humanity still refusing to repent, revealing the depth of human hardness and the justice of God's response.

Chapter 10 presents another unique moment in the Revelation narrative. It stands apart from the sequences of judgment and introduces a mighty angel, distinct in appearance and message. This angel is described as having a rainbow above his head—a symbol that appears here in Revelation in this form. Biblically, the rainbow recalls the Noahic covenant (Genesis 9:12–17), God's promise never again to destroy the earth by flood. Its presence here may symbolize God's enduring faithfulness, even amid judgment. One interpretation suggests the rainbow affirms God's mercy even in wrath—He remains true to His covenantal character. Another interpretation, which some rightly question, is that it could represent a continued offer of redemption. However, considering the timeline of escalating judgment, this latter view seems unlikely. The rainbow in this context likely serves as a reminder of God's sovereignty and covenant-keeping nature, rather than a call for last-minute repentance.

The most striking action in this chapter involves John being told to take and eat a small scroll. This echoes the prophetic commissioning of Ezekiel (Ezekiel 2:8–3:3), who was also instructed to eat a scroll, symbolizing the internalization of God's message before proclaiming it. For John, the scroll is sweet to the taste—God's word is precious—but bitter in the stomach, signifying the painful truths and impending judgments he must declare. The prophecy he is called to deliver will bring both the glory of God's justice and the sorrow of human rebellion.

The final verse of the chapter commissions John to prophesy again: "You must prophesy again about many peoples, nations, languages, and kings" (Revelation 10:11). The translation of the preposition here varies across translations. The NIV uses "about," the KJV says "before," and the ASV says "over." Each translation presents a slightly different nuance. "About" suggests the prophecy is descriptive or thematic. "Before" could imply that John will deliver or present this message publicly. "Over" might hint at a kind of spiritual authority or oversight. While it is difficult to determine the precise intent, the main idea remains: John's mission continues, and his message is meant for the whole world.

These chapters remind us that Revelation is not merely a series of apocalyptic events but also a deeply prophetic and theological work. It records not only judgments but also reveals God's purposes, His faithfulness, and His call to proclaim truth; regardless of personal cost. They anchor the book's message not only in judgment but also in God's mercy, sovereignty, and redemptive purpose.

> **Revelation is not merely a series of apocalyptic events but also a deeply prophetic and theological work.**

Chapter 11 introduces the two witnesses who stand against a sinful humanity to speak on behalf of God for a period of three and a half years. They are eventually murdered by the Antichrist and lay in the street until they are resurrected by God. Notably, the Antichrist does not appear until chapter 13, which occurs three and a half years after the events of chapter 11.

Chapter 12 marks a pivotal shift in the Book of Revelation, introducing one of its most symbolic and theologically rich visions. In this passage, John sees **"a woman clothed with the sun, with the moon under her feet and a crown of twelve stars on her head"** (Revelation 12:1). She is pregnant and in the throes of childbirth. Soon after, a great red dragon appears, intent on devouring her child the moment it is born.

The identity of the woman has been the subject of much debate, but the strongest and most consistent interpretation is that she represents Israel, the covenant people of God. The child she gives birth to is best understood as Jesus Christ, the long-awaited Messiah. Revelation 12:5 tells us that the child **"will rule all the nations with an iron scepter,"** a direct reference to Psalm 2:9, a well-known Messianic prophecy.

This reinforces the conclusion that the child is Jesus, and the vision captures both His incarnation and eventual ascension to heaven (v. 5: "**And her child was snatched up to God and to His throne**").

The dragon is explicitly identified in verse 9 as Satan, "**that ancient serpent called the devil.**" His desire to destroy the Messiah reflects the satanic opposition to Christ's birth, ministry, crucifixion, and resurrection—a theme woven throughout Scripture, from Herod's massacre of infants to the temptations in the wilderness. This dramatic scene serves as both a theological representation of Christ's mission and a universal depiction of the spiritual warfare that underpins human history. It highlights that beyond the political, cultural, and religious events on earth, there exists a profound, unseen battle between the kingdom of God and the forces of darkness.

> **...There exists a profound, unseen battle between the kingdom of God and the forces of darkness.**

After the child's ascension, the woman, representing Israel, flees into the wilderness, where God prepares a place for her (v. 6). This symbolizes divine protection during a time of great tribulation. Some scholars interpret this imagery as indicative of the future preservation of a remnant of Israel during the end times, a theme consistent with both Old and New Testament prophecies (cf. Romans 11:25–27).

Ultimately, chapter 12 provides us with both a retrospective and prophetic perspective. It reflects on Christ's victory over Satan through His death and resurrection while also anticipating an intensification of spiritual conflict in the last days. Yet, throughout these events, God's sovereign hand is evident—safeguarding and advancing His redemptive plan through both Israel and the Church.

Revelation 13 introduces two beasts that symbolize the culmination of satanic influence through political and religious systems. The first beast emerges from the sea, a traditional biblical symbol of chaos and turmoil. This beast resembles a hybrid of the four beasts from Daniel's vision (Daniel 7), combining features that reflect successive empires. It has seven heads and ten horns, representing kings and kingdoms under satanic authority. Empowered by the dragon—identified earlier as Satan—this beast blasphemes God, persecutes the saints, and wields global authority. Those not belonging to God, whose names are not written in the Lamb's Book of Life, are compelled to worship this beast. It embodies a blasphemous world system that demands loyalty through coercive political power and fear-driven dominance.

The second beast arises from the earth and appears like a lamb, a counterfeit of Christ, but speaks like a dragon, revealing its true deceptive nature. Known elsewhere in Revelation as the "false prophet," this beast performs false signs and miracles to deceive the world into worshiping the first beast. It erects an image of the beast and demands idolatrous devotion under the threat of death. Those who refuse are excluded from economic participation. The infamous "mark of the beast" (666) symbolizes a totalitarian system of spiritual compromise, where allegiance to the beast becomes a prerequisite for survival. This chapter presents a sobering picture of end-time deception and persecution, where demonic forces counterfeit divine truth to ensnare the world. It also emphasizes the necessity for discernment, perseverance, and unwavering faith among God's faithful remnant.

Revelation chapter 14 opens with a striking and hopeful contrast. While the previous chapter depicts the rise of the Antichrist and the False Prophet, chapter 14 redirects our focus back to the Lamb, standing triumphantly on Mount Zion. This transition is intentional, serving as a divine interruption in the narrative of evil. It reminds us that no matter how formidable the forces of darkness may seem, they are never beyond God's sovereignty. Chapter 14 offers a glimpse of God's faithful remnant—those who have not succumbed to the beast nor received his mark. It presents a scene of worship, divine proclamation, and impending judgment.

It reminds us that no matter how formidable the forces of darkness may seem, they are never beyond God's sovereignty.

The 144,000 reappear, as they did in chapter 7, sealed and preserved by God. Now, they stand with the Lamb, symbolizing victory, loyalty, and divine reward. Their presence reassures the reader that amidst tribulation, God has not forgotten His people. While chapter 13 concludes with a false prophet marking followers for destruction, chapter 14 begins with God's faithful, marked for salvation.

What follows is a series of angelic proclamations, each announcing aspects of God's impending judgment, calling humanity to worship the Creator, declaring the fall of Babylon, and warning of the dire consequences for those who align themselves with the beast. These messages pave the way for the final harvest—the ultimate separation of the righteous from the wicked.

Thus, chapter 14 serves as both a pause and a preview. It reassures the faithful while clearly declaring that judgment is imminent. Evil may rise, but it will not prevail. The Lamb reigns, and those who follow Him will one day sing a new song known only to the redeemed. This is the rhythm of Revelation: judgment and mercy, warning and hope, wrath and worship. As we progress, the tempo quickens, the imagery intensifies, and God's plan for the end of the age sharpens in focus. Yet even now, the message is clear—Christ is victorious, and His people will stand with Him in glory.

Chapter 15 serves as a solemn interlude that prepares the reader for the final outpouring of God's wrath. John sees a sea of glass mixed with fire, and those who have overcome the beast are standing beside it, holding harps and singing the song of Moses and the Lamb. This song celebrates God's justice, power, and truth, acknowledging Him as the King of the nations whose judgments are righteous and true.

The scene shifts to the heavenly temple—the tabernacle of the testimony—which is opened as seven angels come forth, each holding a bowl filled with the final plagues. They are dressed in pure, shining linen, symbolizing the holiness of their mission. One of the four living creatures gives them the bowls of God's wrath. As the temple fills with smoke from the glory of God and His power, no one is able to enter until the seven plagues are completed. The atmosphere is one of awesome finality—the last warnings have passed, and the full judgment is about to begin.

What was seen in chapter 15 now unfolds in chapter 16 as the bowl judgments begin. With reverent finality, the angels pour out the seven bowls of God's wrath upon the earth. These judgments are comprehensive and unrestrained. The first bowl causes festering sores on those who bear the mark of the beast. The second and third bowls turn the sea and rivers to blood, reminiscent of the Exodus plagues. The fourth bowl intensifies the sun's heat, scorching people, yet even in suffering, they curse God rather than repent.

The fifth bowl brings darkness upon the beast's kingdom, a physical and spiritual thickening of judgment. The sixth dries up the Euphrates River, preparing the way for the kings of the East and leading to the battle of Armageddon. Demon spirits from the dragon, beast, and false prophet gather the nations for this final confrontation. Finally, the seventh bowl unleashes a great earthquake—the greatest in history—splitting the great city and causing massive devastation. Hailstones fall, and Babylon is remembered for judgment. The chapter ends with a stark refusal of repentance and mankind's blasphemy against God, underlining the justness of His wrath.

Chapters 17 and 18 of Revelation are particularly significant due to their vivid and mysterious imagery, centered on the figure of the great harlot, depicted as sitting on many waters and riding a scarlet beast. This woman, referred to as **"Babylon the Great, the mother of prostitutes and of the abominations of the earth"** (Revelation 17:5), has been the subject of intense debate and various interpretations throughout church history. Ultimately, this harlot is destroyed by the very beast she rides—a figure commonly associated with the Antichrist. Her fall is violent and complete, signifying God's judgment against a system or entity that embodies spiritual corruption, false religion, and the seduction of the nations.

The reference to "Babylon" is critical and complex. While some interpreters view it as a reference to the literal ancient city, most recognize that John uses Babylon symbolically. The question then arises: what does Babylon represent? Over the centuries, various interpretations have emerged. Some believe Babylon is a prophetic code for Rome, given the parallels between John's descriptions and the political and cultural environment of the Roman Empire during his writing. Others see it as a representation of the Roman Catholic Church, especially during periods marked by corruption or compromise. Still, others argue that Babylon symbolizes Jerusalem, which, despite being chosen by God, repeatedly turned away from Him and ultimately rejected the Messiah.

The consensus is that the harlot is best understood symbolically, rather than rigidly identified with a single historical or religious institution. Babylon functions as a metaphor for any political, religious, or cultural system that opposes God and seduces humanity into spiritual unfaithfulness. It is a composite image, drawing from Old Testament portrayals of harlotry as symbolic of covenant betrayal, particularly in cities and nations that once knew God but turned to idols.

The phrase "mother of harlots" further suggests that this figure is not only an embodiment of unfaithfulness but also a source of it; either as the origin of such corruption or as its most blatant and influential expression. This designation implies not just the first, but the worst. In this context, Jerusalem—once the dwelling place of God, the city of His temple, and the site of Christ's crucifixion—can indeed be seen as uniquely culpable. As Jesus lamented, **"Jerusalem, Jerusalem, you who kill the prophets and stone those sent to you..."** (Matthew 23:37). To whom much is given, much is required.

Nevertheless, Revelation's Babylon may not be confined to a single city or institution. It can also symbolize the entirety of godless

Babylon represents the culmination of human rebellion...

civilization—economic, political, and religious—that rejects divine authority and exalts human pride. Babylon represents the culmination of human rebellion, echoing the Tower of Babel in Genesis 11, where humanity sought to make a name for itself apart from God. That spirit of self-exaltation continues through history, taking many forms, and will reach its peak in the end times through a global system of deception, wealth, and persecution.

Chapters 17 and 18, therefore, do more than introduce a single figure—they provide a scathing critique of the world's seductive power structures and foreshadow their sudden and dramatic collapse. Whether one views Babylon as a city, a system, or a symbol, the message is clear: every institution or culture that opposes God and entices people into idolatry will ultimately fall under divine judgment.

The destruction of the harlot by the beast, her apparent ally, serves as a sobering reminder that evil is self-consuming. The same Antichrist who benefits from Babylon's influence will ultimately turn against her, fulfilling God's ultimate plan of judgment, even unknowingly. Revelation 17:17 states, **"For God has put it into their hearts to accomplish His purpose..."** Emphasizing that even the schemes of the wicked exist under divine sovereignty.

In the next chapter, Babylon's fall is lamented by the kings, merchants, and mariners of the earth who profited from her luxuries. However, heaven rejoices, as her judgment signifies the arrival of righteousness and the vindication of the saints. Thus, chapters 17 and18 not only reveal the depth of corruption but also prepare the way for the return of the King in chapter 19, who will establish an unshakeable kingdom.

As we transition to Revelation 19, the narrative reaches its climactic moment: heaven opens, and the conquering King rides forth. No longer the suffering Lamb, Jesus now appears as the victorious Lord. He is clothed in a robe dipped in blood—a reminder of both judgment and redemption—and rides a white horse, symbolizing triumph. His eyes blaze like fire, piercing through all pretense. On His head are many crowns, denoting sovereign authority, and His name—King of Kings and Lord of Lords—is emblazoned upon His robe and thigh.

Jesus now appears as the victorious Lord... His name— King of Kings and Lord of Lords...

With the armies of heaven behind Him, Christ descends not in weakness, but in power, wielding the sword of His word to strike the nations. This marks the final confrontation between divine justice and unrepentant evil. The beast of the sea (Antichrist) and the beast of the earth (False Prophet), who deceived the nations, are captured and cast alive into the lake of burning sulfur—a realm often understood as eternal Hell, a place of irreversible separation from God.

This is the first of three significant references to the lake of fire, which becomes the ultimate destination for all rebellion. Prior to this, Scripture identifies four distinct "locations" for human and angelic souls. Humans, upon death, enter either the presence of God (for believers) or Hades (for unbelievers), a temporary place of torment. Angelic beings either serve in heaven or are confined in the Abyss (or Tartarus), a realm of restraint for disobedient spirits. Notably, no humans are ever said to reside in the Abyss—its purpose is solely for fallen angels awaiting final judgment.

Those redeemed by the blood of the Lamb will dwell forever in New Jerusalem...

After the events of Revelation 20, particularly the Great White Throne Judgment, all of creation is divided into two eternal destinies. Those redeemed by the blood of the Lamb will dwell forever in New Jerusalem, where

God and the Lamb are present. In contrast, those who have rejected salvation—Satan, his demonic followers, and all who remain unrepentant—are cast into the lake of fire, the final place of judgment and separation.

Revelation 20 also introduces the thousand-year reign of Christ, known as the Millennial Kingdom. During this time, Satan is bound, and peace prevails under Christ's visible leadership. It is a period of fulfillment, justice, and restoration. However, after this golden age, Satan is released for a final test of humanity. His last rebellion is swiftly defeated, and he too is cast into the lake of fire, joining the Antichrist and the False Prophet in eternal punishment.

Then comes the grand conclusion—Revelation 21 and 22. The old heavens and earth pass away, making way for a new creation, unmarred by sin. At the center of this renewed cosmos is the New Jerusalem—a holy city descending from heaven, prepared as a bride for her husband. Its dimensions are staggering: 1,500 miles in length, width, and height—a perfect cube, reminiscent of the Most Holy Place in the tabernacle and temple. This geometric perfection symbolizes that the entire city is sacred, the dwelling place of God among His people. There is no need for sun or moon, for the glory of God provides its light, and the Lamb serves as its lamp. The gates are never shut—there is no danger, no night, no sin. The river of the water of life flows from the throne, and the tree of life, once guarded in Eden, now bears fruit for the healing of the nations. The curse is lifted. God's people will see His face and reign with Him forever.

There is no need for sun or moon, for the glory of God provides its light, and the Lamb serves as its lamp.

This is not just the end of a story; it is the beginning of eternity. The vision in Revelation does not end in devastation but in divine renewal. What began in a garden with perfect communion between God and humanity finds its fulfillment in a radiant city—the New Jerusalem—where God once again dwells with His people. The pain of the curse is undone. What was lost through sin is restored through the Lamb who was slain and now reigns forever. The final victory is not merely the defeat of evil but the complete restoration of God's intended order, where justice, peace, and holiness reign eternally.

This eschatological hope is neither distant nor abstract; it is deeply personal and powerfully present. It anchors us in moments of suffering, sustains us through trials, and steadies us amid global turmoil. Because the Lamb reigns, we live in confidence. Because the King is coming, we live in readiness. Jesus is preparing a place for all who trust in Him, and His return will fulfill the promise made from the beginning.

CHAPTER

12

Final Thoughts:
God Has Never Let Go

God has never abandoned His creation—and He has never abandoned you.

𝕬s we conclude this journey, I hope you now see with greater clarity what has always been true: God has never abandoned His creation—and He has never abandoned you. From the moment He walked with Adam and Eve in the cool of the garden, God has yearned for communion with humanity. Even after sin fractured that fellowship, His love remained steadfast. Each page of Scripture attests to His relentless pursuit, from Eden to Calvary, from Pentecost to the promise of His return.

In humanity's darkest moments—whether during the rebellion in Eden, the judgment of the Flood, the idolatry in the wilderness, or the exile of His covenant people—God's mercy has never faltered. He has always provided a way. His redemptive plan was never an afterthought or a course correction; it was the eternal design, steadily unfolding through the ages. From the promises made to Abraham, to the Law given through Moses, to the prophetic calls for repentance, and finally to the incarnation of Jesus Christ, every act of divine intervention reveals one truth: God desires to dwell with us again.

Jesus made this desire unmistakably clear in John 14:2–4: "**Do not let your hearts be troubled. You believe in God; believe also in** me. My Father's house has many rooms; if that were not so, would I have told you that I am going there to prepare a place for you? And if I go and prepare a place for you, I will come back and take you to be with me that you also may be where I am." This was not merely a farewell to the disciples; it was a timeless promise to every believer. Jesus is not only the Redeemer who bore our sins; He is the Bridegroom preparing a place for His beloved. The promise is personal, eternal, and unshakeably certain. In Christ, the door to the garden has been reopened. When Thomas, in honest confusion, asked how to follow Jesus to this promised place, the Lord replied with divine finality: "**I am the way and the truth and the life. No one comes to the Father except through me.**" (John 14:6)

These are not words of exclusion; they are words of invitation. Jesus is the singular path not because God is distant, but because He has made Himself near. He did not leave us to wander among many ways—He provided us with the Way. In a world clouded by relativism and competing truths, Jesus stands as the clear, unchanging bridge back to the Father.

As you reflect on all that has been explored in this book—from creation to covenant to Christ's final return—I urge you to embrace the journey of sanctification. This is not just a theological concept; it is the heartbeat of a life in relationship with God. Through the indwelling of the Holy Spirit, believers are daily renewed, reshaped, and restored. Sanctification is evidence that God has not only saved us from something but is also shaping us for something—to reflect the image of His Son and to walk once again in the intimacy for which we were created.

God's plan has always been personal. It has always been about bringing His children back to Himself. In Ephesians 1:4–5, we are told that You were not an afterthought. You were always part of the plan. "**He chose us in Him before the creation of the world to be holy and blameless in His sight... In love He predestined us for adoption to sonship through Jesus Christ.**" This book is not just a roadmap for understanding end-times prophecy or biblical. As you move forward from this moment, may you keep your eyes fixed on eternity and your heart anchored in the unshakeable

> **God's plan has always been personal. It has always been about bringing His children back to Himself.**

hope of Christ, who has promised, **"Surely I am coming soon"** (Revelation 22:20). These words are not merely a poetic conclusion to the biblical canon; they are a divine assurance that has echoed through the centuries, spoken by the risen and glorified Christ to His Church.

The early Christians lived with this anticipation burning in their hearts. The Aramaic phrase *Maranatha*, meaning "Come, Lord," became both their prayer and proclamation—a reminder that history is not aimless but is being drawn toward a purposeful and glorious consummation in the return of Jesus. Church Fathers like Irenaeus and Justin Martyr often spoke of this blessed hope, emphasizing that the second coming of Christ is not just a abstract concept but the fulfillment of God's promise to restore creation and dwell with His people forever.

To be ready means living in a posture of faithful expectation... To be ready means living in a posture of faithful expectation—not driven by fear of judgment, but by the joy of reunion. Paul encouraged believers to **"await eagerly"** the appearance of Christ (Titus 2:13), referring to Him as **"our blessed hope."** This forward-looking faith shapes not only our thoughts about the future but also how we live in the present—with holiness, urgency, and a heart attuned to the eternal.

And when He returns, may you be found ready—not striving, but standing firm; not hiding, but rejoicing; not ashamed, but radiant in His glory. The same Jesus who came in humility will come again in glory, and all things will be made new (Revelation 21:5).

As the title of this book declares, *It Is All About You*; not in a self-centered way, but in sacred significance—because the God who created galaxies also crafted your soul. He formed you in love, called you by name, and has written you into His eternal story. From Eden to the Cross, from the empty tomb to the heavenly city, His desire has remained unchanged: to dwell with His people. To dwell with you.

His desire has remained unchanged: to dwell with His people. To dwell with you.

You were created not for wandering, but for worship. Not for separation, but for communion

Not for despair, but for destiny. Every page of Scripture affirms this truth: God has not abandoned His creation. He is redeeming it. He is restoring it. And He is calling you home.

So walk forward, loved by God, with confidence and courage. The story is not over. The best is yet to come. And when the trumpet sounds and the sky is rolled back, may your heart cry with joy:

"EVEN SO, COME, LORD JESUS."

About the Author

David G. Brown has faithfully served as an ordained elder for over forty years and has devoted more than four decades to teaching Scripture at the adult level. His ministry has been marked by a deep commitment to biblical inquiry, especially in the areas of Revelation, prophecy, and the foundational doctrines of the Christian faith. He is the author of *Miracles, Signs, Symbols, and Judgment: God's Plan for the End Times*—a comprehensive study of eschatological themes, thoughtfully crafted to make complex theology both clear and spiritually enriching.

His theological depth is matched by his hands-on commitment to missions. As a former board member of Haiti Outreach Ministries, David has participated in more than twenty-five short-term mission trips and disaster relief efforts. His life reflects a tangible obedience to the Great Commission, combining local service with global impact.

Concerned by the rise of biblical illiteracy within both the church and society, David presents his latest book, *It Is All About You: From Eden to Eternity—How God Never Forgot His Creation*, as a timely response to growing spiritual confusion and cultural drift. In a world where many question God's presence and plan, he affirms a vital truth: the Creator remains actively involved with His creation. Included at the back of the book is a guided worksheet for each chapter—making it an ideal resource for personal reflection, small-group study, or discipleship training.

In addition, David has developed a complementary study curriculum titled Prophecy Fulfilled: Jesus Is the Messiah, consisting of fifty-two lessons that explore Old Testament prophecies fulfilled in the New Testament. From Genesis to Revelation, every prophecy points to Jesus as the Christ—a yearlong journey through fifty-two prophecies that reveal Jesus as the promised Messiah.

As mentioned within the pages of this latest book, David's first publication is a commentary on the book of Revelation titled Miracles, Signs, Symbols, and Judgment: God's Plan for the End Times. Through the unique format of this text, David provides answers to nearly six hundred questions that have long challenged readers seeking to understand the book of Revelation. The result is a work that not only clarifies these prophetic themes but also emphasizes the importance of developing a personal relationship with God.

David and his wife, Linda, reside in Richmond, Virginia, where they celebrate over fifty years of marriage. He has also served as a football official for more than thirty years and enjoys restoring antique cars, building and refinishing furniture, and engaging in various construction projects. Yet above all, his greatest passion remains unchanged: teaching the Word of God and helping others grow in their understanding of divine truth.

Study Guide: Chapter 1 – God never stopped Loving You

Main Theme: God's unfailing love and personal relationship with humanity.

Key Themes & Instructions:

God's Transcendence and Immanence

Reflect on how God is both beyond all creation and yet intimately involved in your life.

Write about a moment where you sensed God's nearness in a personal way:

_____

_____

_____

_____

Divine Love and Faithfulness

Explore what it means for God's love to be constant, unchanging, and not dependent on your actions.

How does this truth bring you comfort or challenge you?

_____

_____

_____

_____

Identity as Children of God

Consider how being called God's child shapes your self-worth and relationships with others.

What does it mean to you to be called "friend" and "child" of God?

_____

_____

_____

The Redemptive Narrative of Scripture

Trace God's love through the Bible—from creation, through the fall, to Christ's redeeming work.

Write how the story of redemption helps you understand God's character:

_____
_____
_____
_____

Scripture Focus & Instructions:

Matthew 10:29–31 – God cares for even the smallest details of your life.

What does this teach you about your worth to God?

_____
_____

Psalm 139:1–14 – You are fully known and wonderfully made.

Choose a verse that stood out and explain why it resonated:

_____
_____
_____

John 3:16–17; 15:15 – Jesus came because of love and calls you friend.

What does this kind of relationship with Jesus mean to you?

_____
_____

1 John 3:1 – You are called a child of God.

How does this influence how you see yourself?

_____
_____

Romans 8:38–39 – Nothing can separate you from God's love.

Write about a time this promise brought you peace:

_____

_____

_____

_____

Revelation 21:3–4 – God's plan is to dwell with His people forever.

How does this future hope influence your life today?

_____

_____

_____

Reflection Questions:

How does knowing God loves and knows you personally affect your daily life?

_____

_____

_____

_____

What does it mean that God is both near and infinite?

_____

_____

_____

How do you see your value reflected in God's Word?

_____

_____

_____

_____

Application:

Journal Prompt:

Write a short letter to God expressing what His love means to you.

_____

_____

_____

_____

_____

_____

_____

_____

_____

_____

_____

_____

_____

_____

_____

_____

_____

_____

_____

_____

_____

_____

_____

_____

_____

_____

_____

_____

_____

_____

_____

_____

Memory Verse:

Romans 8:38–39 "For I am convinced that neither death nor life, neither angels nor demons, neither the present or the future, nor any powers,"

1 John 3:1 "See what great love the Father has lavished on us, that we should be called children of God! And that is what we are! The reason the world does not know us is that it did not know him."

Prayer Focus:

Use this space to write a prayer of thanksgiving for God's love and closeness.

_____

_____

_____

_____

_____

_____

_____

_____

_____

_____

Final Thoughts:

God has never stopped loving you. From creation to eternity, His love is unwavering and personal. You are deeply known and eternally pursued. Your Thoughts:

_____

_____

_____

_____

_____

_____

_____

STUDY GUIDE: CHAPTER 2 – WHY DID GOD CREATE THE WORLD—AND WHY WERE WE CREATED?

Main Theme: Divine purpose and intentionality in creation.

Key Themes & Instructions:

The Image of God in Humanity

Reflect on what it means to be made in the image of a relational and creative God.

How does this influence your view of human dignity and purpose?

_____

_____

_____

_____

_____

_____

Relationship with a Loving Creator

Explore how God designed humanity to be in relationship with Him.

What does this say about your purpose in life?

_____

_____

_____

_____

_____

_____

Purpose Through Worship and Stewardship

Consider how worship and caring for creation fulfill our divine calling.

In what ways can you better live out this calling today?

_____

_____

_____

Scripture Focus & Instructions:

Genesis 1:26–27 – Made in the image of God.

What responsibility or purpose do you see tied to this truth?

_____

_____

Colossians 1:16; John 1:3 – All things were created through Christ.

How does this deepen your understanding of Jesus' role in creation?

_____

_____

_____

_____

Ecclesiastes 3:11 – God placed eternity in the human heart.

What longings or questions does this verse stir in you?

_____

_____

_____

_____

_____

1 John 4:8 – God is love.

How does this foundational truth shape your understanding of why you were created?

_____

_____

_____

_____

Revelation 21:1–4 – The final restoration of creation.

How does God's end goal reflect His original design?

_____

_____

_____

Reflection Questions:

What does it mean to be made in God's image?

_____

_____

_____

_____

_____

How does God's purpose for creation shape your life?

_____

_____

_____

How is Jesus central to creation and redemption?

_____

_____

_____

_____

Application:

Journal Prompt:

Write out your understanding of your God-given purpose.

_____

_____

_____

_____

_____

_____

_____

_____

_____

_____

_____

_____

Memory Verse:

Colossians 1:16, "For in him all things were created: things in heaven and on earth, visible and invisible, whether thrones or powers or rulers or authorities; all things have been created through him and for him."

Ecclesiastes 3:11 , "He has made everything beautiful in its time. He has also set eternity in the human heart; yet no one can fathom what God has done from beginning to end."

Prayer Focus:

Thank God for creating you with love, purpose, and dignity. Ask for guidance in fulfilling your calling.

_____
_____
_____
_____
_____
_____
_____
_____
_____

Final Thoughts:

God created with purpose and love. You were made to know Him, reflect Him, and live within His eternal plan of redemption. Your Thoughts?

_____
_____
_____
_____
_____
_____
_____

Study Guide: Chapter 3 – Genesis—God's Original Plan

Main Theme: Main Theme: Harmony, relationship, and purpose in God's design.

Key Themes & Instructions:

Intentional Creation and Stewardship

Consider what it means that God created the world with order, beauty, and purpose.

How are you called to care for God's creation today?

_____

_____

The Imago Dei (Image of God)

Reflect on your God-given identity.

How does this truth shape how you view others and yourself?

_____

_____

_____

_____

_____

_____

The Fall, Hope, and Restoration

Explore the effects of sin on God's creation and His plan to redeem it through Christ.

Where do you see God's restoring power in your life?

_____

_____

_____

_____

Scripture Focus & Instructions:

Genesis 1–3 – God's creation, human purpose, and the Fall.

What does this narrative reveal about God's intentions for humanity?

_____

_____

_____

Psalm 8; 24:1 – Humanity's value and God's ownership.

How do these verses influence your understanding of stewardship?

_____

_____

_____

_____

Romans 8:18–23 – Creation longs for redemption.

In what ways do you share this longing?

_____

_____

_____

_____

_____

Colossians 1:15–20 – Christ's supremacy and role in restoration.

How is Jesus restoring what was broken?

_____

_____

_____

_____

Revelation 21–22 – New creation and eternal fellowship.

How does this ending fulfill the beginning of Genesis?

_____

_____

_____

Reflection Questions:

How does being created in God's image impact your life?

_____

_____

_____

_____

_____

What does stewardship look like today?

_____

_____

_____

How is Revelation the fulfillment of Genesis?

_____

_____

_____

_____

Application:

Journal Prompt:

Write how your identity as God's image-bearer influences your choices.

_____

_____

_____

_____

_____

_____

_____

_____

_____

_____

_____

_____

Memory Verse:

Psalm 16:11. "You make known to me the path of life; you will fill me with joy in your presence, with eternal pleasures at your right hand."

John 17:21, "that all of them may be one, Father, just as you are in me and I am in you. May they also be in us so that the world may believe that you have sent me."

Prayer Focus:

Ask God to help you live as a steward of His creation and a reflection of His image.

_____
_____
_____
_____
_____
_____
_____
_____

Final Thoughts:

God's original plan was harmony. Though broken by sin, He is restoring all things in Christ—including you. Your Thoughts:

_____
_____
_____
_____
_____
_____
_____
_____

STUDY GUIDE: CHAPTER 4 – WHEN HUMANITY DISRUPTS THE DIVINE PLAN—WHAT FOLLOWS?

Main Theme: Sin, separation, and the hope of redemption.

Key Themes & Instructions:

The Fall and Its Consequences

Understand how human disobedience broke fellowship with God.

Reflect on how sin has affected your relationship with God and others.

_____

_____

_____

_____

_____

_____

Divine Judgment and Mercy

Explore how God responds to sin with both justice and mercy.

How have you experienced both in your own life?

_____

_____

_____

_____

_____

_____

The Promise of Restoration

Discover how even in judgment, God points toward hope.

What promises from God help you walk through difficult seasons?

_____

_____

_____

_____

Scripture Focus & Instructions:

Genesis 2–3 – The first act of disobedience and its results.

What truths does this passage reveal about human nature and God's character?

_____

_____

_____

_____

Romans 6:23 – The consequence of sin is death.

How does this clarify the seriousness of sin?

_____

_____

_____

_____

_____

2 Corinthians 5:17 – In Christ we are made new.

What old things have passed away in your life because of Christ?

_____

_____

_____

_____

_____

Revelation 21:1–4 – God's plan to renew all things.

How does this hope for restoration shape your perspective today?

_____

_____

_____

Reflection Questions:

What do the consequences of the Fall reveal about God's justice?

_____

_____

_____

How does God show mercy even in judgment?

_____

_____

_____

How does Christ reverse the effects of the Fall?

_____

_____

_____

Application:

Journal Prompt:

Reflect on God's grace in your own story of failure and redemption.

_____

_____

_____

_____

_____

_____

_____

_____

_____

_____

_____

_____

_____

_____

Memory Verse:

2 Corinthians 5:17, "Therefore, if anyone is in Christ, the new creation has come: The old has gone, the new is here!"

Romans 6:23, "For the wages of sin is death, but the gift of God is eternal life in Christ Jesus our Lord."

Prayer Focus:

Thank God for His mercy and the promise of new beginnings. Ask Him to help you walk in the freedom of restoration.

_____

_____

_____

_____

_____

Final Thoughts:

Even in rebellion, God pursues us. Through Christ, He redeems what was lost and restores what was broken. His justice does not cancel His love—it magnifies His grace. Your Thoughts?

_____

_____

_____

_____

_____

_____

_____

_____

_____

_____

STUDY GUIDE: CHAPTER 5 – WHY EVERYTHING POINTS TO MAN'S RECONCILIATION

Main Theme: God's relentless pursuit through covenant and redemption.

Key Themes & Instructions:

God's Covenants with Noah, Abraham, and Israel

Reflect on how each covenant shows God's heart for redemption.

Which covenant speaks most deeply to you and why?

_____

_____

_____

_____

_____

_____

Redemption and Reconciliation Through Christ

Explore how Jesus fulfills the covenant promises.

How does this shape your understanding of God's plan?

_____

_____

_____

_____

_____

_____

God's Unwavering Faithfulness

Consider how God remains faithful despite human failure.

Where have you seen His faithfulness in your life?

_____

_____

_____

Scripture Focus & Instructions:

Genesis 6–9; 12 – God's promises to Noah and Abraham.

What does God's covenant with Noah reveal about His mercy?

_____

_____

_____

Genesis 22:15–18 – God's covenant reaffirmed to Abraham.

How does the promise to Abraham point forward to Christ?

_____

_____

_____

Exodus 2; 14 – God hears and delivers His people.

What does God's deliverance from Egypt show about His character?

_____

_____

_____

Romans 5:8–10 – Reconciled through Christ.

What does this passage say about your value to God?

_____

_____

_____

_____

2 Corinthians 5:18–19 – Ministry of reconciliation.

How can you live as a reconciler in your community?

_____

_____

_____

_____

Reflection Questions:

How do God's covenants point to Christ?

_____

_____

_____

Where have you experienced reconciliation with God?

_____

_____

_____

What part of God's faithfulness speaks most to your current journey?

_____

_____

_____

Application:

Journal Prompt:

Write about a time God pursued you with love and mercy.

_____

_____

_____

_____

_____

_____

_____

_____

_____

_____

_____

_____

_____

_____

Memory Verse:

Romans 5:10, "I have set my rainbow in the clouds, and it will be the sign of the covenant between me and the earth."

2 Corinthians 5:19, "The Lord is not slow in keeping his promise, as some understand slowness. Instead he is patient with you, not wanting anyone to perish, but everyone to come to repentance."

Prayer Focus:

Thank God for reconciling you to Himself through Christ. Ask Him to help you reflect that reconciliation to others.

_____

_____

_____

_____

_____

_____

_____

Final Thoughts:

God's heart is to reconcile. From the flood to the cross, His unwavering love has made the way back to Him. In Christ, reconciliation is not just possible—it is promised and fulfilled. Even in rebellion, God pursues us. Through Christ, He redeems what was lost and restores what was broken. His justice does not cancel His love—it magnifies His grace. Your Thought?

_____

_____

_____

_____

_____

_____

_____

_____

_____

STUDY GUIDE: CHAPTER 6 – THE PROPHETIC INFLUENCE OF GOD ON HUMANITY

Main Theme: God's call to justice, repentance, and hope through the prophets.

Key Themes & Instructions:

Prophets as Divine Messengers

What roles did the prophets play in God's relationship with His people?

Write how you think God still communicates through His people today:

_____

_____

_____

_____

Judgment and Restoration

How did prophets reveal both consequences and hope?

Write about a prophet's message that resonates with your own life:

_____

_____

_____

_____

_____

_____

Fulfillment in Christ

How does Jesus fulfill the prophecies of the Old Testament?

Describe a prophecy about Christ that strengthens your faith:

_____

_____

_____

_____

Scripture Focus & Instructions:

Jeremiah 1:5 – God's purpose before birth.

What does this say about your calling?

_____

_____

_____

Micah 6:8 – God's desire for justice and mercy.

How does this verse shape your daily decisions?

_____

_____

_____

_____

Isaiah 58 – True worship and compassion.

What kind of worship pleases God?

_____

_____

_____

Joel 2:12–13 – Call to heartfelt repentance.

What does true repentance look like for you?

_____

_____

_____

_____

Hebrews 1:1–2 – Jesus as God's final Word.

How does this change how you hear and respond to Scripture?

_____

_____

_____

_____

Reflection Questions:

What distinguishes biblical prophets from religious leaders today?

_____

_____

_____

_____

How can you live prophetically—speaking truth and pointing to hope?

_____

_____

_____

Application:

Journal Prompt:

Write about a time you were convicted to speak truth in love. What happened?

_____

_____

_____

_____

_____

_____

_____

_____

_____

_____

_____

_____

_____

_____

_____

_____

Memory Verse:

Micah 6:8. "He has shown you, O mortal, what is good. And what does the Lord require of you? To act justly and to love mercy and to walk humbly j with your God."

Jeremiah 1:5, "Before I formed you in the womb I knew h you, before you were born I set you apart; I appointed you as a prophet to the nations."

Prayer Focus:

Ask God to give you a prophetic heart—one that speaks with love, acts justly, and lives humbly.

_____
_____
_____
_____
_____
_____
_____

Final Thoughts:

The prophetic voice still echoes—calling us to truth, justice, and hope in Christ, the ultimate fulfillment of God's promises. Your Thought?

_____
_____
_____
_____
_____
_____
_____
_____
_____

STUDY GUIDE: CHAPTER 7 – GOD'S PERFECT REDEMPTIVE PLAN THROUGH CHRIST

Main Theme: The necessity and completeness of Christ's sacrifice.

Key Themes & Instructions:

Atonement and Substitution

Reflect on why sin requires a sacrifice and how Jesus took your place.

How does this deepen your understanding of grace?

_____

_____

_____

_____

Christ as High Priest and Lamb

Consider the Old Testament role of priests and how Jesus fulfills that role perfectly.

What does it mean that He intercedes for you today?

_____

_____

_____

_____

_____

_____

Resurrection and Victory

Think about the power of the resurrection and its role in defeating death.

How does the resurrection give you hope?

_____

_____

_____

_____

Scripture Focus & Instructions:

Romans 5:8 – God's love shown through Christ's death.

How does this verse assure you of God's love?

_____

_____

_____

Isaiah 53 – The prophecy of the suffering servant.

Which verse stands out as most powerful and why?

_____

_____

_____

_____

Hebrews 9–10 – Christ's once-for-all sacrifice.

How is Jesus' sacrifice different from Old Testament offerings?

_____

_____

_____

2 Corinthians 5:21 – Made righteous through Christ.

What does being made righteous in Him mean for your life?

_____

_____

_____

_____

Reflection Questions:

Why did Jesus have to die?

_____

_____

_____

_____

How does the resurrection affirm our hope?

_____

_____

_____

_____

_____

Application:

Journal Prompt:

Reflect on Romans 12:1. What does offering yourself as a living sacrifice look like in your context?

_____

_____

_____

_____

_____

_____

_____

_____

_____

_____

_____

_____

_____

_____

_____

_____

_____

_____

_____

_____

Memory Verse:

Hebrews 10:10, "And by that will, we have been made holy through the sacrifice of the body of Jesus Christ once for all."

1 Corinthians 15:17, "And if Christ has not been raised, your faith is futile; you are still in your sins."

Prayer Focus:

Thank Jesus for His sacrifice and ask to live in the power of the resurrection.

_____
_____
_____
_____
_____
_____
_____

Final Thoughts:

Jesus' death and resurrection were the centerpiece of redemption. He is the Lamb who bore our sin—and now reigns victorious. Your Thoughts?

_____
_____
_____
_____
_____
_____
_____
_____
_____
_____
_____
_____

STUDY GUIDE: CHAPTER 8 – THE APOSTOLIC MISSION— GENTILES FIND REDEMPTION

Main Theme: The spread of the Gospel to all nations through the apostles.

Key Themes & Instructions:

The Great Commission

Reflect on Jesus' call to make disciples of all nations.

What does this look like in your personal context?

_____

_____

_____

_____

Apostolic Boldness and Suffering

Consider how the apostles endured trials and remained faithful.

How can their courage inspire your own walk with Christ?

_____

_____

_____

_____

_____

Gentile Inclusion

God's plan was always global. Reflect on how the early Church embraced all people.

How does this challenge or affirm your view of unity in Christ?

_____

_____

_____

_____

Scripture Focus & Instructions:

Matthew 28:19–20 – The Great Commission.

How are you participating in this command?

_____

_____

_____

Acts 1:8; 10; 15 – The Holy Spirit empowers and directs the mission.

What role does the Holy Spirit play in your witness?

_____

_____

_____

_____

_____

Galatians 3:28 – Unity in Christ.

How does this verse shape your understanding of identity in the Church?

_____

_____

_____

_____

_____

Revelation 7:9 – A vision of every nation worshiping God.

What hope does this give for the future of the Church?

_____

_____

_____

_____

_____

_____

Reflection Questions:

What can we learn from the apostles' mission?

_____

_____

_____

_____

How does your life reflect Christ's call to go?

_____

_____

_____

_____

_____

Application:

Journal Prompt:

Write about one person or group you feel led to reach out to.

_____

_____

_____

_____

_____

_____

_____

_____

_____

_____

_____

_____

_____

_____

Memory Verse:

Acts 10:34-35, "Then Peter began to speak: "I now realize how true it is that God does not show favoritism ^{35} but accepts from every nation the one who fears him and does what is right. ^{36} You know the message God sent to the people of Israel, announcing the good news of peace through Jesus Christ, who is Lord of all."

Acts 1:8, "In the beginning was the Word, and the Word was with God, and the Word was God."

Prayer Focus:

Ask God to give you boldness to share the Gospel and the love to reach across divides.

_____

_____

_____

_____

_____

_____

_____

_____

_____

Final Thoughts:

The apostles carried the Gospel to the ends of the earth. Now it's our turn—empowered by the Spirit, commissioned by Christ.

_____

_____

_____

_____

_____

_____

_____

_____

STUDY GUIDE: CHAPTER 9 – SATAN'S MOVE TO FOIL GOD'S PLAN

Main Theme: Spiritual warfare and ultimate victory in Christ.

Key Themes & Instructions:

Satan's Rebellion and Deception

Reflect on the pride and disobedience that led to Satan's fall.

How do you recognize his deception in the world today?

_____

_____

_____

_____

Sin's Impact on Creation

Consider how sin has affected not just individuals but the entire world.

Where do you see brokenness that reveals this truth?

_____

_____

_____

_____

_____

_____

Christ's Triumph Over Evil

Jesus' death and resurrection broke the power of sin and Satan.

How do you live from a place of spiritual victory?

_____

_____

_____

_____

_____

Scripture Focus & Instructions:

Isaiah 14; Genesis 3 – Origins of rebellion in heaven and on earth.

What does this reveal about the nature of pride and temptation?

_____

_____

_____

Ephesians 6; 1 Peter 5:8 – Be watchful and wear the armor of God.

Which piece of the armor do you most need to strengthen right now?

_____

_____

_____

_____

Romans 8:38–39; John 10:28 – Nothing can separate us from God's love.

How do these verses bring security in the midst of spiritual battle?

_____

_____

_____

_____

Reflection Questions:

What does spiritual warfare look like in your daily life?

_____

_____

_____

How do you walk in the victory Christ has won?

_____

_____

_____

_____

Application:

Journal Prompt:

Describe a recent struggle where you needed to put on the armor of God.

_____

_____

_____

_____

_____

_____

_____

_____

_____

_____

_____

_____

_____

_____

_____

_____

_____

_____

_____

_____

Memory Verse:

1 John 4:4, "You, dear children, are from God and have overcome them, because the one who is in you is greater than the one who is in the world."

1 Peter 5:8, "Be alert and of sober mind. Your enemy the devil prowls around like a roaring lion looking for someone to devour."

Prayer Focus:

Ask God to help you resist temptation and stand firm in His strength.

_____
_____
_____
_____
_____
_____
_____
_____
_____
_____

Final Thoughts:

Though the enemy is real, his defeat is sure. Christ's victory secures our freedom, identity, and eternal hope. Your Thoughts?

_____
_____
_____
_____
_____
_____
_____
_____
_____
_____

STUDY GUIDE: CHAPTER 10 – WHY WOULD GOD GO TO THESE EXTENSIVE MEASURES?

Main Theme: God's redeeming love and covenantal faithfulness.

Key Themes & Instructions:

Grace Over Works

Understand salvation as a gift rather than something earned.

How does this affect your approach to God and others?

_____

_____

_____

_____

Love That Redeems

God's actions are motivated by deep love, not obligation.

Reflect on how His love has personally touched your life.

_____

_____

_____

_____

_____

_____

Relationship Over Religion

God desires restored fellowship—not just ritual or rule-following.

What does authentic relationship with God look like to you?

_____

_____

_____

_____

_____

_____

Scripture Focus & Instructions:

1 John 4:8–10 – God is love; He sent His Son for you.

How does this passage deepen your understanding of love?

_____

_____

_____

Romans 5:8; John 3:16 – God acted while we were still sinners.

How does this challenge your views on grace and mercy?

_____

_____

_____

_____

Ephesians 2:8–9 – Salvation is not earned.

How does this truth bring freedom in your walk with Christ?

_____

_____

_____

_____

Reflection Questions:

Why does God's grace change everything?

_____

_____

_____

How can your life reflect His love today?

_____

_____

_____

_____

Application:

Journal Prompt:

Write about a time you experienced God's grace tangibly.

_____
_____
_____
_____
_____
_____
_____
_____
_____
_____
_____
_____
_____
_____
_____
_____
_____
_____
_____
_____
_____
_____

Memory Verse:

Ephesians 2:8–9, "For it is by grace you have been saved, through faith—and this is not from yourselves, it is the gift of God—9 not by works, so that no one can boast."

Romans 5:8, "But God demonstrates his own love for us in this: While we were still sinners, Christ died for us."

Prayer Focus:

Ask God to help you rest in His grace and extend it to others.

_____

_____

_____

_____

_____

_____

_____

_____

_____

_____

Final Thoughts:

God's plan is driven by love, not obligation. It's not about earning—
it's about receiving. His grace is greater than our sin. Your Thoughts?

_____

_____

_____

_____

_____

_____

_____

_____

_____

STUDY GUIDE: CHAPTER 11 – THE FINAL VICTORY: GOD'S PLAN FOR THE END TIMES

Main Theme: Christ's return, judgment, and eternal restoration.

Key Themes & Instructions:

Second Coming and the Rapture

Understand Christ's return as both hope and motivation.

How does it impact your faith today?

_____

_____

_____

_____

_____

Tribulation and Final Judgment

Explore God's justice and mercy in the context of end-time events.

How does this deepen your trust in His sovereignty?

_____

_____

_____

_____

_____

_____

New Heaven and New Earth

Reflect on the promise of eternal life in God's presence.

What does this hope stir in you?

_____

_____

_____

_____

_____

Scripture Focus & Instructions:

1 Thessalonians 4:13–17 – Christ will gather His people.

How does this bring comfort in times of grief or fear?

_____

_____

_____

Revelation 20–22 – The final judgment and new creation.

Which vision in these chapters gives you the most hope?

_____

_____

_____

_____

_____

Matthew 24; Daniel 9:24–27 – Prophetic signs and God's timeline.

What is your response to the urgency of these prophecies?

_____

_____

_____

_____

Reflection Questions:

What does the return of Christ mean for you personally?

_____

_____

_____

How can you live with readiness and hope?

_____

_____

_____

_____

Application:

Journal Prompt:

Write how Revelation gives you courage and clarity today.

_____

_____

_____

_____

_____

_____

_____

_____

_____

_____

_____

_____

_____

_____

_____

_____

_____

_____

_____

_____

_____

_____

Memory Verse:

Luke 18:8, "I tell you, he will see that they get justice, and quickly. However, when the Son of Man comes, will he find faith on the earth?"

Revelation 1:3, "Blessed is the one who reads aloud the words of this prophecy, and blessed are those who hear it and take to heart what is written in it, because the time is near."

Prayer Focus:

Pray for endurance, watchfulness, and joy as you await His return.

_____

_____

_____

_____

_____

_____

_____

_____

_____

_____

_____

_____

Final Thoughts:

Revelation is not a book of fear but of hope. Christ will return, evil will be judged, and we will dwell with God forever. Your Thoughts?

_____

_____

_____

_____

_____

_____

_____

_____

_____

STUDY GUIDE: CHAPTER 12 – FINAL THOUGHTS: THE FAITHFUL LOVE OF GOD AND THE PROMISE OF ETERNITY

Main Theme: Christ's return, judgment, and eternal restoration.

Key Themes & Instructions:

God's Unwavering Presence

Reflect on God's consistent involvement in your life, even in difficult seasons.

When have you most clearly seen His hand at work?

_____

_____

_____

_____

Jesus' Promise of Eternal Life

Jesus assures us of a place with Him.

What does this promise mean to you personally?

_____

_____

_____

_____

_____

Sanctification and Preparation

The Holy Spirit transforms us daily.

How are you allowing God to shape you for eternity?

_____

_____

_____

_____

A Future Without Sorrow

God promises a world without pain or death.

What kind of hope does this bring to your present circumstances?

_____

_____

_____

_____

_____

Scripture Focus & Instructions:

John 14:2–6 – Jesus prepares a place for His followers.

How does this passage encourage you today?

_____

_____

_____

_____

_____

Revelation 21–22 – A vision of restored creation and eternal fellowship.

Which part of this vision brings you the most peace or joy?

_____

_____

_____

_____

_____

Romans 8:28 – God works all things for good.

How have you seen this promise fulfilled in your life?

_____

_____

_____

2 Corinthians 5:17 – In Christ, you are a new creation.

How does this truth inspire your daily walk with God?

_____

_____

_____

Reflection Questions:

How does eternity shape your present choices and priorities?

_____

_____

_____

What does it mean to be sanctified and set apart for God?

_____

_____

_____

_____

Application:

Journal Prompt:

Write how Revelation gives you courage and clarity today.

_____

_____

_____

_____

_____

_____

_____

_____

_____

_____

_____

_____
_____
_____
_____
_____
_____
_____
_____
_____
_____
_____

Memory Verse:

John 14:2–3, "My Father's house has many rooms; if that were
not so, would I have told you that I am going there to prepare
a place for you? 3 And if I go and prepare a place for you, I will
come back and take you to be with me that you also may be
where I am."

John 14:6, "Jesus answered, "I am the way and the truth and the
life. No one comes to the Father except through me."

Prayer Focus:

Pray with joyful anticipation for Christ's return and ask for strength
to live faithfully now.

_____
_____
_____
_____
_____
_____
_____
_____

Final Thoughts:

The story ends where it began—with God dwelling with His people. You are loved, called, and invited to an eternal home prepared just for you. Your Thoughts?

_____

_____

_____

_____

_____

_____

_____

_____

_____

_____

Index